THE AUTOBIOGRAPHY OF A TIBETAN MONK

Palden Gyatso
with Tsering Shakya

THE AUTOBIOGRAPHY
OF A TIBETAN MONK

Foreword by the Dalai Lama
Translated from the Tibetan by Tsering Shakya

GROVE PRESS
NEW YORK

Originally published in Great Britain by The Harvill Press
English translation copyright © 1997 by Palden Gyatso and Tsering Shakya
Maps by Reginald Piggott

Published simultaneously in Canada
Printed in the United States of America

FIRST AMERICAN EDITION

Library of Congress Cataloging-in-Publication Data

Palden, Gyatso.
    [Fire under the snow]
    The autobiography of a Tibetan monk / Palden Gyatso, with Tsering
Shakya : foreword by the Dalai Lama : translated from the Tibetan by
Tsering Shakya.
        p.   cm.
    Previously published : London : Harvill Press, 1997 under title:
Fire under the snow.
    ISBN 0-8021-1621-3
    1. Palden Gyatso. 2. Lamas—China—Tibet—Biography.
3. Political prisoners—China—Tibet—Biography.   I. Tsering
Shakya.   II. Title.
BQ978.A45A3   1997
294.3'923'092—dc21
    [B]   97-39679

Grove Press
841 Broadway
New York, NY 10003

97 98 99 00 10 9 8 7 6 5 4 3 2 1

Contents

List of Illustrations

(between pages 104 and 105)

Foreword

by the Dalai Lama

Palden Gyatso's testimony is one of the most extraordinary stories of suffering and endurance. He was arrested when he was a twenty-eight-year-old monk, in the early years of the Chinese occupation of Tibet, and was not released until 1992, when he was nearly sixty.

During his thirty-one years in prison, Palden Gyatso endured torture, virtual starvation and endless sessions of "thought reform". Nevertheless, he refused to give in to his oppressors. That he found the courage to do so, and even to forgive those who tortured him, is a tribute not only to the natural resilience of the Tibetan character. I believe it also derives from the Buddhist teachings of love, kindness, tolerance and especially the explanation that all things are relative, which are a source of inner peace and hope.

The Autobiography of a Tibetan Monk provides a vivid insight into Tibet's recent history following the invasion of 1949. Palden Gyatso evokes the horrific years of the Cultural Revolution with deep compassion for others who suffered with him. It was not the threat of execution that most terrified him, but the inhumanity and cruelty he was forced to witness.

His testimony will help those who read or hear it to understand how the structures and traditions of an ancient Buddhist civilisation have been brutally destroyed. The destruction of monasteries and temples, with their books and religious images, is not only a tragedy for Tibet but also a great loss to humanity's cultural heritage. Even more serious are the restrictions placed on those religious institutions that have been rebuilt. Their monks and nuns are no longer free to study and practise as they did when Tibet was independent. And yet individuals like Palden Gyatso reveal that the human values of compassion, patience and a sense of responsibility for our own actions that lie at the core of spiritual practice still survive. His story is an inspiration to us all.

Thousands of Tibetans have escaped from their homeland, as Palden Gyatso has done. Having finally reached the safety of exile, he has not just given up and settled down. His sense of the justice of our cause and his indignation at what has been done to so many Tibetans are so urgent that he has not rested. Having for years resisted Communist Chinese efforts to conceal and distort it, he has seized the opportunity to tell the world the truth about Tibet.

I believe that few readers of this book will fail to be moved by Palden

Gyatso's story and the tenacity and dedication it displays. Like Palden Gyatso, I am optimistic. I look forward to the day when Tibet is restored as a zone of peace, where people can live together in harmony. We will not achieve this alone, but if he has proved nothing else, Palden Gyatso has demonstrated that we are not helpless and that even individuals can make a difference. Therefore, I hope that readers will be inspired by his example to give their sympathetic support to the Tibetan cause.

May 1997
Dharamsala

Acknowledgements

I am indebted to the kindness of many people who have helped me. My greatest thanks must go to my fellow countrymen, who continue to struggle inside Tibet and who risked their lives to help me to escape. Needless to say, they must remain anonymous.

Since coming into exile, many friends have encouraged me to write this book and I am grateful for their advice and suggestions. Gyen Wangchen la, Phara Khamtsen of Drepung Loseling and Gyaltsen Gyaltag la from Switzerland gave me support and advice. I would like to thank Kalsang Takla and Tseten Samdup of the Office of Tibet in London.

I also must thank Kate Saunders, Lhamo Shakya, Dawa Tsering (alias Bobi), Tim Nunn, Robbie Barnett of the Tibet Information Network, Francisca van Holthoon, Margaret Hanbury and Dechen Pemba for their help, and William Fiennes for his work on the final draft of the text. Finally, my thanks to Christopher MacLehose, Katharina Bielenberg, Rachael Kerr and all at the Harvill Press.

Palden Gyatso,
1997

Poem of Dedication

To he who personifies and embodies the compassion of all the Buddhas,
To he who is the manifestation of the guardian deity of the people of the Land of
    the Snows
And the only refuge, the only solace for the suffering humanity of the Kaliyuga,
My heart weighs heavy with gratitude for your kindness and your blessing.

The red hordes of barbarian Chinese, evil incarnate,
Swamped and swallowed the Land of the Snows, trampling even international law.
Unchecked and uncensured, they assaulted our very being – our bodies, our minds
    and our spirit.
Is there any match for the suffering we endured, the losses we felt, the cries we
    made, even in the eighteenth layer of Hell?

And to all of you who inhabit the world who also believe in the virtues of truth,
    justice and decency,
We appeal to you to come forward in your multitude and let your roar of support
Echo along the path of truth and justice and decency.
Help to deliver us.
Help us to be free, to be independent, to be able to do what we choose – in our
    own country.

Palden Gyatso
Translated by Tsering Dhundup

Preface

For most of this century, if not for many years before, Tibet has gripped the human imagination the world over as a Shangri-La. Hidden behind the lofty peaks of the Himalayas, it has enthused explorers, colonial adventurers, writers and mountaineers. Books about Tibet with poetic titles have sold worldwide and scholars have used up a great deal of paper explaining the hidden mysteries of the Land of Snows. Yet amid this thunderous chorus of adulation, the authentic voice of the Tibetan people has until now been heard only as a faint echo.

Palden's story is neither a history nor the mystical revelation of a yogi sitting in an icy cave. It is the story of one man who was faced with the inhumanity of a system perpetrated in the name of progress and ideology. The existence of such horror is not unique to Tibet. If anything, it is merely another example of the brutality that characterises the history of this planet. And as we turn towards the new millennium, it is unlikely that suffering will disappear from the face of the earth.

In October 1950, some 40,000 battle hardened troops of Communist China crossed the Yangtze river and crushed what one observer described, in a reference to the pitiful condition of Tibet's forces, as a "Drury Lane army". The Chinese declared that Tibet had been liberated from imperialism and feudal serfdom, and that it had finally been united with the motherland. The terms "liberation" and "unification" were political euphemisms intended to camouflage what was in fact a military invasion. Two ideas form the basis of Chinese rule in Tibet: Chinese nationalism stressed that Tibet constituted an integral part of China, while Marxist ideology emphasised the idea of material progress. What the Tibetan people felt, was either considered of no consequence or their views were simply not sought. Whichever it was, these twin concepts became the legitimising force of Chinese misrule. As with every colonial rule, conquest was justified in the name of a god, a lofty ideal of liberty or the bringing of civilisation to the native population.

Academics and lawyers can produce persuasive arguments to demonstrate that Tibet was always independent or that it was always a part of China, but for people like Palden and for hundreds of ordinary Tibetans the finer points of international diplomacy and the canons of international law have never been particularly relevant. Palden is convinced of Tibet's separateness and independence because that is his common experience. The two countries are separated by tradition, culture, language and history. For him, that is a fact as clear as the difference between milk and water.

As a child Palden listened to his uncle telling him stories of how in the beginning there was a void and the wind blew, churning the dark emptiness into an ocean from which arose a great mountain peak. This was how the universe began. When all the sea, land and mountains were formed, the first man appeared in Tsethang, an area just south of present-day Lhasa. These mythical stories about the Land of Snows are enshrined in the collective mind of the Tibetan people, fostering their sense of independence, and to the young protesters it is clear that Tibet is as old as the universe.

It is the dusty soil of Tibet, roasted barley, the mumbling of mantras in homage to Chenresig, the Buddha of Compassion, the yaks, their butter and our laughter and the stories that mothers tell their children, that set Tibet apart from China. To Palden these things are more real than international law or the great power rivalry that decides the fates of countries such as Tibet. The ordinary man and woman know instinctively what is just and true.

Tibet's historical relations with China remain complex. On the one hand, all recent Chinese rulers have claimed Tibet as an integral part of China, and on the other, Tibetans have been equally resistant to such claims. For people like Palden, Tibet's unique identity brazenly declares its separateness from China. In Tibet, diplomacy has always been the prerogative of the ruling élite and the people have been content to leave it like that as long as this arrangement does not impinge on their daily lives.

For the majority of Tibetans, their first experience of China was the arrival of the Peoples' Liberation Army. The guns might not have been visible, but Tibetans knew that the loud beat of drums and the clashing of cymbals muffled the sound of gunfire. Chinese propaganda paintings of the time show PLA soldiers mingling gaily with Tibetan peasants and a soldier standing in a field wiping sweat from his brow after harvesting for an old "serf". The reality was very different. PLA soldiers had to coax poor peasants from their hiding places in the mountains to work the fields. It was not a happy encounter.

Since the invasion of 1950, the Chinese have turned the lives of all Tibetans upside-down. The Communist Party declared that the earth and the sky had changed places, and for the Tibetan people this was certainly true. Overnight, the certainties of the Tibetan world were transformed into a bleak insecurity as new ideas and new ways of living were forced upon the people. There was a time when people believed that certain ideals and values were intrinsically superior. Christianity, Western values and ideas of material progress were to be forced upon "backward" people who stubbornly refused to surrender to the march of progress. Such people, alas, are the inevitable victims of modernity.

The Chinese, imbued with these ideas of modernity and the pursuit of a socialist paradise, saw their actions as stages in the march towards progress. Instead, hundreds of lives were lost and whole families were destroyed. Thousands of monasteries were razed to the ground and monks and nuns were sent to labour camps to become a useful "productive force". The loss, in terms of human life and cultural heritage, that Tibet suffered during the fateful years before and during the Cultural Revolution is incalculable. What the Chinese did to Tibet's vibrant and profound 2,000-year heritage was as cruel as burying a man alive.

Today, the Chinese leaders would like us to believe that the Cultural Revolution was an aberration. "Mistakes" were made by the Gang of Four but now the prisoners have been set free and the damaged walls have been repaired. However, Palden can attest that Chinese rule under Deng was little better than under Mao. The soldier on guard in the watchtower was replaced by the video camera; sticks were replaced by electric prods. Only the means, not the existence, of oppression changed. The prison guards at Drapchi might have been better equipped, and received more sophisticated training, but the view from behind the high walls surrounding the prison remained the same.

An older generation of dissidents passed through the flames of Tibet's struggle, handing over responsibility to a new group of young people who defiantly marched into prison under the gaze of the Party. It is bewildering to the Communist Party that Tibetans still continue to campaign for independence; they see this as the ingratitude of pampered natives. It is hard for colonial rulers to understand that a power station, a new sports stadium, the glittering lights of discos and five-star hotels do not restore a people's dignity or allow them to reclaim their heritage. The young protester has not forgotten his parents' suffering and their deprivation.

The Tibetan people cling proudly to the civilisation that flourished on the windswept Himalayan plateau and they lament its destruction. They do so not because they had found a paradise on earth or because their society was perfect, as many of those supporting the Tibetan cause would like to believe. Tibet was no Shangri-La; it had its own imperfections and impurities. Our history is governed by moments of brilliance and profound creativity, punctuated by the follies of leaders, the corruption of the ruling class and the poverty of the common people – the history of nations all over the world.

There is nothing more destructive than a nation enslaved. 2,000 years of Tibetan history have shown that the people are fully capable of governing themselves and that they have a vision of the world they want to create around them. Palden's story shows us the resilience of such a people.

I first met Palden when I was asked to translate for him at various meetings on his visit to London in 1995. He had come in the hope of beseeching the international community to provide help for his country. He had already completed a first draft of his book in a faded notebook. Like most Tibetan books of this type, it consisted of the dates and names of those who had perished. Palden had written this as a testimony and record of those who did not live to tell their own stories. After his tour of England, I travelled to Dharamsala in northern India, where the exile community is based, and together we began the formal process of writing this book.

I hired a room and Palden visited me each day for the next three months. The moment he entered the room, I started the tape machine and recorded every conversation. In the end we accumulated more than 120 tapes, some 300 hours of reminiscences. I had each tape transcribed in Tibetan and these transcripts became the basis of the book.

First I asked Palden to take me through his life history, to sketch out the chronology and the background. Then I asked him for more information about each incident, and about his thoughts and feelings. He spoke frankly and openly, yet it was evident that he was deeply distressed and embarrassed by the unaccustomed attention. And while it was my task to encourage him to speak of his views and feelings, his own natural humility made him shy away from speaking about himself.

We have changed some names and abbreviated descriptions of events to protect the identities of those involved in various incidents and those brave individuals who helped Palden to escape to freedom.

Tsering Shakya,
London 1997

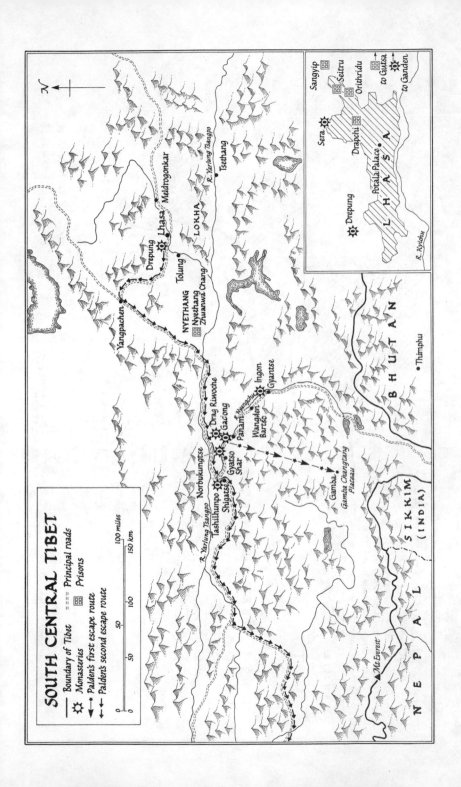

SOUTH CENTRAL TIBET

— Boundary of Tibet   ==== Principal roads
✿ Monasteries   ▦ Prisons
•→→• Palden's first escape route
•--→• Palden's second escape route

50   0   50   100 miles
0   50   100   150 km

Inset labels:
Sangyip ▦
Seitru ▦
Orithridu ▦
Giutsa ▦ ✿
to Giutsa
to Ganden
Sera ✿
Drapchi ▦
Potala Palace ✿
Drepung ✿
LHASA
R. Kyichu

Main map labels:
Meldrogonkar
Lhasa ✿
Drepung ✿
Tolung
Yangpachen
NYETHANG
Nyethang ▦ Zhuanwa Chang
Tsethang
R. Yarlung Tsangpo
LOKHA
Drag Riwoche
Gacong ✿ ▦
Nyingchu
Ingon
Gyantse ✿
Panam
Wangden Bartso
Norbukungtse
Gyatso Shar ✿
Tashilhunpo ✿
Shigatse
R. Yarlung Tsangpo
Gamba ✿
Gamba Changtang Plateau
▲ Mt. Everest
NEPAL
SIKKIM (INDIA)
BHUTAN
Thimphu

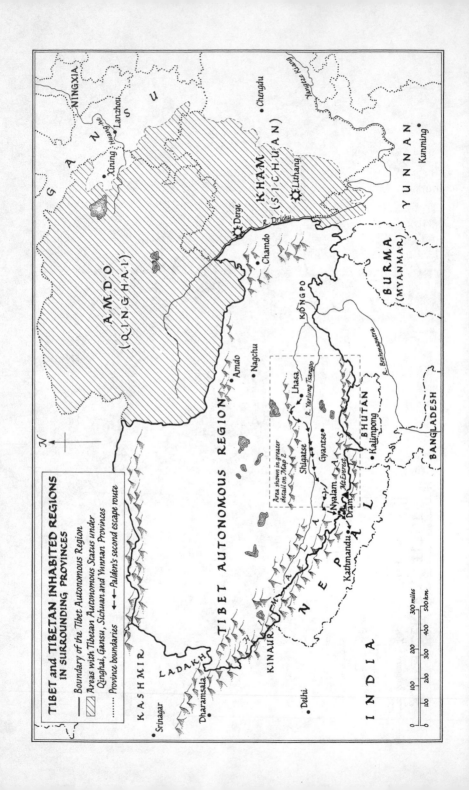

TIBET and TIBETAN INHABITED REGIONS
IN SURROUNDING PROVINCES

—— Boundary of the Tibet Autonomous Region.

▨ Areas with Tibetan Autonomous Status under
Qinghai, Gansu, Sichuan and Yunnan Provinces

···· Province boundaries   ←−← Palden's second escape route

Prologue

It seemed that I had been preparing for this meeting all my life. After waiting outside a gate guarded by an Indian soldier in a khaki uniform, shivering in the monsoon wind and carrying an old Lee Enfield rifle at his side, I was body-searched by a young Tibetan in a blue suit. Then, a minute later, I was in the presence of the Dalai Lama. I had a strange feeling of both joy and sadness. I knew that had it not been for the tragedy that had befallen my country I could never have dreamed of such a meeting with the man we Tibetans call Kyabgon, the Saviour. The shabby guards, the simple bungalow shrouded in a murky mist, made the Dalai Lama's palace in exile a sad contrast to the vision of splendour that my country still conjures up in my mind.

Ever since leaving Lhasa, I had been thinking hard about what to tell the Dalai Lama. Should I begin with an account of my arrest? Should I tell him about all the people who had died from hunger, about the prisoners who had chosen to end their lives? Or should I tell him about the Tibetans who dutifully carried out the orders of the Chinese to curry favour and ensure a comfortable life? Perhaps I should tell him about the younger generation of Tibetans who now hold defiant demonstrations in prison, or about the Tibetan torturers who brutalise the bodies of their compatriots with blows and electric prods. After all, these torturers are Tibetans too, and were nourished by the same Land of Snows.

When I finally found myself in front of His Holiness, however, my mind became empty. At the sight of his maroon-robes and his friendly, grinning countenance I lowered my head, looking up only when he asked me a series of questions. "How did you escape? When were you first arrested? Which prison were you in?" he began. I should have realised that I was not the first prisoner to stand before him. For the last thirty-five years a steady stream of Tibetans have made their arduous escape across the Himalayas and found themselves standing before the Dalai Lama. They all do so in the hope of seeing him and whispering in his ear words they have rehearsed in their minds countless times. Every Tibetan who escapes over the mountains ends his or her journey with a short walk across the tarmac path to the audience room in Dharamsala and has the opportunity to utter the words that are carved on their hearts.

After I had been speaking for twenty minutes, the Dalai Lama stopped me. "You should write your story," he said. At the time I did not realise the significance of his advice. I decided I would write an account of my sufferings, including the names of all the people who had perished in the prison. The document would go to the Dalai Lama, so that these deaths should not go unrecorded. At the time, it never crossed my mind that I would write *a book*.

In Tibet we have a long tradition of writing biographies of great lamas and figures who attain a high degree of spirituality. These books are known as *Namthar*. They are never merely good stories, but are intended to impart spiritual teachings and are read as guides to life. The power of these books is recognised by all. "When we read the *Namthar* of the great warrior King Gesar," the Tibetan saying goes, "even a beggar would be moved to pick up a sword; when we read the biography of the great hermit Milarepa, even a prince would wish to renounce the world."

When the suggestion was made that I should write my story, I was embarrassed and puzzled by people's interest. It was not that I had no desire to tell my story; on the contrary, one of the main reasons for my escape from Tibet was to be able to speak to the world. I had spent thirty years in prison and during that time I had experienced and witnessed unimaginable horrors. Every prisoner lives with the hope that somehow, once the world learns of their suffering, there will be a rush to help those who have fallen into the pit of hell.

In my prison, we used to sing, "one day the sun will shine through the dark clouds". The vision of the sun dispelling the dark clouds and our unbroken spirits kept us alive. It was not only prisoners who were resilient; so were ordinary men and women who lived their daily lives in the shadow of the Chinese Communist Party. Even today, young boys and girls who knew nothing of feudal Tibet and who are said to be the sons and daughters of the Party are crying out for freedom. Our collective will to resist what is unjust is like a fire that cannot be put out. Looking back, I can see that man's love of freedom is like a smouldering fire under snow.

Several days after my first visit to the Dalai Lama, I stood in the open yard of the new temple which faces His Holiness's palace. The Tibetans had named it Jokhang, after the holiest of all the temples in Lhasa. It had been rebuilt on a knoll and housed some of the religious images that had been rescued by devotees and smuggled across the Himalayas. In the Jokhang in Lhasa there is a bronze statue of the Buddha which was brought to Tibet in the seventh century AD as a gift from the Chinese princess who married the great Tibetan king, Srongsten Gampo. This historical event was regarded as of great significance by the Chinese. I remember being told the story again and again in prison, with the emphasis on how the betrothal of Princess Wenchen had brought culture to Tibet and unified the country with the motherland. In the beginning we used to ask, "Does this mean that Tibet also belongs to Nepal, because Srongsten Gampo was also married to a Nepalese princess?" Soon this sort of questioning came to be regarded as counter-revolutionary and was likely to earn you a term in prison.

The temple in Dharamsala was bursting with activity. Dozens of old people were circling the shrine and turning the prayer wheels, recreating that familiar music which in my childhood had mingled with the mumbling voices of elderly pilgrims reciting the six-syllable mantra, "*Om mani pad me hum*". The mist that shrouded the temple slowly dissolved and the plains of India appeared through the clouds. This incongruous sight of Tibetans in a foreign land finally convinced me that I should tell my story in writing, not to advertise my suffering but as a testimony to my country's torment. In this way I could show that while I might be free, my country was still occupied.

As I gazed towards the dusty plains of India, I was overwhelmed by sadness. I vividly recalled the routine of prison life, the regularity of study sessions, the confession meetings and the reward and punishment meetings, which had defined my life for the past thirty years. The scars of prison life remained painfully in my mind.

Dharamsala, with its lush green forests and rain, so different from Tibet, has become the resting place for so many of us. Every day, I meet fellow prisoners who have made the arduous journey to the foothills of the Himalayas. Their delight in being free is combined with a recognition of the past suffering of others. We congratulate each other on the sheer luck of surviving.

I am free in a foreign land, but lingering images of horror still haunt me. I am now living in a small hut nailed together from bits of tin and wood. The room is no bigger than the isolation unit in the prison. The torrents of monsoon rain beating on the tin roof keep me awake all night and the musty odour of damp clings to the walls and floor, although everyone says it will be better when the monsoon is over. In the next hut a group of youths who also made their way over the treacherous mountains listen to Lhasa Radio and cheerfully join in with the latest pop songs. It is strange how people still hanker for news of a place they have fled, and how they long to hear familiar sounds from home, as if to reassure themselves that they are alive.

Dharamsala is special not because it has become home for so many of us, but because it is the spiritual refuge of the Dalai Lama, the Buddha of Compassion. In prison we had uttered the name Dharamsala in hushed tones, developing a sense of reverence and awe for the place. Shortly after my arrival, I was given the task of interviewing other new arrivals to record their testimonies. I could not believe how many of us had the same story to tell. There was not a single individual without a story of horror and brutality, and I realised that all subjugated people share the common experience of bruised bodies, scattered lives and broken families.

Most of those who escape across the snowy peaks are young children. Some are sent away from home by their parents at the age of seven or eight in the hope that they will have a future in a foreign land. These are not the children of rich landlords or wealthy traders; they are the children of the same poor peasants whom the Communists claim to have liberated from servitude.

Dharamsala has a cosmopolitan character, with people from Japan, America, Israel and Europe mingling in the two narrow, muddy streets which form the main market of McLeod Ganj. I befriended many foreigners from countries I never knew existed, including a young English woman called Emily and a Dutch woman called Francisca, who regularly visited my hut to talk to me. It was during the course of those conversations that the story of my life began to unfold. I realised that because I had been lucky enough to survive, I was also duty bound to bear witness to the suffering of others.

Perhaps through the story of my life I can tell the story of my country and give expression to the pain felt by every Tibetan.

THE AUTOBIOGRAPHY OF A TIBETAN MONK

Chapter One

Beneath a Rainbow

I WAS BORN BENEATH A rainbow.

How many times my grandmother told me the story of my birth! With a crooked finger, she would trace the line of a rainbow through the air and describe as she did so how it reached from the river to the fields, with the whole village under its arc. Then she would tell me that my birth was accompanied by many auspicious signs. "Ngodup," she would say, "you might have been the Riwoche trulku!" It was her favourite story and she'd tell it to anyone who would listen.

It goes something like this. A few days after my birth a search party composed of high lamas arrived from Drag Riwoche monastery, which lies two days' walk from our village. The search party announced that I was one of the candidates for the reincarnation of a high lama who had died a year ago. There were many signs to indicate that my birth might be something special. When the monks arrived, the ravens that usually perched on the roof of the monastery were all perched on our house. And one of the chief stewards of the previous lama recalled that the lama had visited our house to carry out a religious ceremony just before he passed away. The lama had mentioned that he felt very much at home. As he was leaving the house, he came towards my mother and placed his hands on her head, saying, "I will return to this house."

According to my grandmother, a few days before I was born my mother had dreamed that she was holding a *dorje*, a symbolic thunderbolt, in her left hand and sitting in deep meditation. The thunderbolt represented the indestructibility of Buddha's teachings. All these signs were thought to be auspicious, since they usually accompany the birth of an incarnate lama.

3

Grandmother would describe how Chang dzo la, the chief steward of the previous lama, had dangled two rosaries in front of my eyes, and how my tiny hands had jabbed forward and snatched one. Grandmother would shake her head from side to side and make clapping gestures, and she would tell me with great excitement that the lama had smiled and confirmed that the rosary I had picked had indeed belonged to the previous lama.

My grandmother was fond of telling me this story. She was a small woman with a tiny face. She had a habit of rubbing dollops of butter on her hair, which made it glisten with grease. Her tiny face shone beneath the tightly combed hair. I loved listening to her. She told me that when the names of all the candidates were submitted to Lhasa for approval, I was not chosen. She insisted that this was because our family had no "back-door" connections with powerful people there. Although I was very young at the time, I could detect traces of disappointment in her voice when she reached the high point of the story.

I, after all, came into the world with a burst of auspicious signs and great expectations. The local astrologer drew up my horoscope and told my father that I would be of great benefit to my family and to others. He did not say how. Perhaps this was what a lowly village astrologer always trumpeted to the ears of wealthy landlords. I think this pleased my father. Later he reminded me of the pronouncement.

I was named Ngodup. In Tibet, parents do not choose names for their children; instead, they usually ask a high lama to bestow a name. I do not know which lama gave me my name, although it was probably the abbot of the nearby monastery. I was born in 1933, the year of the male water monkey, in a village called Panam which lies 125 miles east of Lhasa, the capital of Tibet, and forty-five miles from Shigatse in the west, Tibet's second largest city.

Panam was a small village of no importance, situated in the plains of Tsang. The Nyangchu river meandered through the valley. Mountains reared up on both sides of the river. The wide plain was dotted with

green fields of barley, peas and mustard. The river was deceptive; sometimes it was shallow and you could see only the shimmering ripples
flowing gently towards Shigatse, where the Nyangchu merges with
Tibet's largest river, the Yarlung Tsangpo. When the water was low the
villagers would simply wade across to the other side and take their
animals to pasture. But if a shepherd failed to bring back the animals at
the right time, the river became impossible to cross, and he would have to
make a long detour. It might take him two to three days to find a ford.

In the spring, when the snows melted and the ripples turned into a
torrent, the river became dangerous and the villagers looked at it with
fear. I remember being warned not to play by the river bank; it was said
that even strong beasts like yaks had been carried away by rapids. One of
my first memories is of running to the river bank as a child and seeing a
group of men pulling out a dead yak that had been washed up there.
Along with a number of other children, I stood watching the men cut up
the bloated carcass and divide the meat on to a cloth that was spread
nearby. From then on I was terrified of the river. But we were dependent
on the Nyangchu: the fields were fed from it and areas not reached by the
water were barren and dry. The infertile, cracked land was a constant
reminder of how much we relied on the river. I can't remember a day
when it rained in Panam. The areas the water reached were lush green and
provided us with sustenance. From the river we fetched drinking water,
and small channels were dug to lead water into the fields. All day you
could see a man wandering from field to field, opening and closing the
irrigation channels.

The mountains which make up the Himalayan range rose steeply
towards the clear blue sky on each side of the valley. They soared to a
sloping pasture-ground which stretched out into the sky. The walls of the
mountains sheltered Panam on both sides. When the thaw began in
the spring and the green shoots struggled to emerge from beneath the
ice, the villagers took their animals to graze on the high pasture. But for
almost three months, over winter, the sheep, goats, cows and even some

yaks were kept in the house. Our houses were two-storey buildings made out of mud bricks. The stone foundations were almost three feet wide, forming a broad base on which mud bricks were piled to make a thick wall. These simple mud-brick walls kept the house warm in the winter and cool in the summer.

The first floor was for human habitation. On the ground floor, in the dark, the animals were kept in the winter months. I remember, as a young boy, chasing the animals out of their winter pen. They were hesitant and frightened to emerge into the open. One by one, they would stagger out on unsteady feet and blink, dazzled by the daylight. People would laugh and say that the animals were intoxicated from eating the waste from distilled alcohol: in the winter, in preparation for the Tibetan New Year, every family would brew huge quantities of *chang* and pour the mushy barley waste out for the cows. The animals soon adjusted to the glaring light. Then the older children would shoo them up a narrow path that led towards the high pasture-grounds. The animals and the shepherd spent the summer there, the shepherd occasionally returning to the village with cheese, butter and a donkey laden with dung, which would be used for fuel.

Panam was dependent on farming. Animals provided luxury items like meat, butter and cheese. My family kept over 600 sheep and goats, and were relatively wealthy by Tibetan standards. My father leased large tracts of land from the government and in turn leased them to other farmers. We were called "government taxpayers" (*gerpa*), because we paid taxes directly to the government in Lhasa, whereas other farmers, like my father's tenants, paid taxes to their landlords or to the monastery. My father's tax obligation was complex and I never fully understood what he paid and what duties he had to perform, though one thing I remember clearly is that my family had to supply five men to the Tibetan army. The men did not necessarily have to be family members. In fact, as far as I can remember, my father passed this obligation on to our tenants. It was up to us what arrangement we made with the tenant farmers; the government was satisfied as long as we continued to supply the five men.

My father also acted as the village headman and he was often called upon to settle disputes between villagers. He was regarded as a fair man and our tenants and the villagers called him Bari Jho la, a term that implies endearment and respect. He defended the villagers from absentee landlords who resided in Shigatse and Lhasa and extracted unfair taxes. My family name was Bari Lhopa, meaning "Bari in the South". There was another family in the upper part of the valley called Bari Jang, or "Bari in the North". We must have been related once, but everyone had forgotten how the family became split between the north and south.

In the eighteenth century Panam achieved some fame as the birthplace of the seventh Panchen Lama, the second most important religious figure in Tibet. It was said that when the sixth Panchen Lama died, the oracles foretold that the child would be found "in happiness and sitting in the lap of the sun". Lamas were sent all over Tibet to search for the new incarnation of the Panchen Lama. One such search party arrived in Panam with the oracle's pronouncement fresh in their minds.

The search party approached the first house in the village and found a woman sitting with a newborn infant in her arms. When the search party asked the mother's name, she replied, "Nyima", which means "sun". They did not need to look any further. In the arms of Nyima was the seventh Panchen Lama.

The Panchen Lama was born in the house next to ours. It was the wealthiest house in the village. The family were elevated to the ranks of the Tibetan aristocracy and became rich. The villagers called this *trungzhi*, meaning "birth estate". *Trungzhi* was held in great esteem by all the families in the locality. By the time of my birth, excitement had spread to the whole village. They said that Panam was a blessed village to have seen the birth of another lama. But their excitement did not last long.

My family, like most Tibetans, were very religious and took their religious commitment seriously. Our large house was dominated by the *Kangyur lhakang*, or chapel, which contained the 101 volumes of the *Kangyur*, the teachings of the Buddha. No one else in the village could boast such a collection. I don't know how my family had acquired these priceless volumes, which were hundreds of years old. The *lhakang* was on the top floor of the house and also contained many images of Buddhas, Bodhisattvas and *thangkas*, or religious banners. Some of these were also hundreds of years old. On top of our roof there stood a large solitary brass parasol called a *gyaltsen*, or victory banner. The banner was a unique privilege reserved for a house which possessed a complete set of the *Kangyur*. Whenever other families in the village held religious ceremonies they came to borrow one of the volumes.

Every year the village performed one important religious ceremony. In July, when the crops began to ripen and did not need much tending, it was time for everyone to relax and celebrate what they hoped would be a bumper harvest. But it was also a time to propitiate the local spirits and invite them to protect the crops from malevolent forces. The village observed a ceremony called *Choe-khor*, which means, literally, "circling the teaching of Buddha".

The monks from the local monastery would come down to our house and bring out each volume of the *Kangyur*, wrapped in yellow cloth and raised high above their heads. Outside the house, villagers and family members fought among themselves to carry the volumes on their backs. When all 101 volumes had found an eager back to rest upon, the monks would lead a procession, followed by the villagers, each carrying one volume of the *Kangyur*. The procession traced the outermost edge of the village.

The party would stop in a secluded place we called "the abode of the village spirit" (*yul-lha*). The malevolent village spirit resided here and our wellbeing depended on making offerings to it. It was said that harm would befall the village if the spirit were not regularly appeased. Although the crops were growing well, they still needed to be strengthened by spiritual means. An unexpected hailstorm could fall on the village and destroy all the crops. The farmers in Tibet feared hailstorms as others feared drought. Some villages even had a resident "hailstorm stopper", believed to have magical powers. Whenever someone fell ill in the family, we also made offerings to the spirit.

The spot was marked with a high pile of stones and animal horns half hidden beneath a mesh of tangled prayer flags. The flags depicted the five elements: yellow for earth, red for fire, blue for sky, white for cloud and green for water.

Every year each family would leave a new prayer flag. I never ventured near the spot alone. The musty smell and decaying heap of prayer flags made for a haunting atmosphere. The place made me shiver. Everyone feared the *yul-lha*. The *Choe-khor* ceremony was meant to symbolise the village's faithfulness to the spirit and demarcate the village boundary. After the ritual was completed the villagers felt safe and protected.

When the whole village had been circled, the procession would come to rest in an open meadow near the river. Here, by the river, each family would pitch a tent. For the next few days there would be dancing and singing. The older men would gamble while the young men competed in an archery contest. It was a time to rest and enjoy the summer weather. Two or three months later the crops would be ready for harvesting and each of my father's tenants would have to send a man to work in my father's fields. It was the busiest time in the life of the village and there were many chores to attend to. No one sat idly. When the crops had been harvested, threshing began. Then the grain was piled high and women began to winnow it to separate out the husks. As the villagers were busy winnowing, my father would invite ten monks to the house and they would, simultaneously, begin to read aloud each volume of the *Kangyur.* It would take five to ten days for the monks to read it from first word to last. I remember my father saying that our family had sponsored this ritual every year for hundreds of years and thus our house had been lucky and blessed with the merit of all the good deeds of our forefathers.

But I felt that this luck had not rubbed off on me. My mother died shortly after my birth, leaving my father to care for three daughters and two sons. I do not know how she died. My grandmother once said that my mother looked so healthy and contented immediately after my birth but then one evening fell ill and never recovered. Tibetans believe that when good fortune falls on a family, the same family will also experience misfortune. Perhaps this is an explanation. Since I was considered a possible reincarnation of a high lama, the misfortune fell on my mother.

I never knew my mother's name but she was referred to as *Ama la*. She was only forty when she died. I have no memory of her. Nor do I have a picture of her. In old Tibet there were no photographs and no portraits were painted of a living person. The only photograph I ever saw was one of the thirteenth Dalai Lama which sat on our family altar. Once my aunt took it down and placed it on my head. I wanted to touch it and feel its texture and examine the image, but it was precious and my aunt quickly returned it to the altar. The photograph was bought from a Nepalese merchant; even then only two families in the village could afford it. I don't think a photograph of my mother existed. I once asked one of my relatives what my mother was like and he simply replied, "She was a nice woman." My father never spoke about her and I in turn never raised the subject with him. I think he must have felt a great loss. My father had married at the age of fourteen and my mother was a year younger than him. Like all marriages in Tibet at the time, theirs had been arranged by their families.

My sisters were also very young and could not be expected to look after me, so I was sent to live with my paternal aunt. Her name was Zangmo and she lived in a village six hours' walk from Panam, called Gyatso Shar. She had gone there as a bride many years before. My aunt's family were called Namling and there must have been over twenty people in my new household.

My aunt was in her late thirties when I went to live with her. She had two sons, whom I called *Jho la*, or older brother. They were already grown up; one was sixteen and about to be married. My aunt was a very resourceful woman and in effect the head of the household. She kept a huge bundle of keys to all the storerooms in her *amba*, a fold in the traditional dress which is used as a pocket. Whenever the servants wanted provisions, they had to ask her first. She had a large, round face and wore bright red corals in her ears. Her hair was long and she kept it plaited and tied around her head. I was sent to live with my aunt because a few months earlier she too had given birth, to a daughter called Wangmo. She could breast-feed the two of us.

Gyatso Shar was not much different from Panam. The houses were just the same and, like the rest of the inhabitants of the Nyangchu valley, the people in Gyatso Shar were farmers. Life revolved around farming. Everyone worked on the land. Their skills had been refined over centuries. There were no machines, so everything was done by hand. Today, when I think back, it seems strange that we had no need for the wheel. The Land of Snows had no use for that great invention.

My aunt's family were also *gerpa*, paying taxes to the government. It was said that the accumulated grain from their estate would be enough to dam Tibet's mightiest river, the Yarlung Tsangpo. I grew up thinking of my aunt as my mother. I called her *Ama la* and her house was home. Later, in prison, each interrogation would begin with my name, my age and my parents' names, and I'd have to pause and think carefully to give the right answer. My aunt cared deeply for me. Sometimes she wrapped her arms around me and whispered, "The motherless child."

Everyone in the house was equally generous and I was showered with affection. I can't remember a time when I felt that I had another home, or that my "family" weren't my real family. Once I heard someone refer to "the boy's father". I thought they were talking about my uncle, whom I also called *Pa la*. I'd always regarded him as my father. So when I heard "The boy's father is coming to visit", I was confused. Then I heard people referring to "the boy's home". As far as I knew, I had only one home, and that was where I was living. So I was troubled and knew that some revelation was to come.

I was happy in Gyatso Shar. Life revolved around the village and the family. Childhood was simple. The boys were left to their own devices, while the girls followed their mothers around, working with them, observing and acquiring the skills they had learned from their own mothers. If our parents were working in the fields we followed them and learned by imitation. That was our education. I carried and fetched things. I helped with the weeding. I wandered around the fields, opening and closing water channels.

But my favourite pastime was listening to stories. Tashilhunpo was one of the biggest monasteries in the region and one of my uncles was a monk there. He spent the winter at my aunt's house. He was good with children. He summoned us to listen to his stories. He told us about *Jigten Chag-tsul*: the creation of the world. He described, in a solemn voice, how the world had been covered by water, and how the water slowly evaporated to form the land and mountains. Then Chenresig, Buddha of Compassion, was incarnated in the form of a monkey, and his consort, Dolma, appeared in the form of an ogress. The coupling of the monkey and the ogress resulted in the first human beings. Their six children represented the six types of creatures that lived in the world: gods, demigods, human beings, ghosts, animals and fiends. They multiplied and that was how, my uncle told us, the first Tibetans came into being.

Some of this was terrifying. He told us about other worlds and about hells where people were boiled alive or lived in perpetual hunger. My uncle taught us that when we die, our good and bad actions are weighed against each other in black and white pebbles on a scale. The white pebbles were our good deeds; the black pebbles were all our negative actions. If the scales tipped towards the black then you would go to hell, but if they tipped towards the white then you would go to heaven. My uncle would lean forward, so that his face was close to the faces of the children, and say, "If you don't want to go to hell, you must not accumulate black pebbles."

My uncle was respected by everyone in the village and people sought his advice on all sorts of matters. Once he took me to his monastery,

Tashilhunpo, in Shigatse. This was not so much a religious experience as a genial introduction to the monastic life. And I became aware for the first time of a world outside the village, beyond the mountains. I remember my uncle was sharing a room with a monk from Ladakh who gave me a piece of toffee in the shape of a fish. He told me it was from India. Later that evening I saw a torch for the first time and learned that this too was from India. I thought what a wonderful place India must be, so full of magical things. Tibetans regarded India with the same reverence with which Christians regard Jerusalem. But I was confused by stories about Buddha's life in "the land of Pag-pa". Pag-pa was pronounced the same as the Tibetan word for pig and I used to wonder why India should be called the Land of the Pig. I imagined thousands of pigs roaming through its jungles. When I asked why India was called the Land of the Pig, my uncle and the other monks roared with laughter. Uncle told me it was time I learned to read and write.

All I knew of the wider world was gleaned from my uncle's stories. India was the holiest of all places on earth; everywhere else was to be feared. My uncle's terrifying tales of the outside world, which seemed a place inhabited by people without culture or compassion, tempered my natural curiosity. He told us we were most fortunate to be born in the Land of Snows, and I had no reason to doubt it.

I think now that it was my uncle's stories of Tibet and of the origins of the Tibetan people that first forged my understanding of the essential difference between Tibetans and the Chinese. When the Chinese arrived and told us that Tibet had always been part of China, we did not understand them. We had a different sense of history. Of course, the Communists tried to dismiss these stories as childish tales, but for us they were powerful narratives, part of what it meant to be Tibetan.

Back in the village, my cousin Wangmo was my closest companion. My aunt called us "the inseparables". We had no special toys but just improvised with whatever we could lay our hands on. A stick became a spear and dusty ground became a battlefield on which we could wage imaginary wars. Like anywhere else, the boys wanted to play on their own, but I always tried to include Wangmo in whatever we were doing. She was pretty tough and could fend for herself against any bully in the village.

When we were about five or six, Wangmo fell ill. My aunt did everything she could and lamas were invited to perform rituals to ward off the harmful spirits that were causing the illness. One morning I saw my aunt sobbing in the kitchen and I realised what had happened. My aunt stayed in her bed for days. I could be of no comfort to her.

The grown-ups went on as if nothing had happened. I suppose they thought that I would be saddened if I heard them talking about Wangmo and that if they avoided the subject then soon all would be forgotten. Sometimes I think we Tibetans tend to avoid uncomfortable subjects in the hope that pain will vanish of its own accord. Even today, the memory of my aunt and of Wangmo brings tears to my eyes. Those were the happiest days of my life. Wangmo and I played together without a care in the world. We used to play in puddles and make figures out of mud, coming home covered in dirt. Aunt would scream at us and call one of the servants to clean us up.

It wasn't long after Wangmo's death that I met members of my real family. My grandmother, my sisters and my brother came to offer their condolences to my aunt. Everyone started to cry when they arrived. My father had sent new clothes and a pair of leather boots, made in India. I don't remember meeting him until the day my aunt called me inside and wiped the dust from my clothes before taking me inside to the family prayer room. There was a man sitting on a raised seat, sipping tea. He had large, piercing eyes. He wore a long turquoise earring which hung down to his shoulder.

My aunt nudged me forward. "Meet your father," she said. I behaved as all children do when meeting a stranger: shy and nervous, but at the same time excited at the prospect of receiving a gift. I went forward to meet him. He reached deep into his pocket and brought out what appeared to be a rock of white crystal. I cupped my hands and stretched them towards him. My father placed the rock of crystal in my cupped hands.

My father began to speak but all I could do was gaze at the gift in my hands. It was what we call *shel kara*, or "sweet glass". I kept it in my pocket for days, bringing it out occasionally to have a good lick.

Despite our separation, there was still a natural bond between father and son. One day I stood up for my father when one of the older boys in the house commented that he looked like a piece of shit on account of the cloak he wore, a *chuba* the colour of earth. I chased the boy round the house and thumped him hard on the back.

I was summoned to meet my father whenever he came to visit my aunt. Our talks were short and to the point. "Have you been good?" he'd ask. I'd nod. "Listen to your aunt and be good." Then he'd stuff my pockets with toffee or dried meat. I showed off his gifts to the other children, knowing that it would make them jealous. There was a sense of mystery, of importance, about my father which the other children envied. Father was entertained lavishly when he visited. He slept in the best room in the house.

My aunt never got over Wangmo's death. She devoted herself to her work. In the summer she worked in the fields and in the winter she spent all the time weaving and spinning wool. And on top of this she took care of the household chores. She became, if anything, more devoted to me.

One day my father arrived and I knew that he had come to make plans to take me home with him. I saw my aunt sobbing. I was nine years old when my father decided the time had come for me to move back to Panam for good.

On a summer's morning my aunt woke me up with a cup of tea and a bowl of *drel-sil*, a mixture of rice, sweet potatoes and sugar. She was using the old Chinese bowl with two dragons embracing from each side, the bowl that was usually kept on the family altar. *Drel-sil* is served to mark an auspicious day. My aunt handed me a white ceremonial scarf called a *khata*. She told me to place it on the rug on my bed, where I had been sitting. She said that this meant I would come back to the house. My cup was filled to the brim with tea and this too meant that I would return soon. She pointed to a pile of new clothes and told me to put them on. These clothes had been specially made for the occasion and my aunt fussed about me as I got dressed.

So I was finally to leave this house. I was sad and I could see the sadness in my aunt's face too. She regarded me as her own son. Her daughter had died but I had fed at her breast and grown up before her eyes. She did her best to put on a brave face. She nudged me along and watched as I put on the new clothes, sometimes reaching forward to tuck in and to tidy the loose ends.

Outside in the courtyard the whole family was getting ready. Six or seven ponies were being saddled and loaded with wooden boxes. My father was supervising the work. I stood watching. The family came up to me one by one and draped *khatas* around my neck. It wasn't long before I felt myself disappearing beneath the heaped scarves. My aunt was the last to drape one around my neck. She came towards me with her hands wide apart carrying the finest silk *khata* you can imagine. When she embraced me the tears on her cheeks wetted my own cheeks. Though I was buried beneath all the scarves, I reached out and held on to my aunt and let out a loud, involuntary cry. Even the neighbours heard my cry and came into the courtyard to take part in the occasion. Some of them draped more *khatas* around my neck.

Someone said, "Ngodup is being sent away like a bride!" I composed myself and wiped my eyes. I was placed on a pony and the village children began to chant, "*Na-ma, Na-ma*!" or "Bride, Bride!" I wanted the pony to take me as far away as possible. When we set off, the chants soon faded and the children stopped following us. My father and grandmother led the procession. The *khatas* around my neck drifted out behind me like flags. My aunt came with us until, some distance from the village, she ordered the muleteer to stop. She rode towards me and lifted all the *khatas* from my neck.

Now and again my father turned to glance at me. I tried not to catch his eye. When we got home all the family and neighbours were waiting for us. I was taken down from the horse. A man approached me and gave me another *khata*. My aunt stayed for a few weeks before going back to Gyatso Shar. When she left she was weeping.

My new life in Panam was the beginning of my adulthood. In Tibet in those days we grew up very quickly. My father and brother had both had to take responsibility for a family when they were just fourteen. But in the house there was not much for me to do. My sisters and my brother took care of all the chores. I got bored. I stayed away from my father, who, as he grew older, became more dignified and solemn. I can remember the sound of him reciting his prayers, a low murmur that made him even more distant and unapproachable.

I think now that my father's love for me was coloured by the instinctive sadness we feel for a motherless child. If he avoided me it was only because I brought back memories of my mother. I think he felt helpless in the knowledge that he was not able to look after me. He never spoke about my mother, never even mentioned her name. This didn't mean that he had forgotten her, rather that he could not bring himself to face the fact that she was not there.

Father had remarried a year after my mother died. My stepmother had had two children by the time I came back to Panam and one of them was already a monk at Gadong monastery. My stepmother was not aloof like my father. She was kind and affectionate and always ready to embrace me warmly; she didn't want to be the archetypal stepmother. When my father died and my older brother assumed the role of head of the household, he moved in with my stepmother. She was still young and my family felt that a new bride in the house would only mean quarrels. To keep family wealth intact it was quite commonplace for several brothers to share one wife, but in our case my brother moved in with our stepmother. She was young and could still bear him children.

But the greatest compensation for my move back to Panam was Gadong monastery. It was less than an hour's walk from our house. Two of my father's brothers were monks there. Sometimes I was taken to see them and sometimes, when I had nothing to do, I went to the monastery on my own. My grandmother noticed how much time I was spending there. She told me the story of my birth again and suggested that I should think of becoming a monk. I liked the idea. I was lonely in the village, but in the monastery I found companionship and even the adults seemed to have more time for me.

Chapter Two

Cutting Ties with the World

I T WASN'T LONG BEFORE my grandmother began to fret about my future. My father still saw me as a child and hadn't given any thought to what I was going to do with myself, but Grandmother pestered him, telling him it was time to "pave the way for Ngodup's future".

In Tibet in those days there wasn't much choice for a village boy, even for a well-off one. Either he worked on the family land or he entered a monastery. The oldest son inherited the farm and all family obligations. By the age of fourteen my older brother had taken over much of the responsibility of running the estate. He would stride around, handsome and confident, making sure that everything was running smoothly, allocating work to hired labourers and dealing swiftly with complaints from tenants. Some days I accompanied him and saw how much the villagers respected and admired this model son.

My grandmother had suggested I become a monk because she was very religious. She visited the monastery on the eighth, fifteenth and thirtieth day of every Tibetan month, each visit taking a whole day. She'd get up early and put on clean clothes. She'd take a large block of butter with her and a tin of sunflower oil from India – the finest oil and a rare luxury. I started to go with her to the monastery. Although she was over seventy, she was strong and could still walk all the way up the steep hill. Then she'd wander slowly around all the shrine rooms, adding some oil or dollops of butter to the lamps. Whenever she came to the image of a deity, she'd stand with her hands clasped, mutter some prayers, then lean forward and touch the base of the image with her forehead.

At noon she punctuated her tour by visiting one of her two sons. My uncles would have prepared a lunch of *tsampa*, or roasted barley flour, and dried meat. My grandmother might take a nap, and I'd wander about and play with the younger novices. They were learning to read and write and I envied them. After her rest, my grandmother would make her last offering at the central temple. She'd look towards the main shrine room, bring her tiny wrinkled hands that were like a bird's claws right in front of her face and with slow, deliberate gestures begin to recite a prayer. When I asked her what she prayed for, she said that she prayed for the welfare of all sentient beings and that no one should be in bad health. She always said that good health was the most precious thing, something money cannot buy. Illness, she believed, was indiscriminate and came to both rich and poor.

Now, looking back, I think that her concern reflected the situation in Tibet. Although traditional Tibetan doctors called *amchi* practised in some places, there weren't any in Panam. You had to walk for a day or two to see an *amchi* in Shigatse or Gyantse. When anyone fell ill, there was very little a family could do. We all relied on spiritual means for curing sickness, and sometimes people did make what seemed like a miraculous recovery.

An expanse of green fields separated the village from the monastery. Where the fields ended, the lower slopes of the mountains rose steeply and the monastery perched on its own mound, with a commanding view of the valley. You could see the Nyangchu river meandering towards Shigatse. Sometimes, from my father's house, I could see the whitewashed walls of the monastery glinting in the bright sunlight.

The monastery was over 900 years old. It was founded by the great Indian scholar-saint Khache-Sakyashri, who came to teach Buddhism in Tibet in the eleventh century.

The monastery's name is the subject of much dispute. It was commonly believed that the name Gadong was derived from the local name for the mountain below which the village was situated. The mountain was called Ga, which means saddle. *Dong* means "in front", and so Gadong monastery was "in front of saddle mountain". But scholars have argued that the monastery was actually called "Tree of Happiness". The theory is that soon after the monastery was founded, Buddhism began to decline in Tibet and the indigenous Bon religion reasserted itself. After many years the remaining monasteries failed to observe the Buddhist rules of monasticism. It was said that only in Panam did the monks continue to adhere to strict codes of monastic discipline. Later, the monks from our monastery were to travel all over Tibet to teach and revive the old monastic rules. And so the monastery was called the "Tree of Happiness".

At one time there were nearly 200 monks there. As far back as anyone can remember, one member of our family had always been a monk at Gadong. The monastery and nearby villages were bonded by the fact that almost every family in the vicinity had a son at the monastery. It was *our* monastery.

When my father called me, I went up to the small room at the top of the house where he spent most of the day reading from sacred texts. A pot of tea stood on a clay stove. My uncle, the monk, was there too. We were joined by my grandmother. Father lifted his cup. He blew over the surface of the tea to cool it, then took a sip. He turned to me and said, "*Bu*, your uncle and I think you should join the monastery." He looked at Grandmother, as if hoping that she would finish the conversation on his behalf, but as soon as I heard father's words I nodded and said, "Yes."

I had wanted to go to the monastery for ages but had had no idea how you became a monk. I was reluctant to raise the subject with my father in case he thought I was just unhappy at home. Grandmother started telling the story of my birth again, as if none of us had ever heard it before. But this time she had a point to make: I should be a monk at Drag Riwoche, since the chief steward had said that if I ever became a monk he would be happy to have me there. She was still convinced I was the Riwoche Lama, that I'd only lost out because we didn't have the right contacts in Lhasa. But father dismissed Grandmother's suggestion and insisted that I was to go to Gadong. Looking at my uncle, he said that our family had been connected with Gadong for centuries and that we should not break with tradition. My uncle nodded. Father brooked no further discussion about the matter.

Given the choice, I'd have said I wanted to go to Tashilhunpo in Shigatse, one of the greatest monasteries in Tibet. It was the home of the Panchen Lama, the second highest lama after the Dalai Lama. The people in our region had a special reverence for him. I had visited Shigatse with my aunt and it had felt special to me. And I also had many relatives in Tashilhunpo. This isn't to say that I didn't like Gadong, which was a magnificent monastery, and something like a home from home, but I didn't see it as a great centre of learning. Despite its antiquity and fame in years gone by, in 1943 Gadong was a simple monastery which catered for the simple spiritual needs of village people. But anyway, I had no say in the matter.

And so it was decided that I should join "our monastery". I should not be the one to break the connection between the monastery and our family, a connection that stretched back centuries. My uncle was keen for me to come to Gadong. He was old and had few students. He had inherited a huge *shag*, or monk's quarters. The *shag* had been passed down in our family line for generations. My uncle in Gadong was more serious than my uncles in Gyatso Shar. He spoke to me about important family matters, as if I were no longer a child. Our relationship would be that of teacher and student.

My grandmother arranged for new sets of monk's robes: one for summer, one for winter, a third for ceremonial occasions. Every few days the tailor would arrive with something else. My new clothes were laid neatly in a pile in the shrine room. Sometimes Grandmother summoned me and held the clothes up against me to measure them. Two days before I was due to depart for the monastery, my aunt arrived. When she saw me she got off her pony and came rushing towards me, arms outstretched in greeting. I tried not to cry. I was secretly hoping that she had come to take me away. I remembered Wangmo and my time in Gyatso Shar, and I think my aunt did too. She clung to me for a long time and we walked hand in hand back to the house.

My aunt began to fuss over me and check all my belongings. Grandmother was glad to have her take charge. Everything was packed into two wooden boxes covered in yak hide. The cases were loaded on to two stout ponies and taken to my uncle's *shag*. My aunt's arrival made me uneasy about going away to live in the monastery. Seeing her wandering around the house brought back all sorts of memories. And her demeanour was somehow different. I think that she too no longer saw me as a child.

I wasn't apprehensive about becoming a monk. I knew the monastery well and almost all the monks there were familiar to me. My family was held in high esteem and some of the monks referred to my father as *jin-dag*, or patron. My father had been very generous to the monastery. When I became a monk he made a large gift of grain and butter.

I remember that day clearly. My aunt came to wake me up. She brought a cup of buttered tea. Grandmother followed with a bowl of rice mixed with sweet potatoes. They helped me on with my fine woollen *chuba*. My stepmother was busy serving everyone tea. My uncle was there too, because Father had asked him to take me in his charge.

So, according to custom, I went to live in my uncle's *shag* and there, under his tutelage, I was initiated into monastic life. His name was Lobsang Wangpo, but everyone called him Wangpo la. He was in his fifties but believed himself to be extremely old. He looked like my father and they shared the same mannerisms, but you could tell them apart by my uncle's shaven head and his monk's robes. He had a reputation for being strict with children but he was gentle and lenient with me. He never scolded me.

I think it was in 1943, the year of the male water horse, that I went to live at the monastery. Some neighbours came to present me with *khatas*. My father and stepmother draped them around my neck. My stepmother began to cry. She stuffed some roasted barley into my pockets, saying that it was bad luck to leave the house with empty pockets.

I was put on a pony and led towards the monastery. Slowly the noise from the house faded behind me. I didn't look back. I heard only the sound of the horse's hoofs on the soft ground. Uncle walked ahead, glancing back now and again to check that we were following him.

More relatives were waiting for us in Wangpo la's *shag*. My half-brother was two years younger than me but he had become a monk the previous year. He was living with another uncle. Wangpo la gave me a tour of the monastery. He showed me round the *shag* and we examined every nook and cranny of it like explorers. There were four rooms and a kitchen. There were cupboards full of china and wooden bowls and ritual implements. From two of the rooms you could look out down the Panam valley and the course of the Nyangchu. I could just see my father's house in Panam village. I could make out tiny figures going into the house. I could see the shadowy figure of my stepmother scurrying about the yard. I recognised my family and the neighbours simply by the way they walked.

My uncle became my teacher and I had to call him *Gyen la*, teacher. He was now responsible for my wellbeing. That afternoon a monk came and shaved my head, leaving a tiny lock in the middle of my scalp. The next morning I formally became a *getsul*, or novice. My uncle woke me up very early. He showed me how to put on my woollen robe, so heavy I could hardly walk in it. Uncle explained the etiquette of the monk's robe. The lower section was not to be folded at the back with pleats, since this was a sign of vanity. The upper shawl should not cover the head or face, since this would indicate arrogance. There was a great art to wearing a robe. But today I notice many monks who do not observe the proper rules.

We were taken to the main prayer hall. I could feel the eyes of all the other monks on me as I walked down the aisle behind Uncle. The abbot sat on a raised seat. He was called Kunsang Doden, but we knew him as *Khen Rinpoche*, or the Precious Abbot. He was about forty and he was always grinning. He had studied in Sera, one of the great monasteries in Lhasa, and was treated with great deference.

Now and again, during the ceremony, the abbot reached out his hands in slow, deliberate gestures to seize a bell or *dorje*, the symbolic thunderbolt, from the table in front of him. I remember his deep, melodious voice rising above the chorus of the other monks. His body swayed gently as he chanted, as a field of barley will sway when a breeze disturbs it.

When the chanting stopped I found myself standing right in front of *Khen Rinpoche*. He reached out and touched my cheek. An attendant monk handed him a pair of scissors on a small tray. With one hand he lifted the lock of hair that remained on the crown of my head. He picked up the scissors with his other hand and snipped off the last of my hair.

"*Khyoed chos-la tro-ham?*" he asked. "Will you be happy in religion?"

"*Tro-la,*" I replied, which means, "Joy."

Then I was given a new name, the name by which I am known today: Palden Gyatso. The ceremony signified that I had severed all ties with my worldly life. Although I had not yet taken any religious vows, I was told that from now on I should conduct myself like a monk and concern myself only with religion.

I took the novice's vows a year later. There are four basic vows: never to take a life, to abstain from stealing, to abstain from falsehood and to practise celibacy. These vows are broken down into ten precepts and these I understood better. There is such a multitude of living things; it is impossible to avoid taking the life of, say, the insects beneath your feet. Yet this too is regarded as taking a life. So there had to be different degrees of killing. A novice or fully ordained monk breaks his vow only if he kills a human being or takes the life of an animal intentionally. A monk must eschew gold, silver and other fineries. He must avoid intoxicating liquors and abstain from dancing. He must not see spectacular shows. These were all viewed as worldly matters which would distract a young mind from its studies.

For a while I was allowed to roam around the monastery, observing its various activities. Many of the boys were younger than me; it was customary for boys as young as seven to become novices. It was said that a boy could become a novice as soon as he could chase a raven.

My first years in the monastery were like attending school. I began to learn how to read and write. I had to trace over what my teacher had written on a hard wooden board. This was called "dry writing". With a bamboo pen I would follow the strokes and curlicues of my teacher's letters. But I was not allowed to dip the pen in ink. After a week of tracing my teacher's script, I graduated to "wet writing". I still had to copy the teacher's letters, but now I was writing them on to a wooden board dusted with a thin layer of soot. This procedure lasted for several months. It was a year before I was allowed to write on paper, though that was itself a rare experience, even for older monks. Making paper was a laborious, expensive process and so the results were never wasted.

Learning to read was another hard struggle. Each monastic order had its own set of Buddhist liturgical texts which all monks were required to recite from memory every morning. Another uncle, called Choden la, taught me *pe-cha*, or scripture. Each day I'd have to recite a text I'd memorised the day before. If I made a mistake I'd have to hold up my left hand so that my teacher could hit it with a cane. Choden la kept a number of leather whips hanging on a pillar. He used to say, "If you work hard, the whips will stay where they belong." More often, though, he used the bamboo cane. He'd say, "Think of the cane whenever you are memorising."

A novice's life was hard. But the camaraderie that developed among the young monks and the great care shown by my uncle and teacher Wangpo la made things a bit easier. Soon I was either engrossed in my studies or doing simple chores such as cleaning lamps and fetching water.

The day started early. Monks were up by four in the morning and had to finish all private studies by sunrise. I would recite and memorise texts for two or three hours every morning. I can remember my uncle telling me that that was the best time to learn, because it was then that the mind was at its most receptive. A conch shell was blown at sunrise. This summoned all the monks to the morning assembly. My uncle and a few other older monks did not have to attend, but this was a privilege reserved only for monks who had held senior office.

The assembly began with all the novices lining up at the entrance of the hall. The long brass horn was blown and the elders took their seats. The young novices would then recite a prayer of dedication to Je Tsongka-pa, the founder of the Gelgugpa sect to which Gadong monastery belonged. After this we could take our seats. We offered prayers for the long life of the Dalai Lama, prayers that the whole world would be free from famine and plague, and prayers that all people could live in peace. Two cups of tea were served during the assembly. One of the duties of a novice was to serve the tea: he had to carry it hundreds of yards from the kitchen to the hall in a vast brass pot. Sometimes the pot was bigger than the novice.

I never had to do the tea round. A novice might avoid doing certain heavy duties if he came from a wealthy family that had made large dona-tions to the monastery. But I still had to attend to such chores as sweeping, cleaning windows and lighting the hundreds of butter lamps. During festivals there were thousands of butter lamps to light, and after-wards we had to clean and polish them. And my uncle was always giving me errands to run.

Most of my time was devoted to my studies. There were three ways that a monk could live in the monastery. Those with the intellectual aptitude could devote themselves to studying. Others specialised in ritual, and they would become experts in the different ceremonies and offerings and in the intricate sand mandalas which represented the abodes of various deities. Monks who were not intellectually inclined and who found ceremonies tiresome became officials who looked after the monastery's economic interests. They were the business managers who collected loans and taxes from tenants. Some of them conducted trade on the monastery's behalf.

One day, when I was twelve or thirteen, I went back to the *shag* for lunch and heard my uncle calling me into his room. My immediate thought was that I had done something wrong. My uncle told me to sit down and offered me tea. He pointed to a pile of tea, butter, *tsampa* and cloths. He said that these were gifts from my aunt's home. Then he

27

lowered his voice and told me that my aunt had died. I can remember how I shivered and how I thought of all the times she had fussed over me. She was the only person I had truly loved. It was with her that I felt most at ease. But now I had grown up and even had responsibilities of my own, such as the supervision of other novices as they carried out their chores.

I forgot about the world outside the monastery and devoted myself to my studies. I memorised more and more texts. I had a good incentive to work hard, because I had noticed that illiterate or lazy monks ended up with the lowliest duties. I found memorising very hard, though some students accomplished it effortlessly. Whenever a student had memorised a particular text, his teacher would ask the abbot to allow the novice to recite the entire text in front of the assembly. This was pretty terrifying. After the daily liturgy, the young monk would stand in front of the assembly and recite his text. I had to do this several times and I remember the silence in the hall, broken only by the slurping of tea. Monks who managed to recite all the liturgical texts like this were said to have passed their examination. But if a monk dried up in front of the assembly, it was considered a disgrace not only for him but also for his teacher. Luckily, I managed to scrape through.

Since these prayers are recited every day, monks tend to remember them for life. But my experience is different. My long confinement in prison has meant that I can no longer remember many of the prayers we recited in Gadong.

Once a monk had mastered all the basic prayers he could go on to further studies. Either you learned directly from your *pe-cha* teacher, alone or in groups of three or four, or you could learn from sermons given by a respected scholar. Gadong was just a simple village monastery and it didn't have a high reputation for scholarship. But the abbot established what we called *she-dra*, or a philosophy class. He invited a learned lama from Lhasa to spend a few weeks at Gadong in order to instruct the monks in philosophy.

Geshe Rigzin was one of the noted teachers at Drepung monastery, near Lhasa. Geshe had even taught our own abbot. I began to attend his classes. Simplicity and asceticism were manifest in his manner and appearance. His voice was very soft, sometimes almost inaudible. He spoke in a clear Lhasa dialect but you could detect traces of a foreign accent. Geshe had been born in Kinaur, in the Indian state of Himachal Pradesh, and had come to study at Drepung when he was sixteen. We called him *Gyen*. Every day for four months he preached sermons and introduced the more complex aspects of Buddhist philosophy. He said that those of us who really wanted to learn should enrol at one of the three great monasteries in Lhasa. He said Gadong monastery was like a well: there was water there, but not enough to swim in and if we really wanted to swim we'd have to find an ocean.

Even when I was eighteen I still had no idea of the world outside the valley. We had no inkling of the civil war then raging in China. I cannot recall ever talking about events elsewhere. The outside world seemed to us a wonderland of fabulous events and inventions and magical machines. Even Lhasa seemed a long way away and we knew nothing of Tibetan politics. Later, in prison, the Chinese would show us films about the Chinese war against the Japanese and about the Second World War, but at the time we in Panam knew nothing of these. In Panam only the shifting of the seasons marked the passing of time.

This tranquillity was shattered in October 1950. We began to hear rumours that the Chinese were about to attack Tibet and that the Dalai Lama had fled Lhasa for India. One morning some of the monks said that they had felt the tremors of an earthquake. Much later we learned that there had indeed been an earthquake which had affected areas in Kham and Kongpo. This was seen as a bad omen. The earthquake, coming so soon after the Dalai Lama's flight, seemed to confirm our worst fears.

I remember a rush of religious ceremonies. We held rituals invoking protective deities to ensure the safety of the Dalai Lama and the Land of Snows. But a few months later we heard that the Chinese had crossed the

Drichu, the river that marks the border between Tibet and China, known in Chinese as the Yangtze. That winter, the men from our village returned from Chamdo and we heard first-hand accounts of the battle fought by the tiny Tibetan army in Kham.

Two men came to see my uncle. A man poked his head through the door, stuck his tongue out as a sign of respect and asked if this was Kusho Wangpo la's *shag*. I asked them to come in and immediately recognised them as my father's tenants Yugyal and Topgyal.

"We've just come from Chamdo," they said.

I went to fetch my uncle. Soon the *shag* was crammed with monks eager to hear what Yugyal and Topgyal had to say. They told us about Zhango Dora, another of my father's tenants, a fearless, muscular man who wore an amulet that protected him from bullets. He had led the attack against the invading Chinese army, but the small Tibetan force was no match for them and soon Zhango, armed only with a long sword, found himself in hand-to-hand combat. Yugyal and Topgyal took turns to tell the story, pausing only to take sips of tea. When Yugyal stopped, Topgyal picked up the story without missing a beat. He waved his hands in the air to represent the swordplay of Zhango Dora. We all listened silently. Zhango killed many Chinese soldiers, but he was exhausted and sat down to rest beneath a bridge. Blood trickled from the bridge on to his amulet, causing it to lose its protective power. Then a shell exploded near the bridge and Zhango was killed.

We listened to this story as though it were an epic poem, not real life. There was no sense of panic, no realisation that our country had just been invaded and was on the brink of being conquered by the Chinese. I don't remember any feeling of anxiety. A few days later, Zhango's family came to the monastery to see the abbot and make an offering. But otherwise life went on as if nothing had happened.

A few months later we heard that the Dalai Lama had returned to Lhasa. In July 1951 he came to give a sermon in Gyantse, a small town just a few days' walk from Panam and the centre of trade with India.

My father came to the monastery and said that we must all go and see the Dalai Lama. He said it was the chance of a lifetime. It would be our first glimpse of the man we revered as a living incarnation of the Buddha of Compassion.

We set off early. News of the Dalai Lama's arrival had spread fast and we met dozens of small groups of monks and villagers heading for Gyantse from all directions. I could hardly believe the number of people I saw gathered there. People were camping in every open space and each party had built improvised stoves – three large stones placed in a triangle with pots resting upon them. At night people huddled up close and slept out in the open. A special clearing had been set aside for monks, so we found ourselves a level spot of ground and made it our base.

I've never seen so many people. Everywhere you looked there were people camping around makeshift stoves and columns of smoke rising into the air. Women were wearing their finest jewellery and elaborate head-ornaments in the shapes of bows, inlaid with coral and turquoise. Enterprising merchants had set up stalls selling all kinds of trinkets brought over the border from India. I paced up and down the dusty paths. Merchants sat cross-legged on either side, tempting passers-by with their displays of Chinese tea bricks, mirrors, cooking pots, spices, woven garments, boots and toys.

Suddenly there was a big surge through the crowd and the merchants quickly folded their goods into bundles. I could hear a military band and saw Tibetan soldiers marching. The soldier leading the band was wearing a tiger skin. The soldiers were followed by a group of Tibetan aristocrats dressed in fine yellow silk brocades, waving their arms from side to side. The aristocrats were followed by monks carrying incense burners and bundles of incense sticks. And behind the monks, in a richly decorated yellow palanquin carried by several brawny bearers, came the young Dalai Lama, looking out at the crowd.

It was my first glimpse of him. His radiant face peered from the palanquin. I won't forget it. All Tibetans look to him as the Kyabgon, the saviour. We believe that the Dalai Lama is the incarnation of Chenresig, the Buddha of Compassion. His presence in the Land of Snows gave all Tibetans a spiritual and political focus, being seen to protect not only the teaching of Buddha but also the wellbeing of all people.

Before that trip to Gyantse, I had never been exposed to the bustling, commercial energy of a frontier town. There I met people from the most far-flung corners of Tibet. Where previously I had thought of my village as the centre of the universe, now I saw Tibet as a nation. But no one in that thronging crowd of pilgrims and merchants and monks could have predicted that our world was on the point of such a cataclysm, and that the next time so many of us were together would be in the prisons and labour camps, beneath the eyes of Chinese guards.

We heard rumours that some of the wealthier aristocrats in Lhasa were moving their assets to Kalimpong in India. They were worldly enough to know what was in store. But the mood in Gyantse was festive: people were mingling and doing business and praying. Most of all, praying. I remember the contentment on people's faces. They would never forget their glimpses of the Dalai Lama.

We stayed in Gyantse for several days. I strolled around the makeshift bazaar. A crowd had gathered to watch a procession and people were whispering, "*Gya-mi, Gya-mi*", "The Chinese, the Chinese". It was the first time I'd seen anyone from China. They were riding stout Tibetan ponies, festooned with decorations. They wore the simple blue suits that would later be known as the Mao suit. This looked very incongruous. The crowd parted to allow the procession to pass: five Chinese riders, followed by Tibetan officials in robes of fine silk brocade and elaborate head-pieces. Later I would learn that one of these men was Zhang Jingwu, the Chinese representative in Tibet. But it did not look like the grand entrance of a conqueror; no army marched behind him and no one carried guns.

Much later, when I was in prison, the Chinese published a picture of people gathered at Gyantse when Zhang Jingwu had arrived. The caption read: "Tibetan masses welcoming the central government representative." What a lie! We had come to get a rare glimpse of our leader, the Dalai Lama. Not one Tibetan had gone to Gyantse to welcome Zhang Jingwu. But we would become familiar with how ingenious the Chinese authorities could be at making up all sorts of "facts".

We made our way back to Panam like children returning from a great adventure. My father said that it had been the best experience of his life and that even if he died tomorrow he would be happy. Tibetans believe that simply hearing the Dalai Lama teach brings benefits in the life to come. Back in Panam there was a big banquet to celebrate our good fortune and the fact that the Dalai Lama had assumed the political and spiritual leadership of Tibet. During his minority, Tibet had been ruled by a regent, but now that the Chinese had arrived and it seemed that difficult times lay ahead, the Tibetan aristocracy had asked the young Dalai Lama to assume power. He was not yet eighteen.

A year later we heard that the Panchen Rinpoche, the second most important figure in Tibet, was to return to Tashilhunpo monastery in Shigatse after an absence of twenty-three years. His predecessor, the ninth Panchen Rinpoche, had fled Shigatse after some dispute with the Lhasa government and had died in China. His incarnation was found in Amdo. It was announced that on his way to Shigatse the new Panchen Rinpoche might stop for a night in Gadong. We all worked together to clean up the monastery and make it beautiful. One group of monks whitewashed the walls. Another cleared the paths. We put up tents. I was to walk behind the Panchen Rinpoche holding a large parasol. But when the day came, the Panchen Rinpoche and his retinue stopped briefly near the monastery and did not even visit Gadong. We were disappointed but the villagers were thrilled to have glimpsed the Panchen Rinpoche. My father said how fortunate these years were, that we should get to see two great lamas with our own eyes.

Tibetans know the Dalai Lama and the Panchen Rinpoche as the sun and the moon. It seemed that all would be well now that both the sun and the moon were shining over the Land of Snows.

Chapter Three
The Revolt

THE TRIP TO GYANTSE made me more determined than ever to go on with my studies and devote my life to religious practice. I'd reached the age when a young monk had to decide whether to remain a novice or be fully ordained. I was nearly twenty and still very much the simple village monk. Education in Gadong was a private affair; how hard we worked was left to our own discretion. Some monks remained illiterate and served the monastery in practical ways. My teachers had encouraged me to memorise all the requisite texts. I'd learned how to perform complicated rituals and how to play some of the instruments that accompanied the rituals. I had worked hard and passed all the examinations. But in Gadong there was nothing more for me to do. I had a choice: either I could go to Lhasa and continue my studies, or I could assume some administrative responsibility at Gadong.

My uncle asked me if I had thought about taking the *gelong*'s vow. Almost all novices eventually take it. My teachers urged me to do so, saying that if I didn't then my studies would come to an end and I would be fit only for servile jobs in the monastery. I was worried that I might not be able to observe all 253 rules which make up the *gelong*'s vow. But in 1952, along with twenty other novices, I took the vow in front of our abbot and so became a fully ordained monk. Today I am the only one of those twenty still alive. Some were to die in prison. Others were beaten to death during the Cultural Revolution.

Rumours of the growing Chinese presence in Tibet began to seep into the monastery. We heard that anti-Chinese protests had been held in Lhasa. Families in the village began to hide their valuables. My own family decided to hide some of their jewellery and it was clear that some of the senior monks were engaged in hiding many of the monastery's priceless objects. We received daily reports of PLA soldiers in other villages. The Chinese, keen to make their presence known, had been staging theatrical shows and even screening films. I can't imagine what the villagers made of this marvel of modern technology.

The first Chinese troops arrived in Gadong in the eighth month of the Tibetan calendar in 1952. I was reading in my room when a monk burst in and told me that the Chinese were coming. Outside, three Chinese officials in Mao suits were reining up their horses. Monks peered out at them from behind their windows.

The Chinese delegation went to see the abbot. One of the officials carried several rolls of silk on a tray. Behind him another official carried a tray full of the best Chinese tea. They were accompanied by a Tibetan interpreter and I could tell from his accent that he was from Kham, in the east. He had exchanged his traditional Tibetan attire for the same dark blue Mao suit. I didn't witness the actual meeting, but later I watched them leave, followed by the abbot and other monastic officials. The abbot and the others were now wearing a small badge showing Mao's head on the left side of their monk's robes. The Chinese seemed very pleased that the abbot had agreed to wear the badge.

Our *changdzo*, or treasurer, was being particularly courteous to the Chinese. He said in his most grovelling voice, "We will cherish the gift from *Pon-po la.*" I was shocked that he had used the words *Pon-po la*, which means "leader" or "chief". Since most Tibetans could not tell the difference between senior officials and ordinary soldiers, all the Chinese were referred to as *Pon-po la*. This was only one element in the new vocabulary that was to creep into our language like a virus. The Tibetans were already afraid. Whenever they encountered the Chinese, their demeanour was subservient. Even today we continue to refer to all Chinese officials as *Pon-po la*.

As soon as the Chinese were out of sight, the abbot and the others took off their badges. The *gye-kod*, or disciplinarian master, took off his badge, looked at it disapprovingly and flicked the trinket over the monastery wall. Later, in prison, I worried that someone might have reported this incident. The Chinese called this sort of act "not showing a pleasant face". This was code for "is opposed to socialism".

The Chinese began to make demands on the monastery that the abbot found hard to refuse. The same delegation, accompanied by the interpreter, came back and requested a loan of grain. The Chinese assured the abbot that once the roads were finished, there would be an abundance of grain to pay back any loan with interest. The abbot agreed to loan some grain.

Then the Chinese set up an office in Panam and began to organise meetings. One fine summer's day a group of Chinese came beating drums and clashing cymbals, followed by children from the village. Dancers carried huge red flags, which they waved gracefully in the air. They went from house to house announcing that a show would be held that evening. They marched to the gates of the monastery and invited the monks to the show. I couldn't tell if they were men or women because they all wore the same uniform and their hair was covered by the same cap.

That evening almost everyone in the village turned out to watch the performance. I was too curious to stay away, even though monks are not normally allowed to see things. I found every other monk from the monastery already there, waiting for the show to begin. The Chinese had set aside a special seating area just for the monks.

We watched the dancers applying their make-up in a makeshift tent. This in itself was a tremendous show. An interpreter told us to leave, saying that if we all stared like this the women dancers would not be able to change. There was a loud drumroll and clash of cymbals and dancers dressed in the PLA uniform ran on to the stage carrying wooden machine-guns. They leapt high in the air. Their agility was at first impressive but soon repetitive. The storyline was not that hard to follow. The theme was always the same: the PLA are helping poor peasants with the harvest.

The PLA are rescuing a young girl from the clutches of an evil landlord. We would be forced to sit through this sort of thing many, many times.

Groups of PLA soldiers travelled to remote villages to hold film shows. Like the dance groups, these attracted huge crowds, huddling together in the open air, waiting excitedly for this magical display of light to begin. Some Tibetans were baffled by the illusions of the light: they would go round to explore behind the white screen stretched between two poles, expecting to find actors hiding there. Most of the films showed the PLA fighting the Guomindang and the Japanese. They always ended in victory for the Communists. I remember someone asking me why the Japanese never won.

The Chinese, you see, had *a message*. The film screenings and the dance shows demonstrated the power of the Communists. And there was a social message too. Chinese officials visited poor families and showed great concern for their welfare. They issued interest-free loans to poor farmers. Nor did they neglect the rich. In 1952 the Chinese began to set up offices in the Panam area and they invited influential Tibetans to serve on various committees.

They were generous too. Tibetans who worked for them were paid in pure silver coins called *da-yuan*. Even our monastery received huge quantities of these coins. The silver was later melted down and made into lamps and bowls for the offering of water to the deities.

The theatrical shows became political meetings. A Chinese officer would stand on a box before his audience and make a lengthy speech about how he and his troops had been sent by Chairman Mao to help the people of Tibet and how, once they had finished, they would return to China. They never mentioned Communism. The subject of the speeches was the development of Tibet and the improvement of our quality of life.

It wasn't long before we all felt the Chinese presence. Panam was situated between the three major towns in Tibet and we witnessed daily arrivals of more Chinese soldiers. They had been on the march for months with very little food. You could tell from their mannerisms that they were just boys of eighteen or nineteen, but they had the look of old men. Their faces were chapped by the wind. Their lips were dry and cracked.

I saw some women offering lumps of butter to a group of Chinese soldiers. They did not know what they were meant to do with it. One of the women rubbed her hands together and then pretended to rub her face. The young soldier nodded his head and mimicked the old woman's gesture, smearing butter all over his hands and face. All the women burst out laughing.

Day-to-day life in the monastery went on pretty much as it had done before. It seemed that the Chinese were being careful not to intrude upon religious study. By now I had learned to construct intricate sand mandalas which represented the conceptual universe of different deities. Mandalas are made from fine, coloured grains of sand and require patience and nimble fingers. That winter, Gyen Rigzin Tenpa, one of the most learned monks from the Drepung monastery in Lhasa, came to Gadong and advised the abbot that some older monks should be sent to Lhasa to obtain the *geshe* degree, the highest scholarly qualification a monk can obtain.

The abbot accepted Gyen's advice. It was considered very prestigious to have studied at one of the "Three Greats": Drepung, Sera and Ganden. These were the great monastic universities of Tibet, all situated several miles outside Lhasa. Only a few of the monks at Gadong had studied at one of these centres of learning. Monks who had returned from Lhasa were allowed to sit at the head of a row during morning assembly.

I suppose that anyone entering a monastery dreams that one day he'll go to one of the Three Greats. I was no exception. But when the abbot announced the names of the monks who were to go to Lhasa, I was not on the list. I remember being bitterly disappointed. Even monks have pride. Only now do I know that my uncle had requested that I be kept behind, presumably because he felt that my future lay in Gadong, that I might take up a responsible position there, become treasurer perhaps or ritual master. These offices did indeed hold considerable prestige, but I was young! I was earnest! How I longed to join one of the famous monasteries in Lhasa! Running away seemed to be the only option.

A few days later the three selected monks got ready to depart for Lhasa. I went to say goodbye. I placed *khatas* round their necks and wished them well. But secretly I had planned to travel with them. I had packed all my belongings into a single bundle. A few hours after the monks had left I slung the bundle over my shoulder and went after them. I left through the back gate so no one would see me and followed the path up the mountain towards the high pasture-grounds. I ran hard to catch up with the three monks. When I finally stopped running I was relieved to see that no one was following me.

When the three monks saw me they knew immediately what I had done. They knew that I was a runaway. For a couple of hours they tried to persuade me to turn back, but I told them I'd made up my mind. I can be very stubborn.

My mind drifted on thoughts of Drepung. Now and again, as we walked, one of my companions reminded me that I'd left the monastery without the abbot's permission. He'd say, "Palden, come on. Don't you think you should go back to Gadong?" I'd shake my head and keep on walking. I knew how much trouble I'd be in if I went back to Gadong. But if I pressed on to Drepung, perhaps my teacher and my new abbot would see that my intentions were honourable. Until then, I was a runaway!

It took thirteen days to reach Drepung. We had heard much about its splendour and our pace quickened as we drew near. I remember reaching the end of a ridge and looking up and there, in the distance, was the great monastery. We stood still, looking with wonder at the monastery, its shape distorted by the glistening light, so distant that all we could see were specks of white, like grains of rice. *Drepung* means "a heap of rice" and each of the buildings that make up the monastery looked to us like a grain of rice. The sunlight bouncing off the gilded roofs was so bright I had to shade my eyes. The white buildings stood out from the grey sweep of the mountains and the darker patches of the trees below. This place was to be our home for the next ten years. We approached through a park where, in the cool shadows of willow trees, monks came to read and meditate.

The monastery spread out like a town halfway up the mountain. Three mighty peaks rose up behind it. But you cannot really appreciate its size from a distance, such is the maze of narrow streets and cloisters contained within the whitewashed walls.

We set down our bags and stood in a straight line facing the monastery. We raised our clasped hands high above our heads and brought them down slowly in front of our faces, then held them in front of our chests. We prostrated ourselves three times – once each for the Buddha, the Teachings and the Community of Monks.

"We have arrived," one of my companions said.

We picked up our bags and began to walk towards the monastery.

It wasn't hard to find other monks from Gadong, since all the monks in Drepung are divided into different colleges according to the region they come from. There were four great colleges or *dratsang*, each of which was further divided into hostels or *khamtsen*. Monks from Gadong usually joined Loseling College, which had thirty-two *khamtsen*. We would have to enrol in Tsangpa Khamtsen, the hostel for all the monks from the Tsang region. In 1995 I visited Oxford University and was reminded by the different colleges and the students milling around of Drepung and its collegiate organisation.

When Drepung was built in 1416 it was perhaps the largest religious establishment in the world. In the 1950s more than 10,000 monks from all over the Buddhist world were living and studying there. Some had come from as far as Kalmukia on the banks of the River Volga in the Soviet Union. There were monks from Ladakh and monks from Gyalthang on the Burmese border. There were even monks from Japan and China.

For a few days we lodged in the dark, sparsely furnished quarters of an older monk from Gadong. I was worried about finding a teacher and a *dratsang* that would admit me as a pupil. The other monks already had a letter of introduction from the monastery and would have no difficulty in gaining admission, but I, the runaway, had nothing.

A group of us left for Lhasa, four miles east of Drepung, the city that is for all Tibetans the centre of their spiritual world. Everyone hopes to make the pilgrimage to Lhasa at least once in their lifetime. Soon, walking along the gravel track, I could see the gleaming roof of the Potala Palace rising from the floor of the Lhasa valley. What colours! The golden roof, the red walls which indicated the residence of the Dalai Lama, and below these the whitewashed walls that made up the base of the palace. This was the home of the patron saint of Tibet.

As we approached the city I saw an elephant. I had never seen one before. From a distance it looked like a huge boulder moving towards us, sending up clouds of dust from the ground beneath it. People around me took off their hats and stuck out their tongues as a sign of respect. The elephant stood in front of us. "*Salam!*" the *mahout* commanded, and the elephant folded its trunk and raised it in the air. The crowd threw bread and money. The elephant picked up the money and passed it to the *mahout*.

I spent a few days buying provisions and visiting other holy sites. I joined the long queue of pilgrims outside the Tsuklakhang, home to the most sacred of all the images in Tibet. The statue of Jowa had a graceful golden countenance and was studded with hundreds of precious stones — coral and turquoise and jade. Two attendants stood below the image receiving offerings and moving the pilgrims forward. The flickering lights from the lamps sparkled in the precious stones.

The shrine room was hot from the hundreds of butter lamps and smoky with their fumes. I promptly fainted. I was carried out by the crowd into a courtyard where the icy Lhasa air smarted on my face. One of my companions tapped me on the shoulder and we made our way to the Barkor, the road which circled the Tsuklakhang.

Lhasa thronged with people. The Barkor was lined with shops and stalls. Buyers haggled with merchants. Traders from Nepal rubbed shoulders with merchants from Kashmir. I noticed a mosque. It amazed me to see Tibetan Muslims. We called them *Kache*, a mispronunciation of Kashmir, since most of their ancestors came from that province. And the Chinese were here too: Chinese soldiers strolled through the Barkor followed by groups of noisy Tibetan children, mimicking their speech. A few jeeps and trucks had made it over the rugged paths from eastern Tibet. Outside Lhasa the Chinese were busy building roads.

There were some practical considerations to be worked out at Drepung. It was customary for monks from Gadong to join the Tsangpa Khamtsen but I was not admitted to the college. Fortunately, rules for admission to a hostel were not so strict, as long as you could find a "guarantor teacher". An older monk from Gadong called Shenrab Thonmi took me to see his teacher, Gyen Yongzin. Gyen Yongzin was the private tutor to a young incarnate lama called Tirab Trulku. Shenrab recommended me to him. I prostrated myself before him and handed him a *khata*. Gyen Yongzin looked at me thoughtfully, as though inspecting goods. He said he could recommend me only to his own *khamtsen*, which was the Kongpo Khamtsen. I was duly admitted. My name was registered and I became a full member of the monastery.

Then I had to find a room. Shenrab let me share with him. Several monks already lived in his house. My tiny room was bare but for a small mud stove in one corner and a few piles of dung and wood. The uneven floor was covered by a threadbare rug. A tiny window looked out on to a whitewashed wall. There were two narrow mattresses and two wooden tables.

Now that I was a member of a college and had somewhere to live, I could attend all the lectures in Drepung. I went to hear a lecture by

Gyen Pema Gyaltsen, the most famous lama at the monastery. We went to his *shag* and were led into a large room where he was already sitting on a hefty chair. He gestured towards rows of mattresses covered with fine Tibetan rugs and indicated that we should sit down. I can remember him telling us to study hard. He said that we had travelled from afar with "the hard earth and the clouds" as our only guides.

Life wasn't that different from Gadong. I got up at about five. At dawn you'd hear the voice of a young novice monk chanting the *Cho-khad*, followed by the note of a conch shell summoning all the monks to morning tea. Each monk took his own *tsampa* and was served four cups of tea. The fourth cup was a creamy colour and tasted slightly sour. The story was that this was because in the past the tea at Drepung had been made from the milk of the snow lion, the mythical creature supposed to roam the mountains of Tibet.

The morning was given over to private studies. I'd pray for the long life of the Dalai Lama and other great teachers. I'd end my prayers by devoting all the merit I had accumulated from my actions to the benefit of all sentient beings. Then I would revise the philosophical texts that my teacher had explained the previous day.

At midday we gathered in a *choe-ra*, an open and secluded part of the monastery shaded by willow trees. Each *dratsang* had its own *choe-ra* and monks would gather there to hear the teaching of the abbot or other senior lamas. Afterwards the monks would split up into groups and discuss a chosen subject, either the teaching they had just heard or some philosophical text. As new students, we were grouped together so that we could begin to learn the art of debate.

Soon we had slipped into the routine. But we could not ignore the worsening political situation in Lhasa. We heard news of more demonstrations. We heard that anti-Chinese posters had appeared in the streets. Chinese officials visited the monastery to hold meetings with the abbots and the high lamas. Later, some senior lamas were also obliged to attend political meetings in Lhasa.

In the winter of 1953 a large group of monks arrived from Kham and Amdo and we heard news of what was happening on the other side of Tibet. We learned that the Chinese had confiscated land belonging to lamas and monasteries.

I tried to concentrate on my studies but events outside the monastery began to impinge on our lives more and more. At the beginning of 1954 we learned that the Dalai Lama and the Panchen Lama were to travel to China. This made many of us anxious: how did we know that the Chinese were not going to keep them in Beijing? The monks who'd escaped from Kham and Amdo had described how the Chinese had invited lamas and village leaders to meetings only to arrest them.

A friend lent me a small, dog-eared booklet which contained the last testament of the thirteenth Dalai Lama, who had died in 1933. I was struck by one of the lama's prophecies: he warned of the rise of the "red ideology", which would seek to destroy the political and religious system of Tibet. He said that this had already taken place in Mongolia. (Weeks later an elderly monk from Mongolia would tell me how the Chinese had destroyed the monasteries in his country and imprisoned all the monks.) The lama prophesied that the Chinese were now infected by the "red ideology" and would one day destroy Tibet's religion.

So the Dalai Lama and other high lamas left for China. Every day there was news of more fighting. More and more refugee monks arrived at Drepung from eastern Tibet. In Lhasa the leaders of anti-Chinese demonstrations were arrested. The senior abbots and lamas were required to attend meetings and what the Chinese called "study sessions".

I had received a letter from Panam informing me that my father was very ill, so I made the long trek home. I went into the house and sat down with my stepmother. She did not seem at all worried. When I asked how *Pa la* was, she just offered me some tea. I braced myself for bad news. Suddenly my father walked into the room. He looked perfectly healthy and I was confused. But then it became apparent that my father and my uncle had summoned me under false pretences. They wanted me back because my uncle was old and needed someone to look after him. My uncle and my father did all they could to persuade me to stay in Gadong. I could not say no. I felt a sense of obligation, both religious and familial. I had no choice but to remain in Gadong.

Of course it was very disappointing not to be returning to Drepung, where my studies had been going so well and I'd had the privilege of sitting at the feet of some of the greatest lamas of our time. I could carry on studying in Gadong, but there was no one there to guide me. I kept myself occupied by doing chores in the monastery and going out to visit homes and conducting rituals.

I remember the flood of June 1954. It was a beautiful summer's day. All the monks were in the assembly hall when a novice came running in and spoke to the disciplinarian who was sitting in his usual place near the door. The disciplinarian stood up and interrupted the ceremony. He told us that the river had burst its banks and flooded the village. We rushed outside. The whole of Panam was under water. The water had reached the waist of my house.

A lake some fifty miles to the west, near Gyantse, had burst its banks. By the time the flooding reached Panam, most people were awake and able to escape to higher ground. But in the upper reaches of the valley hundreds of villages had been washed away and later we would see many bodies washed up on the banks of the river. Water covered the entire valley. The dry mud houses absorbed the water and began to crumble away. That afternoon the water slowly subsided and we went into the houses to salvage whatever we could.

We had no harvest that year. All the crops had been destroyed and we had to rely on reserve grains. The flood forced many poor farmers to work on the roads being built by the Chinese. While they rebuilt their houses many villagers moved into the monastery with their relatives. My *shag* became the new family home. But women were not allowed to sleep in the monastery and in the evening they wandered in threes and fours down to another building.

When I was in prison the Chinese announced that they had helped during the flood. None of them came to help in Panam. The Chinese were everywhere but they were far more concerned with setting up offices and a firm institutional foundation for their rule. Like a spider, China was spinning a web around Tibet and there was nothing we could do about it.

In 1955 the Chinese announced the formation of the Preparatory Committee for the Establishment of the Autonomous Region of Tibet. Chinese cadres came to our village to make the announcement. My brother had been appointed Secretary of the Local Committee. He was a good administrator and everyone in Panam respected him. The Chinese even gave him a salary of eighty *da-yuan* a month. My father said that the Chinese were like fishermen: they were putting out bait for Tibetans but one day we would be wriggling on the hook. He wanted to fight the Chinese and throw them out. He argued that once the road was built, it would be impossible to force the Chinese out.

A number of Chinese officials visited the monastery and distributed white enamel mugs to all the monks. Each mug bore the slogan "Celebrating the Inauguration of the PCEART", written in Tibetan and Chinese. This mug would become a symbol of Chinese rule. We used to say that we would never trade a Tibetan wooden bowl for a Chinese tin mug. The enamel mugs were useless, because when tea was served in them they conducted heat so efficiently that you invariably burned your lips on the rim.

The Chinese became more daring in their propaganda. To incite the poor against the landowners, their shows and films portrayed evil landlords. We were shown a film called *White-haired Girl* which told the story of a beautiful girl who was enslaved by a cruel landlord and then escaped into the mountains, where she was rescued, of course, by Communists. The Chinese were clever. They never said outright that there should be land reform in Tibet. Nor did they neglect those supposedly evil landlords. Whenever they established offices, they ensured that property owners sat on all the committees.

Inside the monastery walls we tried to go on as before. Gyen Rigzin Tenpa became a frequent visitor. The abbot expanded his philosophy class and introduced debating classes throughout the winter. Monks at Gadong began to receive a good education again. Gyen was a famous teacher and was always being invited to other monasteries, but he had found something of a home in Gadong.

That autumn, the autumn of 1955, my uncle and teacher Gyen Wangpo la fell ill. One morning he told me that he couldn't move his toes. Then the paralysis crept up his legs and trunk until he was completely immobile and could not leave his bed. I felt that his care was my responsibility. "All things that are born in this world must one day face death," he said. A few days later he asked me to cover him with his yellow ceremonial robe, and he told me to place the *Lhamrim Chenmo*, one of the most important Buddhist texts, near him. He began to recite from it. I sat on the floor listening as he recited from memory. His voice began to fade and then became a groan. When I looked up, I saw his hands clasped together as if in prayer and I knew that he had died.

We learned that the following year the Dalai Lama and the Panchen Rinpoche were to visit India to celebrate the 2,500th anniversary of the birth of Buddha. It seemed likely that the Dalai Lama would visit Gadong either on his way to India or on his return, so I could not go back to Drepung just yet.

The visit came sooner than expected. In February 1957, a few days after the Tibetan New Year, the Dalai Lama and his entourage arrived. Our small monastery was swamped with visitors. Young men carried their old parents or grandparents on their backs from the surrounding villages to see the Dalai Lama. We had to vacate our *shag* in order to make room for visiting dignitaries. The courtyard was filled with more than

1,000 people. I stood beside the Dalai Lama's throne. I remember that when His Holiness asked me if I had been to Lhasa, I was too frightened to speak and just stood there trembling. Nudged by an official, I managed to utter a "yes". His Holiness asked me the name of my teacher and I told him, "Gyen Pema Gyaltsen." The Dalai Lama said, "You must go back and continue your studies."

So a week later I headed back to Lhasa. My family now accepted that I had to go; they could hardly disagree with the command of the Dalai Lama. By 1957 the Chinese had completed a road between Shigatse and Lhasa and I travelled along it for the first time in a Chinese army truck. The journey took two days. It would have taken fourteen on foot. The truck was packed with supplies and the passengers were jostled about in the back like beans in a box. By evening, I ached all over and everything was spinning when I jumped out of the truck – the world kept on moving. We arrived in Lhasa the next day covered in dust.

I was still enrolled at the Kongpo Khamtsen but if I wanted to rejoin the college I'd have to serve as a *Mang ja*, which involves offering tea to all of the monks in the *khamtsen*. And as one of the older monks, I'd also have other responsibilities in the *khamtsen*. I worried that I would have no time left to study. I decided to try to join another *khamtsen* where, as a freshman, I would not have any responsibilities. I joined Tsa Khamtsen, a large college that was mainly for monks from Kham. Monks from central Tibet were not allowed to hold office, and this suited me just fine.

It wasn't, however, all that easy to settle down to my studies. In Tsa Khamtsen we were the first to hear of the destruction of the monasteries of Lithang and Derge. Refugees came from the east bringing news of the closure of more and more monasteries by the Chinese. We heard that monks were being sent to work in the fields.

The news became more alarming by the day. By 1958 the conflict had spread from Kham into central Tibet. Thousands of Khampas poured into Lhasa. Morning debating classes were interrupted by news of what was going on in the capital. Every day we heard more about fighting between the Khampas and the Chinese.

In central Tibet we had always viewed the Khampas as forthright and quick-tempered, but now we admired their courage and strength. Khampa refugees arrived at the monastery in increasing numbers. They were large people and strode about with a confident demeanour. The men carried weapons with them all the time; the women had bright red cheeks and decked themselves out in jewellery. In the east, the Khampas were getting themselves ready for a guerrilla war. They came to Drepung to seek the blessing of the high lamas. They arrived on ponies with weapons slung across their backs. The lamas gave them protective amulets.

This was supposed to be an auspicious year as the Dalai Lama was to take his final examination. The New Year celebrations were followed by *Monlam Chenmo*, the prayer festival. In previous years this had been a focus for anti-Chinese protests, but this time the *khamtsen* master of discipline had instructed us to be on our best behaviour and return to the monastery as soon as the festival was over. Monks came from all over Tibet to attend *Monlam Chenmo*. They came to see the award of *Geshe Lhamrim*, the highest degree it is possible to attain. Of all the Dalai Lamas, only the thirteenth and fourteenth had obtained the *Geshe Lhamrim*.

The *Monlam* ceremony began at the end of February, on the third day of the Tibetan New Year. I joined the crowd and sat praying among the monks and lay people. You could sense the tension in the air. The Chinese kept their distance. All the talk was about how well the Dalai Lama had fared in the exams, but trouble lay ahead.

On 10 March I was instructed to go to Lhasa to attend to some monastic business. Ten of us set off in the early morning. As we approached Norbulingka, the Dalai Lama's summer palace, we saw a man coming towards us on a bicycle as fast as he could, puffs of vapour blowing from his mouth. He stopped a few feet away and jumped off the bike. You could tell from his clothes that he was a young government official. He told us he'd been sent to summon all the monks to come to Norbulingka. He said that the people of Lhasa were gathering outside the palace to protect the Dalai Lama. Apparently the Chinese had "invited" him to a new military camp and he had "accepted". The official's voice began to tremble as he told us that the Chinese were to take His Holiness to China.

We rushed to Norbulingka, where, sure enough, a huge crowd had gathered in front of the gates. This, in hindsight, was the beginning of the Tibetan uprising. The crowd was out of control. Everyone was shouting. A jeep was making its way through the protesters. A Tibetan cabinet minister called Sampho, accompanied by a bodyguard, was being driven into the palace. Someone threw a stone from the back of the crowd. It landed on the canvas roof of the jeep, but then another stone hit Sampho on the head and he had to be taken to hospital. The crowd then turned their anger on another Tibetan official called Chamdo Khenchung. They were pushing and punching him, calling out his name. An elderly monk was trying to stop the crowd from hurting Chamdo Khenchung, but they ignored the monk's protests and carried on pummelling the official.

The crowd had become a mob. Chamdo Khenchung had disappeared, as though swallowed up. We headed away from the crowd towards Lhasa. I saw a blind man being led to the demonstration and remember thinking how strange it was that even a blind man had been drawn into things, as though he too had heard the story of the Dalai Lama and wanted to play his part in protecting his spiritual leader from the Chinese.

In Lhasa itself there were more demonstrations. Crowds had gathered and people were chanting, "Chinese out of Tibet! Chinese out of Tibet!" The mob that had been outside the palace came marching into the city centre. They were dragging the body of Chamdo Khenchung.

We walked back to Drepung in silence, scarcely able to believe what we had just seen. When we got there it seemed to be deserted: no novices in the courtyard, no one in the *choe-ra*, just a slow drumbeat coming from the Temple of the Wrathful Deities. I found a number of monks gathered in my *shag*. None of us could sleep. We went up on to the roof and looked out towards Lhasa.

The next morning the master of discipline told us he was looking for volunteers. I put myself forward immediately. The monastery began organising monks into groups of 100 and we were told to stand guard. My group was instructed to watch the areas at the back of the monastery. Some of the monks had been issued with English rifles. The Chinese had dispatched soldiers to lay siege to Drepung. You could see them encamped below the monastery, where the slope of the hill starts to flatten out.

One morning the abbot of Loseling College sent me and some other monks to Norbulingka. Our only instruction was that we should go to the north gate. Tibetan armed guards were stationed every ten or fifteen yards along the approach to the palace. And in the palace itself monks had exchanged their robes for laymen's clothes and rifles.

We waited several hours in the palace. Then five of us were told to go to the Shol Parkhang, one of the oldest printing houses in Tibet. On the steps we were met by a fat man in his late forties who began to lecture us on how it was our duty to defend the teaching of Buddhism from the assaults of the faithless Communists. But I just wanted to know why we'd been sent here. The fat man brought out a sheaf of posters and several buckets of paste. We marched around the centre of Lhasa pasting up posters which I only read once they were on the walls. They called for the Chinese to leave Tibet and asserted Tibet's independence.

The city around us was in chaos. People were looting shops. As we hurried back to Drepung we could hear more chanting: "Chinese out of Tibet!" and "Long Live the Dalai Lama!" I learned later that the women of Lhasa had held their own protest, led by Kundaling Kunsang la. I was later to witness her execution in prison.

Drepung was now full of newcomers: monks in laymen's clothes who were only recognisable as monks by their shaven heads. Some wore swords at their waists. Through the night I heard the cracks and rattles of gunfire and the explosions of mortar shells. We stood on the roof looking out towards Lhasa. The cracks of guns and the bursts of mortars lit up the sky like fireworks.

At dawn you could smell gunpowder in the breeze. The noise of gunfire and mortar shells went on relentlessly. We were told to return to our quarters, keep quiet and do nothing that might alarm the Chinese soldiers now camped below the monastery. We had no way of knowing what was going on in Lhasa, whether the people were gaining ground or the Chinese had crushed the revolt.

That afternoon a lone figure walked up the path to the monastery. He brought a message indicating that the people of Lhasa had taken over the Chinese military camp. The messenger added that the monks should remain in the monastery. But it did not take us long to realise that the messenger was a spy sent by the Chinese. I learned later, in prison, that other monasteries had received similar messages.

We knew that the Chinese would attack the monastery. It was only a matter of time. We could see that the Chinese camp less than a mile below Drepung was being reinforced. We could see a line of trucks. Monks began to flee up the mountain behind the monastery. I didn't know what to do. I tried to get some sleep in my *shag* but could not rest because of the constant firing of guns. In the morning this gave way to a menacing quiet. The silence of the monastery was broken only by the noise of the shelling in Lhasa. Everywhere I went monks were getting ready to escape or were already on their way. Most of the monks had fled during the night. Only two other monks from Gadong were still in the monastery.

The three of us hurried to Gyen Rigzin Tenpa's *shag*. I still regarded Gyen as my mentor. All the monks from Gadong held him in special esteem. Normally he would have spent the winter in Gadong, but this year he had been invited to Lhasa to attend the Dalai Lama's graduation ceremony. He was seventy-two and quite frail.

"Are you still here?" Gyen asked, with a smile. We told him that most of the monks had already fled the monastery. He nodded his head, saying, "Bad times are on the way." We asked Gyen to come with us to Gadong. He told us he was too old, that he would be a burden to us, but we persuaded him that he should at least move to a place of retreat in the mountains behind Drepung. I picked up some *tsampa* from my *shag* and Gyen told me to pack some of his books. That was all I took with me on the path leading up the mountain from the monastery, with the sound of the shelling in Lhasa behind us and the traffic of monks and villagers alongside us on the path, all of us hurrying away.

By now Drepung was completely cut off from Lhasa. Chinese soldiers guarded the paths leading to the monastery. Farmers from the villages below had moved into the monastery buildings with their animals. The path up the mountain was filled with monks and farmers and children shooing their family's cattle. Gyen was having trouble breathing and his heart was beating erratically. Every few minutes we would have to stop and rest. We reached the top of the pass some time after sunset and spent the night in a cave.

The next morning we were woken by another, louder explosion. The Chinese were shelling the monastery. We stood there watching the shells land on the monastic compounds. I looked at Gyen and saw that he was crying. Smoke and dust rose in billows every time a shell landed on the *khamtsen* and courtyards and temples. But we could not linger. Gyen could no longer walk and the three of us took it in turns to carry him on our backs.

In a few days we came to a monastery called Chimcha Ling, which was used as a retreat centre by the monks of Drepung. The abbot, a former student of Gyen Rigzin Tenpa, welcomed us warmly. We heard that the Chinese had entered Drepung and arrested all the monks they found there. They were being held in the assembly hall with their hands tied behind their backs. I knew we had to press on to Gadong. We would find our way by the landmarks of mountain peaks.

March is a cold month in Tibet and the journey was exhausting. The snow was fresh on the high passes and the dawn chill was bitter. During the day the sun beat down on our heads and our enfeebled bodies were soon drained of energy and strength. It took us almost twenty days to reach Panam, where the shapes of the mountain peaks were as familiar to me as an old friend. Gyen seemed to have relaxed and our companions were more talkative than they had been at any stage on our journey. But still we did not know what to expect. Were the Chinese here too? We paused for a moment at the edge of the village. There was no indication that anything unusual was going on. It was late afternoon and most of the villagers were inside their houses.

We walked slowly up the path to the monastery. We passed through the gate. A monk was standing in the middle of the courtyard stroking a dog. He seemed puzzled by our appearance. Then monks began rushing from all sides to greet us. They were amazed to see that this frail old man was Gyen Rigzin Tenpa. In the past, Gyen's arrival would have been marked by a fanfare of trumpets and lines of monks seeking his blessing. Now there was just this spontaneous, informal greeting. But the abbot, mindful of the dignity of ceremony, came down the stone steps, prostrated himself before Gyen and presented him with a *khata* of white silk.

The monastery knew very little of what had been going on in Lhasa. The monks there were used to shutting out the rumours that were always drifting in from the city. A man had actually been chased out of a neighbouring village for announcing that Lhasa had fallen and the Dalai Lama had fled. Tibetans believe that such auguries are bad omens. But now we had to tell the monks everything we had seen. We all prayed for the safety of the Dalai Lama. My companions and I were congratulated by the abbot. Monastic officials draped white *khatas* around our tired necks.

Chapter Four

The Arrest

WE FELT SAFE IN Gadong. People in Panam were going on with their lives as if nothing had changed. They thought that if they could just keep their heads down and get on with tilling the land, then life in the village would continue as it had for centuries, no matter what turbulent events were taking place in Lhasa.

From the top of the monastery I could look down the valley over the whole village. I watched old men sitting in the sun and women weeding the fields and younger men tending to the irrigation channels. I had looked upon these things ever since I first joined the monastery. The scene held no foreshadowing of all that was about to occur.

Gyen recovered quickly and resumed teaching. Nearby monasteries invited him to teach their monks too and in May of that year I travelled with him to Ingon monastery, in a remote area north of Gadong. The monks there did not seem at all perturbed by the crackdown in Lhasa. Gyen spent a month teaching at Ingon. I went back to Gadong, visited my family and then went into retreat. I was sure that before too long I would be going back to Lhasa with Gyen Rigzin Tenpa.

In June 1959 three Chinese officials came to the village, accompanied by an interpreter. They announced that everyone had to exchange their Tibetan currency for Chinese paper money. The Chinese officials set up a temporary office dominated by two large metal trunks full of new Chinese banknotes, and the villagers queued up to hand over their Tibetan money in exchange for these crisp new denominations.

We heard that the Chinese had taken over Gyantse monastery and arrested all the monks. But still I felt secure in Gadong. Our monastery had not participated in the revolt and my own involvement in the Lhasa uprising was insignificant. Of what could the Chinese possibly accuse us? In July I went back to Ingon to fetch Gyen Rigzin Tenpa and he was welcomed back to Gadong with great ceremony. Strange to think that only a few months before we had walked into the monastery like beggars.

One morning I was reciting a text in my room when I heard a slow drumbeat coming from the Temple of the Wrathful Deities. I stopped chanting. Then someone knocked on my door. A novice came in and told me that all the monks had to gather in the courtyard. He was very agitated. Outside, in the courtyard, the monks were looking up at the Chinese soldiers standing along the outer walls of the monastery, their guns fitted with bayonets. Some monks were bringing a table out into the courtyard. An old monk told us to place flowers on the table and a novice was sent to fetch pots of flowers. The Chinese officials said nothing; they just observed the preparations we were busy making for them. We offered them tea, as is customary. They declined.

The monks sat down on the dusty floor of the courtyard. I was sitting beside Gyen Rigzin Tenpa. The Chinese officials sat facing us behind the low Tibetan tables. We did not recognise them. These were not the same Chinese who had made up the cadres that had been stationed in the Panam district and who had got to know the monastery quite well. The soldiers watched us from their positions on the roof and the outer wall. The sun flung their shadows on to the whitewashed walls, the guns with their bayonets making sharp silhouettes. More soldiers were guarding the gate.

The senior Chinese official stood up. He announced that "reactionary bandits" had betrayed the unity of the motherland and kidnapped the Dalai Lama. He spoke fast, brandishing a fist. He said that Gadong monastery had to declare where its loyalties lay. Then a local Tibetan called Samling stood up beside the official and said that Gadong had been associated with reactionaries. He said that the monastery too had "betrayed the unity of the motherland". Samling, speaking in the Lhasa dialect, said that monks must cleanse their minds and learn to identify the real enemies of the people. He scolded us as a teacher would a child who had been making mischief. He paced up and down as he made these bizarre accusations.

At first I didn't understand what Samling was saying. Often he paused, as if waiting for a response. And then he drew a small notebook from his pocket, showed it to the Chinese official and began to read out the names of the monks who held office in the monastery: Tenpa Choephel, the *changdzo* or treasurer; Choedrak, the junior treasurer; Trinlay, the ritual master; the master of discipline. As Samling read out their names, they were told to step forward. Then soldiers approached. They pointed their rifles at each monk's face while another soldier shackled their hands behind their backs in tight metal cuffs.

Everything happened so fast. In Tibet there is an expression "the heart jumping out of the mouth" and that's how I felt. We were gripped by fear. I looked at Gyen Rigzin Tenpa. His eyes brimmed with tears. But the shackled monks before us gave no indication that they were afraid. There was a question in their expressions: "Why are you doing this to us?" These were the faces of innocent men.

The Chinese official stepped forward and Samling translated what he said. He pointed his finger at the monks and accused them of being in league with bandits. The monks stood silently, their heads bowed, while the official walked past them, screaming abuse. Then he warned, "There are some among you who have still to confess their crimes and submit to the will of the masses." He told us we were wolves dressed in sheep's clothing but that soon he would root us out. It was only a matter of time. The monks were led away at gunpoint. They were locked in a room in the monastery.

We had to attend a "study session". More Chinese officials had arrived, guarded by young soldiers. The officials wore blue Mao suits with a pen stuck in the right-hand breast pocket like a badge. Some had several pens in their breast pockets and it seemed to us that the pens were an insignia of rank: whoever had the most pens must surely be the most senior. The Communists said that everyone should wear the same uniform as a sign of equality. But they displayed seniority by other means. The suit of a high-ranking officer simply had more pockets. The Chinese were far more conscious of rank and status than the Tibetan officials they were in the process of ousting.

The "study session" was conducted by a Chinese official called Zhu xi. He was the local Committee Chairman and his dark complexion and chapped skin suggested that he had been in Tibet for a long time, for that dry, broken skin is the signature of Himalayan winds. Zhu xi's lesson concerned the recognition of "the three exploitative classes".

"The Tibetan people," he said, "have lived beneath the weight of three mountains. Today we have cast aside those three mountains. We have arrived at a new chapter in Tibetan history. The exploited masses have overthrown their master, a master who has lived for centuries on the fat of the masses. Now the sky and the earth have changed places!"

Again we were bewildered. We were simple village monks and the official's jargon meant nothing to us. Exploited masses? Three mountains? What *was* he talking about? He began to explain.

"Listen carefully," he continued. "The three burdens which weigh on the backs of the masses like mountains are the old feudal government of Tibet, the aristocracy and the monasteries. These three classes have oppressed and exploited the Tibetan masses for centuries."

We still didn't have any idea what he meant by "exploited".

"Do you recognise your exploiters?" the official asked. We shook our heads. The official paused, searching for an analogy. Then he said, "The exploitation of the masses is like a carpenter using a plane to shape a block of wood. The masses are the wood. The exploiter is the carpenter."

Our faces remained blank. The official lost his composure. He interpreted our incomprehension as obstinacy. The session ended with another warning that we should cast away "old thoughts". We were told we had "green brains". This was another phrase coined by the Chinese. It would later become a term of abuse.

The following day we were summoned for a repeat performance. The word "study" suggests a noble pursuit but in Chinese hands it was demeaned into something quite different. A "study session" involved keeping groups of us in a kind of quarantine and then subjecting us to a barrage of accusation and intimidation. Soldiers patrolled on all sides. We were confined to the monastery for a whole month and forced to attend study sessions every day. From my window I could see that the villagers had been forced in groups out into the fields for study sessions, herded and penned there like cattle.

The end of July and the beginning of August would usually have been a busy period. The villagers would have been getting ready for the impending harvest. But now no one was tending to the fields of barley. The Chinese had decreed that there were more important things to do than harvest crops. I worried about my family in the village. The elderly and infirm had to attend study sessions and so did children.

The second lesson explained the difference between "oppression" and "exploitation". Samling translated for the Chinese official. He talked of the exploitation of the "three big mountains". He took out some notes and began to read from them. He raised his voice. "The masses live under oppression as the ox moves beneath the yoke," he declared. "The ox is controlled by the yoke. He cannot escape from the yoke. The Tibetan masses have lived under the yoke of feudalism. But now, with the assistance of the Communist Party, they have shaken off the yoke."

It seemed very important that we should understand the fine distinction between oppression and exploitation. Were monks the exploited or the exploiters? The Chinese inquisitors were not easily satisfied with the answers we gave to their questions. They had been well trained and were sophisticated in their arguments. They had had village study sessions throughout China in which to perfect their techniques.

At noon we were divided into groups of ten and told to discuss the morning's lesson. I took Gyen Rigzin Tenpa's hand and led him to a group. None of us knew how to start a discussion. We just sat there, looking at one another. Then a Chinese officer and a young interpreter came to join our group. We sat on the floor; the Chinese all sat on small wooden stools. The officer explained to us how miserable the old feudal system had been. Then he began to explain the nature of class and the class struggle.

The officer told us that there were four classes: landlords, rich farmers, middling farmers and poor farmers. He asked us which class we belonged to. I replied that I was a monk. The officer did not approve of this reply. He said that there were class distinctions even in a monastery. He said that we had not quite got to grips with the Marxist concept of class and the class struggle. Later we would be categorised into rich monks, middling monks and poor monks. Because of my family back-ground, I was a rich monk. This meant that I had no future in the new proletarian society. Each person's class label would be printed on their identity pass. And before long the class label would determine everything, including access to education and employment.

The group meetings became a dangerous forum. No one was exempted from answering the Chinese officials' questions. We had to say whether we were the oppressed or the exploited. Most important of all, we had to declare whether we were the oppressors or the exploiters. For a few days we tried to evade the questions. Eventually we admitted that we really did not understand the subjects being discussed.

One day another young officer came to our meeting. "Monks aren't oppressed," he said. "How could they be? All you have to do when the conch shell is blown at dawn is take your empty bowls to the assembly and wait to be served." He laid particular emphasis on the word "empty". "But where does your tea come from?" he asked. He paused, pretending to wait for an answer. But we had learned by now that silence was the best course of action. So the officer answered the question himself: "Everything in the monastery is the fruit of the exploitation of the Tibetan masses!"

Meetings and study sessions were held every day. Our silence began to frustrate the Chinese. They thought we were just being obstinate. They were expecting monks to denounce one another and arrive at a sudden understanding of the class struggle. So they adopted a new method. All the monks who came from poor family backgrounds were summoned to separate meetings. They were told that they were from the "poor" class and should therefore identify with the oppressed Tibetan masses. But the monks said that the monastery had been kind to all people. Then a Chinese officer announced (with some glee) that the villagers had denounced the monastery, declaring it to be a prime exploiter and oppressor of the masses. We had no way of knowing if this was true, because we were allowed no contact with our families in the village. Later we would learn that, at about the same time, the villagers were told that we had confessed to swindling the local people.

Having failed to elicit denunciations and confessions, the Chinese began to punish individuals. Their first victim was an elderly monk who came, like me, from a wealthy family. The Chinese brought all his belongings into the courtyard. Next to his possessions they heaped the contents of a poor man's *shag*. The two monks stood quietly beside these piles of their worldly goods. The Chinese official launched into a volley of accusations, jabbing his finger at the piles of belongings. Questions were put to the elderly monk through an interpreter. A Chinese officer lifted a thick maroon woollen gown from the elderly monk's pile.

"Where did this come from?" he asked sternly.

"Wool," replied the monk.

The Chinese officer was perplexed by the simplicity of this answer. He assumed that something must have been lost in translation and looked towards the interpreter. The interpreter repeated the question.

"Where did this come from?"

"A sheep," said the monk, who was beginning to cry.

We all thought he was doing very well to have answered the questions so correctly and intelligently. But his answers were incorrect. He had failed to take into account the labour of the serfs. According to dialectical materialism and the theory of class causation, the monk should have replied that the source of the gown was the labour of the exploited serfs.

We were faced with this conundrum all the time. Once we were asked, "Who nurtured you?" We answered, of course, "Our mothers." This was the wrong answer. We should have said that proletarian labour had nurtured us. The Chinese attributed our slowness to our "green brains", but we were simply not prepared to digest all the new terms that were fired at us in the study sessions. It was not until much later that I learned how to cloak my answers in the language of dialectical materialism and class causation.

After months of keeping us away from the villagers, the Chinese decided that we should now meet them face to face. One morning in August I heard the sound of voices chanting "*Nga-dag sum tsa-med zo*" ("Destroy the three exploiters!") and "*Log chod-pa tsa-med tong*" ("Destroy the reactionaries!"). From my window I could see that the villagers were marching towards the monastery in groups of four, carrying vast banners emblasoned with slogans in Tibetan and Chinese. Two of the children from the village walked a few yards ahead of the procession carrying a large red flag. As the procession reached the narrow path that led to the monastery gates, the neat column of people fell into disarray. The villagers were stamping their feet hard on the ground and throwing clouds of dust into the air. They were shouting and brandishing their clenched fists above their heads. Normally visitors adopted a humble demeanour as they approached the monastery gate, coming in reverence with their heads bowed. I could tell that some of the villagers were embarrassed and made uncomfortable by the clamour of their arrival.

The Chinese had turned the monastery into an exhibition hall. The villagers had been marched up the valley to Gadong in order to view a display of the belongings of Changdzo Tenpa Choephel, our treasurer. The entire contents of his *shag* were there for all to see: rolls of fine wool; silver lamps inlaid with jewels; rolls of exquisite Chinese brocade and silk; elaborate ritual instruments; a set of wooden bowls lined with silver.

And next to Changdzo la's belongings were those of a poor monk: a broken teapot; ancient, rudimentary wooden bowls; a patched blanket; a pair of worn-out boots.

"Look at these possessions!" said the young Tibetan who was giving an enthusiastic commentary on the exhibits. "The exploiters live in the lap of luxury. The exploiter wears silk. He drinks from silver cups fashioned from the sweat and tears of the working class." Then he pointed to the poor monk's belongings, saying, "This is how poor monks live. The poor monk has only this thin blanket to cover himself on cold winter nights."

The villagers, now expert in the theory of class causation, appeared to be shocked at what they were seeing. They shook their heads at appropriate moments. They gasped with astonishment, right on cue. We too were made to line up and view the display in the courtyard. The commentator spoke indignantly about the inequalities in the monastery.

Changdzo la was not there to defend himself. He and the others were already prisoners of the Chinese. We had seen them being forced to work in the temporary camp the Chinese had set up just below the monastery. Two tin buckets dangled from the ends of the bamboo pole Changdzo la carried on his shoulder. This method of carrying things was new to Tibet. All afternoon we could see the treasurer going to and from the river with his tin pails and his bamboo pole. He provided a continuous supply of water to the Chinese in the camp.

We referred to this period as "*Gya-mi dong-pa ngos-su toen*", or "the time the Chinese showed their true face". We were sustained by the hope that the Dalai Lama would return and ensure that everything was restored to its proper place and habit. The sun, we told ourselves, will reappear from behind the cloud.

That summer, 1959, was a crush of meetings. There were denunciation meetings, confessional meetings, meetings to criticise reactionaries, meetings to oppose imperialists and even meetings known as "bitter memory" meetings in which we would sit and listen while a "serf" told stories about his suffering at the hands of landlords. We were expected to cry during such meetings.

In Panam the Chinese were beginning to redistribute land. They confiscated all my family's possessions. We were classed as "rich landlords", which meant that we didn't stand a chance. As the son of a rich landlord I was of course a fully fledged member of the exploiting class.

But you would have been hard-pressed to identify a sudden surge of revolutionary zeal among the poor farmers. I remember a very poor young man called Kunchok. He lived in a ramshackle house and made a living by travelling from village to village taking whatever work he could find. He often carried farmers' grain to the watermill. When the Chinese gave Kunchok his own land he wasn't at all happy, because he didn't like farming. He composed a song whose lyrics, as I remember, ran something like, "The Communist Party is generous, but I have no need for land! Please let me go where I want to go!"

The meetings came to an end in November 1959. I think now that it was just getting too cold for the Chinese officials. One day we were lined up and issued with a piece of paper. The writing on the paper was Chinese and none of us understood it. We were told that we should keep this piece of paper with us at all times and show it to any visiting officials. Months later a young Tibetan from Gyantse translated the Chinese for me. The writing on the paper said, "Name: Palden Gyatso. Age: 27. Class: son of a rich landlord. Political background: not yet investigated."

That last entry showed yet another way in which people were categorised. Some Tibetans were called *tsang-ma*, which means "clean". If you were *tsang-ma* then you were probably from a poor family and had never participated in any anti-Chinese activity. Others were called *tsang-ma med-pa*, or "unclean". I had not yet been classified. The authorities had not yet passed judgement on my political pedigree.

The Chinese officials who had come to Panam and Gadong to conduct the study sessions began to pack their bags and leave for Gyantse, leaving the village to administer itself. They were as anonymous when they departed as they had been when they arrived. We knew them simply as *Gya-mi*: the Chinese. They had never introduced themselves. When they referred to each other they used a title such as *zhurzi* (chairman) or *zhuren* (deputy chairman) or *shuji* (secretary).

Any hope that life was going to go back to normal was soon dashed. Higher authorities in China had decided that the officials had not been sufficiently thorough in rooting out reactionaries or eliminating the enemies of the Party and the motherland. So, at the beginning of 1960, the Chinese launched a campaign of "reinvestigation". This meant more meetings and study sessions. As someone whose political background was "not yet investigated", I knew I would be a target in this new campaign.

I remember a Chinese officer swaggering into the courtyard and announcing that monks had been clinging to outdated feudal ways. We had to reconcile ourselves, he said, to the fact that the feudal serfdom of old Tibet had been vanquished. The might of neither imperialist America nor our old gods could bring it back. But this was just a preamble. The Chinese officials then asked if we had been in Lhasa during the uprising. No one spoke. Clearly frustrated, the Chinese decided that the whole monastery was guilty of supporting reactionary bandits. They instigated a search for hidden weapons, moving from *shag* to *shag*. They found nothing.

I had inherited my uncle's *shag*. Gyen Rigzin Tenpa had the best room and the abbot had entrusted me with his care. I made him breakfast and provided whatever comforts I could. Gyen was hardly a demanding guest. He had simple tastes. Our lives had become entwined and we were very close. He was an Indian citizen and could have asked the Chinese to repatriate him. Many monks from Ladakh and Spiti, who were living in Tashilhunpo and Lhasa, had already been repatriated to India, but Gyen chose to remain in Gadong.

The new investigation team came from Lhasa. There were rumours that the previous investigating officials had been disgraced and had themselves been subjected to study sessions. The new lot were more authoritative and more crisply dressed. Gyen and I waited in the court-yard while the *shag* was searched. Gyen's belongings caused the Chinese to get very excited. We saw a young Chinese soldier thrusting a photo-graph into the hands of a senior officer. They disappeared into a room. Twenty minutes later they emerged and came towards us. The officer in his smart blue suit and supercilious manner told us that, incredibly, there were still those who refused to admit to their crimes and continued to conceal their treacherous activities from the Party and the people. It was clear that he was referring to me and Gyen.

Gyen told the interpreter that he was an Indian citizen and that he had come to study in Lhasa when he was very young. He said that I had helped him reach Gadong from Lhasa. Then he politely requested that he be repatriated to India. But before the interpreter had even finished translating Gyen's request, the officer was holding out a faded black and white photograph of a group of people. The officer demanded an explanation.

The photograph showed a group of Tibetans standing in a formal pose with the leaders of the Indian Independence movement. In March 1946 the Tibetan government had dispatched a high-ranking delegation to India and China whose purpose was to congratulate the victorious Allies after the Second World War. Gyen Rigzin Tenpa had been selected as an ecclesiastical representative and had travelled with the delegation to India, where they had been received by Viceroy Lord Wavell. Since India was on the point of gaining independence, the Tibetan delegation had also met with the Indian nationalist leaders. Nehru and Gandhi were both visible in the photograph the Chinese had now confiscated.

I was allowed to accompany Gyen back to his room. We packed some of his books and belongings into a small bag. I watched as he was marched out of the monastery and ordered into a waiting jeep. I rushed over to say goodbye to him. All he said was, "I shall be staying in Sikkim for some time." Two Chinese guards lowered their guns at him and commanded, "*zho, zho*", "move, move." He got into the jeep. I was never to see Gyen Rigzin Tenpa again.

A soldier took me to a small room which had belonged to a monk but was now being used solely for the purpose of interrogation. It was bare but for three wooden stools and a high wooden box which served as a table. Folded papers had been placed under one side of the box so that it sat level on the uneven stone floor. Two guards stood at the door.

The officer introduced himself as Liao. His face and lips were dry and chapped – that signature, again, of the Himalayan wind. There were wide gaps between his teeth. He smoked cigarette after cigarette, lighting one from the embers of another. Gyaltsen, the officer's Tibetan interpreter, sat on one of the rickety stools, waiting for instructions.

Liao's manner was severe and indignant; he spoke in a kind of bark. "You have concealed your identity for a long time," he said. "You had ample opportunity to confess your crimes. Our party workers have been extremely lenient. Still you have chosen to hide your crimes from them. This is very serious. And now I learn that you opposed the motherland and took part in the Lhasa demonstrations."

He paused to suck on his cigarette. "The Communist Party will be lenient so long as you admit to your errors. The Party will ignore your – misjudgements."

Liao took out another cigarette. Then he pointed at the photograph lying on the makeshift table. "This we cannot forget," he said.

He wanted to know everything about Gyen, every detail of my relationship with him. I told him all that I knew about my teacher's background. This was common knowledge at Drepung. Liao was unimpressed.

"We know that your teacher was spying for the Indian government," he said angrily.

I protested that Gyen did not have the slightest interest in politics. But the Chinese had already made up their minds: Gyen Rigzin Tenpa was a spy.

"You have to acknowledge that your teacher was a spy," Liao insisted.

But I was resolute. I refused to make the false allegation the Chinese were attempting to draw from me. Several hours passed. Liao became irritated by my persistence. Then he said something that I would later recognise as a standard caution. I would hear it many times during my imprisonment. Liao's voice was suddenly gentle and I could hear the translator take on that tone like some secret passed from one man to the other.

"Do you know the Party policy?" he asked.

"No," I replied.

Liao stressed that the Party's policy was leniency: they would be willing to forget my crimes if only I confessed to them. But if I resisted, he said, then the Party would "fight back". I said once more that Gyen Rigzin Tenpa was not a spy. Liao's voice sharpened. He insisted that Gyen Rigzin Tenpa *was* a spy.

"You can say what you like," I said.

Before I could breathe in, Liao's open palm had caught me on the side of the face, knocking me backwards. The two guards who had been standing by the door came forward and grabbed my arms. I saw the interpreter, Gyaltsen, step back. He looked frightened. The guards began to kick me.

"Do you confess?" asked Liao. "Do you?"

"Do whatever you want with me!" I shouted. I was enraged. I'd lost my senses.

The guards held my arms behind my back, tied them with a rope, then threw the end of the rope over a wooden beam. They pulled down on the rope, hoisting my arms up, wrenching them from their sockets. I screamed. I began to urinate uncontrollably. And I could no longer hear anything beyond my own screaming and the thuds of the guards' fists landing on my body.

After a while a guard untied the rope and before I could think straight Liao began to question me again. He wanted to know if I was ready to confess. I said that I had nothing to add to what I'd said earlier. Liao signalled to the guards. They put me in handcuffs and shackled my feet together with a chain. "Think carefully," said Liao, looking me straight in the eyes. "Confess."

They took me to another room and left me there alone. Later that afternoon a Tibetan man brought me some food. "Why don't you confess?" he whispered. "They'll kill you if you don't confess."

The interrogation went on for several days. I went over my story again and again, explaining my connection to Gyen Rigzin Tenpa. The Chinese were not interested in my involvement with the uprising. All they wanted was for me to implicate Gyen as a spy. But how could I do that? In Tibetan Buddhism the bond between teacher and student is based on devotion and trust. I looked to Gyen as my mentor. How could I betray him and live with a clear conscience? And what if the Chinese had not sent Gyen back to India at all? If the Chinese were keeping Gyen prisoner somewhere and I denounced him as a spy, what then? I had nothing to confess.

One morning I was woken early. Guards dragged me into another room. A tall Chinese official came in, wearing a long padded woollen jacket that indicated a senior rank. This man would later become chairman of the notorious Drapchi prison. He was known as Chairman Yin and I would always recognise him by his large nose. Yin was followed into the room by a young girl who, to judge from her two gold teeth and soft Lhasa accent, seemed like the daughter of a wealthy Lhasa merchant. But she had forsaken traditional dress for the uniform of the Chinese cadres. Later I would discover that this young girl was in charge of a prison in Lhasa. Her name was Dolkar.

The Chinese officer had a pistol in a holster on his belt. Dolkar began to ask me questions, beginning with my name. She took out a notebook and recounted some details about me. I nodded, confirming that the details were correct.

"We know all about you," she said. Dolkar looked at me and, seeing the bruises that darkened my face, asked me what had happened. I didn't reply. Dolkar spoke quietly to Yin in Chinese and ordered the guard to take off my handcuffs and the chain that shackled my legs.

Dolkar was much more confident than other Tibetan interpreters. She even seemed to have some influence over Yin. She did most of the talking. She told me to run through my life story from the age of eight, while another Chinese officer sat behind me taking notes. She only interrupted me in order to translate what I was saying for Yin and the other officer. Everything was written down in Chinese. Dolkar questioned me about my story for days. Some details were gone over again and again. The officer sat with us in the room, checking everything I said against what was in the notes, looking for inconsistencies. I was made to explain the slightest discrepancy between different versions of the story. Then the officer inserted a correction into the notes and I was made to sign my name against it.

The authorities cross-checked my confession against those of the other monks and villagers. The Chinese did this with everyone. They compared any statement you made with the testimony of your brothers and sisters and anyone who had even the slightest connection with you. They built up detailed dossiers on everyone. And they made sure you knew just how thorough they were. "But your brother said this," the interrogator would say. "Why don't you remember?" So your mind would start racing: *Do they really know everything? Did my brother really say that? How much should I reveal?*

For ten days Dolkar and Yin never once lost their composure. Dolkar was especially polite, speaking just as a well-brought-up Lhasa girl should. One day I was asked to sign the notebook. Dolkar began to read from it at random in order to reassure me that the notes were accurate. I signed the book and pressed my thumbprint on to the last page. They took the book away.

"There is still one problem we have yet to resolve," said Chairman Yin. "That problem is your involvement with the Indian spy Rigzin."

The atmosphere in the room was changing. Dolkar began to call me *logchod pa*, a reactionary. Yin reprimanded me about my role in the Lhasa uprising.

"I've already told you everything!" I said.

Yin hit me hard in the face. The two guards forced me to kneel on the floor. They pushed my head down. Yin leaned over me, repeating the word "confess". He took out his pistol and pressed it against my temple.

"This is the only path left for you," Yin said.

And then, as if feeling it would be better to die than go on with this suffering, I shouted, "Kill me! Kill me!"

Yin seemed taken aback. Dolkar began to kick me. The guards spat out abuse and tied my arms with a rope. Then again they threw the rope over the beam and hoisted me off the ground. I must have fainted because the next thing I remember I was lying on the floor with my hands and feet in shackles. Yin was standing in the room.

"Your case is very serious," he said. "We have not finished with you."

"You are an insolent reactionary," added Dolkar. "I would not hesitate to shoot you."

Some time in the summer of 1960, the interrogation finally ended. Yin and Dolkar stopped questioning me about Gyen Rigzin Tenpa and I was taken out into the monastery courtyard. The first thing that struck me was how exhausted the monks looked, as if some flame had died in them. They looked bewildered. No one spoke. I could hardly recognise my old friends. Could my old friends recognise me? We were all dressed in *chubas*, the clothes of lay people.

Seven of us were led down the path from the monastery, our hands tied behind our backs and all of us bound together by a long rope, as mountaineers are. We approached Panam and I heard the sound of people crying. I glimpsed my stepmother and my father, my brothers and sisters, for the last time. I walked with my head bowed low.

We were taken to a small monastery called Norbukhungtse, a few hours' walk from Panam. And so my imprisonment in "the new society" began.

Chapter Five

Flight

I'D SEEN NORBUKHUNGTSE ONLY from a distance and all I knew of its history was that it had once been abandoned. The Chinese had built two wooden watchtowers on the monastery's roof. Soldiers still in their teens leered at us as we were pushed up the path at gunpoint. More soldiers waited for us in the courtyard. We were handed over to a senior officer. Two guards began to search our belongings.

I'd brought my bedding and the few clothes my family had found for me. And I'd brought my prize possession — the gold Rolex watch my brother had given me when I set out for Drepung in 1956. "Lhasa is a long way away," he'd told me. "If you get into any trouble, you can sell the watch." Monks are not allowed to wear watches or jewellery and I had never worn the Rolex. But I had heeded my brother's advice and kept it with me at all times. Now, in Norbukhungtse, the Chinese took the watch from me. I was given a slip of paper and told that it was a receipt for the watch. The guards confiscated many of our possessions. They took away our belts and the long sashes Tibetans use to tie their *chubas*. We were given lengths of string with which to tie up our trousers.

I was escorted into a large rectangular room. Seven mattresses were spread on the dusty floor. You could tell that the room had once been richly decorated: there was faded paint on all the ornaments. My bedding threw up a cloud of dust when the guards dropped it on the floor. Other prisoners rushed towards me, stretching out their hands and offering to carry my bags. It seemed that they were welcoming me as a guest in their own homes. An old man found a space for me on the floor and laid out my bedding.

All my fellow prisoners were wearing laymen's clothes but I recognised three of them as monks from their cropped hair. They were all keen to know where I came from and why I'd been arrested. Most of them had been arrested for their "involvement" in the Tibetan uprising. Though we had participated only on the fringe of that movement, the Chinese still insisted that we were guilty of opposing the Communist Party and the motherland. This was a serious crime. In Gadong we'd been told that the Communist Party would crush its enemies without mercy.

There were 200 prisoners in Norbukhungtse, most of them from nearby villages. I would be held there for several months, and my hands and feet were never without their cuffs. My hands were cuffed behind my back and I could not even eat unassisted.

The next morning I was woken by the shuffle of feet. A guard opened the heavy wooden door and a kettle of black tea was brought in. We lived on this black tea and anything our families could provide.

My oldest brother was also a prisoner in Norbukhungtse. We were not allowed to talk to one another, but we exchanged glances whenever we passed in the courtyard. I worried about how my family would be able to supply enough food for both of us, as well as fuel for cooking it. Somehow they managed to supply us with *tsampa* and butter and the fried biscuits called *khabse*. We were not allowed to see them; they simply handed over the provisions to the guards.

This clever system meant that the cost of keeping prisoners was met by ordinary Tibetans. Families were told that a prisoner's treatment would depend on his family's willingness to co-operate with the authorities. Families believed that by giving food regularly they could ensure that their loved ones were well treated. But it didn't work like that. The longer families stayed in touch with a condemned and politically dubious prisoner, the more they exhibited behaviour that would be cited during the Cultural Revolution as evidence of reactionary ideas.

At about ten o'clock on that first morning, I was summoned to another interrogation. The Chinese officer wore the earth-coloured jacket of the soldier's uniform, but his trousers were the blue of a senior official. I can see him now, his cropped hair and large, round face. An interpreter introduced himself as Dhundup. Like many of the Tibetans working for the Chinese, Dhundup seemed nervous, a little unsure of himself. He wore the blue suit of the Chinese cadres.

The interrogation started gently. They began with the usual question: *Do you know the Party's policy?* What came next was as inevitable as a refrain. If I confessed, the Party would be lenient. If I refused to confess, the Party would be violent. The interpreter gave these phrases the gentle, rhythmic quality of poetry.

"Do you understand the meaning of leniency?" the Chinese officer demanded.

I did not reply.

"Leniency," he went on, "does not mean that the Party can turn a blind eye to every crime committed by a reactionary. If someone deserved to be executed and the Party chose to sentence them to life imprisonment, that too should be regarded as leniency."

I nodded my head, though not because I agreed.

The next day I was taken into another, darker room. A shaft of light shone through a single, narrow window and by this light I could make out the tools that lay on the table by the wall, the large stick and the lengths of rope. In the corner of the room there was a heap of handcuffs, chains and leg irons.

The Chinese officer launched into a volley of questions about my life since the age of eight. Once more my answers were noted down and compared with statements I had made previously. The interrogator listened quietly, occasionally asking me to clarify some minor point. The tools remained on the table, the shackles in their pile in the corner of the room.

By the fourth day we had got to the events of 1959. The officer was more alert now and analysed every statement I made. He was especially interested in discovering if the Lhasa uprising had been organised and, if so, by whom. He repeated certain questions over and over again:

Who instructed you? Who were your friends? I did not realise then that every person I named immediately became a suspect.

I insisted that no one had told me to go to the demonstration outside Norbulingka, the Dalai Lama's summer palace, on 10 March. Without warning, the officer banged his fist violently on the table. He picked up a handcuff and dangled it in front of my face. I blinked at every slight motion of his hand.

The officer began to question me about Gyen Rigzin Tenpa, accusing him repeatedly of being an Indian spy. But strangely the mention of Gyen's name was a source of strength to me. When the officer said he had evidence against Gyen I knew that he was bluffing. I told him he should question Gyen directly. I refused to say anything more. The officer tapped on a notebook, saying, "All the evidence is in here." Still I refused to corroborate their accusations.

The officer picked up a pen, placed it on the edge of the table and pointed to it. He told me that I too was on the brink and that confessing was the only way to save myself. This was my last warning. Two guards began landing blows on my back with the butts of their rifles. I slid from the chair on to my knees. My whole body was shaking.

The Chinese officer shouted, "Confess! Confess!" Dhundup, who had joined the Chinese in beating me, translated the officer's commands into our native tongue.

The Chinese were demanding that I denounce my own spiritual teacher. But how could I do anything that would bring harm to Gyen Rigzin Tenpa? I had no idea what had happened to him, whether he had been detained or deported to India. As far as I was concerned, I had done nothing that could be considered politically significant. I had nothing to confess. And no amount of beating could induce me to implicate Gyen Rigzin Tenpa in these preposterous accusations.

It was only later that I realised what great emphasis the Communists placed on confession. All meetings began by extolling the virtues of confession and the futility of resisting the People's Liberation Army.

I remember a Chinese officer comparing Tibetans resisting the PLA to eggs smashing against the face of a cliff. But every prisoner had to confess his guilt. The Chinese did not believe their work was done until the prisoner confessed.

Whenever a Tibetan was arrested some charge would be found to keep him in prison. Then the Chinese would use every trick in the book to extract a confession from him. They would talk to his family, his friends, anyone who had had the slightest contact with him. And if this didn't work they would find someone prepared to denounce him as a reactionary. Sometimes they blackmailed those closest to him in the whole world.

In Norbukhungtse there was a prisoner from Panam called Sumshi Wangyal. Sumshi was very stubborn and refused to admit that he had committed any crimes. The Chinese officer never even told him why he had been arrested, so Sumshi had no idea what he was meant to be confessing to. "I have done nothing wrong," he said, over and over again. Then one day he was told that his wife had made a full confession and denounced him as a reactionary bandit.

The Chinese had discovered that Sumshi had been having an affair with a woman in Panam. They revealed this to his wife and she, in a rage, told the Chinese that they had given lodging to some Khampa guerrillas. Sumshi probably didn't even know if these Khampas were refugees or fighters, but the information was just what the Chinese needed.

At first I was baffled by the authorities' insistence on obtaining admissions of guilt. Soon I realised that it was an important element of Communist Party policy. An admission of guilt was like saying, "The Party is right and I am wrong." It did not matter to the Party whether the confession was genuine or not. All that mattered was that it proved to the Party that one more enemy of the people had been eliminated.

I admitted that I had been present at the Lhasa uprising. This did not seem very important to me. After all, if the Chinese intended to arrest everyone who had taken part in the Lhasa uprising then they would surely have had to round up the entire population of Lhasa. But no amount of beating could induce me to denounce Gyen Rigzin Tenpa. So I was charged with taking part in the March uprising in Lhasa.

One morning we were all made to line up in the courtyard. A number of new Chinese officials had arrived. One of the senior officers stood on a step and announced that the investigations had been completed. We had been found guilty by the military court. Since the Lhasa revolt, the whole of Tibet had been under military control and the jurisdiction of military courts.

My name was called and I stepped forward to receive a single sheet of paper. The headings were written in red ink; the rest was in bold black Chinese characters. "Gyantse Military Division" was the only thing written in Tibetan. I had no idea what the document was. When the meeting came to an end we all rushed towards the young Tibetan interpreter with our pieces of paper. The young man glanced at the papers one by one and read out the number of years specified on each document. When he looked at my piece of paper he shouted, "Seven years."

I wasn't frightened by the announcement of my sentence, because all this time I had a strange, abiding feeling that this predicament would soon be over and I would be released. I was not alone in this: the prisoners shared the belief that we would all be freed as soon as the Dalai Lama returned to Lhasa from India. I had no inkling then that I would be imprisoned for more than thirty years.

We received our formal sentencing from a Chinese military court. There had been no hearing and the flimsy document was the only sign of any kind of procedure. All decisions had been made behind closed doors. There was no right of appeal. I had been sentenced to seven years' imprisonment and classed as a reactionary, a label which would apply for three years after the end of my sentence, as would the deprivation of all political rights.

Now that the Party had won, the official interrogation came to an end and there were, for the moment, no more beatings. But the questions went on and on. We were interrogated daily, asked what we were thinking and whether we still opposed socialism. Under Communism, we were told, imprisonment was not just a punishment but also an opportunity to reform ourselves through labour. This was our first task: to reform the way we thought. I was to let go of all that I remembered of the old Tibet and learn to cherish the new socialist society. Our labour was to contribute to the building of that new society.

So we were put to work. Every morning we lined up in groups for a roll call, then marched out to an open field which was normally used for grazing horses. The villagers had identified the field years ago as barren and difficult and had reserved it, wisely, as a grazing area. But the Chinese decided that the land should be ploughed and cultivated. In the cold spring of 1961 six of us were forced to carry a huge metal plough to the field. We had to devise a means of pulling the plough. We tied ropes to its axles, three of us pulling on each side. A young PLA soldier stood on the back of the plough, adding his weight so that the blades would sink into the ground.

The soldier was enjoying himself. He rode the plough like a chariot and when he felt we were not pulling hard enough he cracked a whip of flex-wire across our backs. Our only break was for lunch, but even this included socialist education. One of the officials would read from the *People's Daily* and then talk about other socialist countries and their leaders. We had to learn the names of our "fraternal" nations: Albania, Bulgaria, Czechoslovakia, Poland, Romania, Yugoslavia. The Soviet Union was on the list too; it was still a friend of China at that time. We also had to memorise those countries which were considered the enemies of socialism. These were headed, of course, by imperialist America and Britain.

We had to learn the names of the great socialist leaders: Marx, Engels, Lenin, Stalin and Mao. Huge portraits of these men hung in prominent positions in the prison. Stalin was particularly revered. Later, during the Cultural Revolution, Mao's portrait occupied the most prominent wall.

We worked that same field for nearly five months, pulling the plough day after day across the rocky ground. We came to hate the sound of the ploughshare grating against the stones in the shallow soil. Our one consolation was the food brought by our families.

It must have been in July 1961 that we were transferred to Lhasa. One morning, without warning, I was summoned from the field and marched back to the prison. Other prisoners were already waiting in the courtyard. The soldiers told me to pack up my bedding.

When I came out with my bundle of blankets, forty or fifty Chinese soldiers had surrounded the prisoners in the courtyard. Five army trucks had pulled up outside the monastery. Our blankets were piled into one of the trucks. The soldiers tied our hands behind our backs with coarse rope. I didn't know whether to laugh or cry at the sight of the prisoners trying to climb into the trucks, their hands useless in the coarse cuffs. They staggered; some were laughing. But the soldiers became impatient. Two of them grabbed a prisoner by his shoulders and threw him into the back of a truck. I was sent flying into the truck in just the same fashion. Thirty of us were crammed into the back. We did our best to make ourselves comfortable by shifting our bodies from side to side.

Four young, nervous-looking soldiers sat at the back fiddling with their guns. There were more soldiers above us, on top of the truck. Still more sat on a raised platform between us. On each side of the windscreen they had fixed two huge red flags. More red flags fluttered from the roof of the truck. Once we reached the road the truck soon picked up speed. Soldiers began to bang drums and clash cymbals. They indicated that we were to sing. We were only allowed to sing one song. It was called "Socialism is Good" and it had become a sort of anthem. Its lyrics were hardly what you'd call catchy:

> Socialism is good.
> Socialism is good.

In a socialist society people are held in high esteem.
Eradicate reactionaries.
The Imperialists are running away –
Like dogs with their tails between their legs.
People of China unite.
Let socialism rise like a mighty wave.

We had to sing this with great enthusiasm if we were not to be accused of harbouring negative attitudes towards socialism. We sang "Socialism is Good" at the top of our voices. Later the song would become famous for another reason. A Tibetan prisoner we knew had no way of telling his family that he had been arrested. When he saw another villager called Dhargyal working in the field, he sang his own version of "Socialism is Good":

Brother Dhargyal la,
Brother Dhargyal la,
Can you take a message to Lhobdrak?
Tell my family I've got food to eat and clothes to wear.
Take care of the children.
They should not worry.
Tell them I've been taken to Lhasa,
Taken to Lhasa.

Since the Chinese guards knew only the tune, they could not tell that the words were a little unorthodox.

The truck sped on, red flags flying, the engine drowned by the clamour of drums and cymbals. People working in the fields waved at us, imagining perhaps that we were some kind of theatrical troupe. They had no way of knowing that the trucks were full of prisoners.

Two days later we arrived in Taglung Drag, a village outside Lhasa which the Chinese had turned into a huge military camp. We were issued with our first uniforms. These were old army garments with the pockets torn out and dark blue dye thickly splashed over the khaki.

From here we were driven to Drapchi, a former Tibetan military garrison on the outskirts of Lhasa. That night we were packed into a hall and slept wherever we could find a space. We hadn't eaten all day and we were all exhausted from the journey in the trucks.

The following morning a large man opened the door and ordered two prisoners to come and collect tea from the mess. I had with me a bag of *tsampa* my family had sent and I mixed this in with the black tea. Soon the atmosphere in the hall was more relaxed. Everyone was chatting. The door was kept open so we could wander in and out at will. At first we were reluctant to walk out of the room, but slowly, one by one, we began to explore our new prison.

Prisoners were crammed into every inch of space, shoulder pressing up to shoulder. You could see the remnants of the Tibetan army, now prisoners of the Chinese. And you could see hundreds of monks, recognisable only from their closely cropped hair. We guessed that there were more than 6,000 people imprisoned in Drapchi.

For a few days we were left alone, with no interrogations or meetings or work details. We began to relax. I met many former monks from Drepung and we sat in the sun talking, telling each other what we'd been through, exchanging whatever information we could. One evening, when I returned to the makeshift dormitory, my companions told me that I'd missed a meeting during which a Chinese official had taken all their names and other details. These names were called out the next morning and my companions were told that they were going to be transferred. My name was not on the list.

The prisoners were being transferred to various prisons in Tibet and China. My companions from Norbukhungtse were moved to Kongpo, a remote prison in the thick jungle of southern Tibet. Kongpo would turn out to be a death camp. Many of my companions would die there of starvation and illness. The only thing that saved me from Kongpo was the fact that I'd missed the roll call. I was put in a labour group that was moved from site to site along the Lhasa valley, working on construction projects for the Chinese army.

We camped in an open field in rows of canvas tents. We had nothing with us apart from a few private belongings and our bedding. We had to have our own bedding, because the Chinese never issued blankets to prisoners in that early period. The tents were encircled by a mesh of barbed wire, so thickly tangled you could not pass your hand through it. A movable bundle of barbed wire served as a gate, guarded day and night by two soldiers. Other guards walked the perimeter of the camp, rifles slung over their shoulders. Each morning we were marched from the camp to one of the construction sites. The Chinese were wasting no time in building roads and institutions in Tibet.

I'm not sure if our lack of food and other essentials was actually a part of our punishment, or whether the Chinese were simply not prepared for the vast number of prisoners they would have to cope with. We had to find our own utensils – not an easy task, since most of us had been arrested unexpectedly and had had no time to worry about packing spoons and mugs and bowls. No container meant no food. Some prisoners had brought their own wooden bowls, but these soon cracked and were unusable. Tibetan butter tea greased the bowl and made it shine. But the rations of hot prison broth took away the shine, broke down the grease and the bowls began to fall apart.

Food soon became a serious problem in Taglung Drag. My family could no longer supply me with provisions as they didn't know where I was. I couldn't stop thinking about food. We were all preoccupied by the search for things to eat. We were served black tea in the morning and a bowl of thin soup with shreds of cabbage in the evening. This menu never changed. We were given a ration of four ounces of *tsampa* in the evening which we were meant to use the following day. But many prisoners just couldn't wait that long and would gobble it down there and then. This meant that they would have nothing for lunch the next day.

In the evenings we returned to the compound for our ladleful of soup. If you were lucky enough to have a big bowl, then you'd get the entire contents of the ladle. If you had only a small bowl, you might get only half a ladle. There were no second helpings; it all came down to the size of your container.

This made eating utensils the most prized possessions in the whole prison system. Some prisoners had obtained old tin cans which had originally contained the rations issued to Chinese soldiers. We scoured rubbish heaps for these precious cans. They rusted very quickly: holes would appear after a month or so, rendering them useless. Prisoners tried to patch up the cans by beating them into a new, smaller shape. But the most sought-after utensils of all were the galvanised cans with the yellow stain inside; the yellow stain that meant they were proof against rust.

We learned not to wash the cans too frequently or brush them with anything abrasive. If you rubbed off the yellow stain then the can would rust and you'd be left with the same holes you got in the cheap cans. The galvanised cans originally contained pork and sometimes there would be tiny strings of meat caught in the seams. Such cans were savoured as though they were extraordinary delicacies.

I found one such can near an army barracks and I treasured it so much I even made a woollen case for it so I could keep it with me at all times. You could exchange a galvanised can for coral or turquoise or a gold ring, for such precious stones had no value to prisoners whose sole concern was survival.

The shortage of food soon became critical. There was no way we could survive on our meagre ration of *tsampa*. I could hardly bear the weight of my own body. This is how starvation begins. I woke up one morning to find that two prisoners had died during the night and it was not long before we were going to sleep unsure of which of us would be alive when we woke.

Life in the monastery had helped me to discipline myself. I divided my ration of *tsampa* into minute portions and allowed myself a mouthful at regular intervals. We boiled up the leather from our boots into a thick porridge. Prisoners ate anything they could lay their hands on. Some even ate grass, which made them bloated and extremely ill.

We endured this deprivation for more than a year. Later the Chinese would explain how the Soviet Union, previously a good socialist ally of China, had cancelled all her aid to China and demanded repayment of her loans. One of the Chinese officers declared that the Soviets had demanded their repayments in grain and that this was the reason the whole of China was facing severe famine. The Chinese never conceded that the failure of their agricultural policies might have been to blame for the shortage of grain.

Towards the end of 1962 we gathered again at Drapchi. We were made to attend mass meetings at which we were asked to give an account of our experiences. Prisoners had come to Lhasa from all over Tibet and we began to discover that many of those arrested in 1960 had died in the previous two years. But the authorities continued to read out our names from the old lists. A name would be read out, there would be no reply, then prisoners would shout back, "Died of starvation."

The senior Chinese officers knew that something was wrong but could not admit it. We were warned that we were not allowed to refer to death by starvation. How could anyone starve in a socialist society? It was a great embarrassment for the Chinese. The names were read out again. Long silences followed the names of the dead. Officers waited for a response, scanning the crowd, but none came. Then someone answered, "*U-chi log-la don-pa-re*", which means "the breath left him". The Chinese officers seemed happy with this response, because it implied no responsibility on the part of the new socialist society. So, as the roll call went on, whenever they read out the name of someone who had died, we simply replied, "The breath left him."

After this we were put into smaller groups and a Chinese officer came to talk to us through a Tibetan interpreter. He seemed genuinely moved by our stories and told us that we would all be sent back to our local district prisons, which would, in my case, mean Norbukhungtse. The Chinese did nothing without good reason and it soon became apparent that the Tibetan prisoners were being dispersed in these small groups in order to prevent them rioting. India and China were on the verge of war and the Chinese were well aware that hundreds of thousands of Tibetan prisoners represented a serious threat to their internal security. So what seemed like compassion was just another strategy, a device to keep us calm.

A few months before I was returned to Norbukhungtse, the prison meetings began to concentrate on a new theme: the denunciation of "expansionist" India and her leader, Nehru, whom the Chinese referred to as "the running dog of the imperialists". The more the officials denounced India, the more hopeful we were that Tibet would soon be liberated. We had no idea of what was going on outside the prison walls, but the vehemence of China's denunciations of India convinced us that the Dalai Lama had been able to muster international support. We prayed that we would soon be free again. Everyone in the prison kept whispering, "It will be soon."

Some time in November a group of us were prodded into the back of another truck and transferred back to Norbukhungtse. We could tell that the Chinese officials were alarmed at what was happening. The way they were so indignant about India "eating away" at Chinese territory just made us laugh. Some of the braver prisoners actually said, "But this is just what you have been doing to Tibet." The Chinese were surprisingly tolerant of these remarks. Whenever there was a dangerous period outside the prison, rules inside the prison were relaxed. We began to hear more news of our families. I learned that mine had suffered badly and that all our land had been confiscated.

The Chinese even began to release prisoners. Every day another batch of five to ten were allowed to return home. The prospect of freedom was a fresh resource of strength to us. We would gather in the courtyard to say goodbye to those lucky enough to be going to join their families once again, and they would tell us not to worry, that it would be our turn soon. Between October and December 1962 our spirits were high. It seemed that all we had to do was wait.

I had no reason to think that I would not be released. I'd decided to go back to the monastery at Gadong. I'd heard that a number of monks were still living there. Every day I imagined that it was my turn to say goodbye to the other prisoners, to walk out of the gate and climb into the truck for the journey home. Then, one cold morning in December, five of the twenty prisoners who shared the room were told to pack their bedding. I was one of them.

I packed my things into a bundle. I could hear laughter and chattering. Everyone was smiling. I walked out into the open yard where the others were already waiting. We thought it was only a matter of a few formalities and we would be on our way home. But we waited and waited and nothing happened.

Two army jeeps drove into the courtyard carrying a group of high-ranking officials, recognisable from their blue woollen suits. The prison officers rushed out to welcome them. They were all laughing and shaking hands. We just waited. We waited for several hours but still nothing happened.

In the afternoon, a Tibetan interpreter told us to return to our room. He said we would be released in the evening. I waited in the room. We were starting to get anxious. I wasn't sure if I should unpack my bedding. Then a guard came to lock the cell. He told us that we wouldn't be going home tonight.

The next morning we were given a copy of the newspaper. A banner headline declared "Victory to China!" That was all we needed to know. My hopes of release vanished and I thought of what was now in store – the hunger, the meagre rations, the work and the beatings. But I had to keep my anger inside; there was nothing I could do.

We were summoned to a meeting in the courtyard where we found the Chinese in a celebratory mood. They walked with a new, proud briskness. One of the officers made a victory speech. He told us how powerful China was and praised the magnanimity of the PLA in declaring a cease-fire. Then he denounced the Dalai Lama.

We all noticed a sudden change in Chinese attitudes towards Tibet's spiritual and political leader. In the past the Communists had been careful not to condemn the Dalai Lama personally, but now he was freely denounced as a reactionary. We were told that sooner or later the Indians would send him back to Tibet. One of the officers said, "Your hope of separating Tibet from the motherland has been extinguished for ever."

I knew now that I was not going to be released and I began to think about escaping. After careful questioning, without alerting all twenty prisoners in the cell to my plans, I was able to identify six other prisoners who were prepared to attempt escape. There was a sixty-eight-year-old man called Gyalpo and his son, Wangyal. Gyalpo said that he would rather die trying to escape than remain in prison. There was another monk from Gadong called Loden Kalsang. I didn't know Loden very well but since we were from the same monastery I felt that I could trust him. There was a young man, a nomad, called Dhargye. His knowledge of the mountains and the high plateau could be invaluable. The rest of his family had already escaped to India and Dhargye wanted to join them.

It was agreed that I should be in sole charge of organising the escape. It was clear that we could not escape during work periods; the only option was to flee during the night. I knew the layout of Norbukhungtse very well and thought there was a way out of the prison. Our cell had previously been used as a kitchen and, at the back, there was a door through which wood and yak dung had been brought into the monastery. When I first came to Norbukhungtse I was set to work blocking up this opening and I knew it would be easy to remove some of the mud bricks.

One morning, when the guard came in to take us to work, I said that I was feeling sick. I was in luck. He made no comment but left me alone, locking the door behind him. I went to the back of the cell and began to dig into the soft mud bricks with a stick. The mud crumbled easily and soon I could feel the bricks moving. I knew I couldn't push them out, as the noise would have alerted the guard. Instead, I made enough space to get my fingers round the bricks so that I would be able to remove them one by one. We would have to go that night, before my excavations were discovered. When my cellmates returned from work that evening, I told the old man that we were going tonight and asked him to pass on the message.

At about midnight I crept to the back of the cell and removed the mud bricks from the old doorway. When I saw a single star shining through the hole I knew I would be able to get my shoulders through it. The old man climbed through after me, followed by his son and the other prisoners. I told them to stay close to the wall. Guards paced to and fro above us, but the wall was too high for them to notice us in the dark. The last prisoner came through the hole in the wall and we began to walk down the hill.

Dogs barked as we approached the village and I was afraid the noise might alert the guards. I imagined the light of their torches picking us out as we made our way down the hillside. We walked all night under a bright moon, heading for the mountains. By sunrise we had reached the top of a ridge and looked down at the whole valley filled with the orange glow of that early light. We stopped to rest in a small cave and soon fell asleep.

Dhargye woke me up. He took me to the mouth of the cave and pointed to the group of Chinese soldiers riding on horseback towards us. Looking down the valley we could see soldiers converging on the village from all directions. They were after us. We decided immediately to head further up into the mountains and make for the Bhutanese border, a journey of about four or five days.

It was the middle of winter and the passes were covered in snow. We left a trail of footprints in the snow which I knew would give us away to the Chinese soldiers pursuing us. We had to walk during the night and rest all day. Once the sun had disappeared, the temperature fell below zero and our scanty clothes would not have kept us from freezing to death. Walking kept us warm and the moonlight was enough to see by. The days were warm and we squinted at the glare from the sun reflecting off the packed snow. All we had with us was *tsampa*. We added a little water to it and that was our sustenance.

We walked across the mountains for four nights and five days, knowing that a search party was on our heels. Dhargye was our guide and he knew the mountains like the back of his hands. On the fifth day we descended a high mountain pass into a valley called Gamba Changtang. Dhargye told us that all we had to do was cross a small pass and then we would be over the border and safe. But just as we looked out towards Bhutan we saw a group of soldiers riding through the snow on dark horses towards us from the east, and at the same time gunshots rang out behind us. My companions began to run. I jumped behind a low stone wall, a corral built by nomads. A bullet hit a stone near me and the sudden whistling sound of its impact was deafening. I pressed myself as close to the wall as I could and held my breath, listening to the gunshots and the footsteps of the soldiers running towards me through the snow. The next thing I knew, the butt of a rifle was landing on my head and back. I lost my hearing – there was just a ringing sound deep in my head – and before I could regain my balance two young soldiers had tied my hands behind my back and hauled me up by the shoulders. My companions had also been caught and I could see the old man being beaten by three soldiers. Others soldiers were beating his son.

We were taken to a village called Wangden Bartso. People crowded on either side of the narrow mud track, shouting, "Down with reactionaries!" and waving their fists above their heads. We were paraded in front of the villagers and some called out, "Reactionaries should be punished!" They were just afraid of the Chinese and knew that if they did not condemn us then they would be accused of helping reactionaries to escape. I tried not to think of what lay ahead.

That night we were herded into a cowshed. In the middle of the night we heard soft footsteps approach the shed, pause, then recede. At dawn we found that some food had been left for us and this we devoured with the hunger of animals.

Chapter Six

No Escape under the Blue Sky

WE ARRIVED AT NORBUKHUNGTSE at sunset and the prison seemed very peaceful in the evening light. The main gate creaked as the guards pushed it open and that sound was enough for the other prisoners to know that we had returned. The prisoners were assembled in the courtyard to watch as the guards went through the formalities of handing us over. Warders paced back and forth. But for their footsteps, the prison was silent. One of the guards ordered us to bow, so we lowered our heads. Then the prisoners began to shout, "Down with the reactionaries! Down with the reactionaries!" We had heard this before, but not the slogan that followed. "*Log chodpa tsa-med tong*," the prisoners cried. They were calling for the execution of reactionaries.

The noise subsided and a prisoner I knew called Yamphel took a few steps towards us. He was a good man, much respected by the other prisoners, but it became apparent that he had been instructed to carry out a *thamzing* or "struggle session". He made the obligatory denunciation about reactionaries betraying "the kindness of the Party", shaking and stumbling over his words as he did so. Then another prisoner stepped forward, one of the very few prisoners with a beard. He too made a rousing denunciation of reactionaries. He raised his fist, leaned close to us and said, "Your time is up on this earth." I was shaken by what he said, afraid that now the Chinese would be able to say that fellow prisoners had demanded our execution.

That night we were kept outside, with no bedding or blankets to protect us from the extreme cold. My body ached. The sharp cold steel of the cuffs bit deep into my wrists and ankles. I tried to tuck my sleeves and my trousers between the steel and my skin but they slipped out straight away. We were too exhausted to struggle against the hunger and the cold and at some point I fell asleep. I was woken by the warmth of the sun on my face.

We were transferred to Gyantse prison, one of the main prisons in the Tsang region. Seven of us were prodded into two carts. Guards travelled with us. We were not allowed to speak and it took the whole day to cover the distance to Gyantse. There was no light there. A few warders came out with torches and pushed us briskly into a room. I told my companions that it was a fact we had escaped; we could not deny that. The important thing was that we should not blame each other or implicate anyone else.

It was in Gyantse that I had first witnessed the Chinese invasion of Tibet and now I had returned as a prisoner of those invaders. But I also had fond memories of the town, because it was here that I had first seen the Dalai Lama. The prison used to be a Tibetan government manorial estate. It was built from the traditional mud bricks and the Chinese had made only a few modifications in order to convert it to a prison. The Chinese kept over 2,000 prisoners in Gyantse, most of them members of what used to be the Tibetan army.

I was separated from my six companions the day after we arrived at Gyantse. From now on I would see them only during meetings in the prison yard. I was placed in *tsuk* (cell) number one, along with eleven others. They welcomed me as though I were a guest in their own homes. The cell was new and clean and I guessed that the prisoners had had to build their own prison, as an act of what the Communists called "contributing to socialist construction".

The cell was a simple rectangular room built from mud bricks with raised platforms on each side covered with thin straw mats to serve as beds. I remember the smell of fresh mud. Two notices were pinned by the door, one each in Tibetan and Chinese. These listed the rules of the prison. Rule one: Obey the guards at all times. Rule two: Prisoners must not spread gossip or defame socialism. Rule three: Prisoners must not communicate with relatives or friends outside the prison. Rule four: No sticks, stones or ropes to be brought into the cell. And so on.

Two narrow openings high up on the wall served as windows. Each man's space on the platform became his private domain. It was an unwritten rule that one prisoner should not intrude upon another's space, for we all knew how important that was. Some time later the authorities would move us from cell to cell at regular intervals and the security of that private space was ours no longer. Two huge sanitary buckets were kept in the corner of the cell and during the summer the smell of fresh mud would give way to the stench of human waste. Each morning, by rote, two of us would empty the buckets. We went out to work during the day and at night the door of the cell was locked behind us.

I was interrogated again, this time for a month. The interrogation began on my second day at Gyantse. I was led into a room in which several Chinese officials were already waiting. They wore the dark uniforms of the judicial office. The senior officer's name was Fang Yuan. Fang was tall and his teeth were yellowed from cigarettes. He questioned me, through an interpreter, for six days and not a moment passed when his lips were without a cigarette. Fang delivered his questions to the interpreter in a peculiar, precise manner. For three days the questions focused on my past and once more I found myself telling my life story from the age of eight onwards. Parts of this story, you see, I have had to tell many times before.

On the fourth day Fang revealed the main thrust of his interrogation. "Why did you escape?" he asked abruptly.

I had been waiting for this question ever since my arrest and I knew that this was my chance to speak my mind. I'd been waiting for this opportunity for two years. I told Fang that it should be obvious why I had wanted to escape. I explained how I had been beaten during the interrogations of 1960; how prisoners had starved to death during my stay at Taglung Drag; and how those of us who had survived lived only with the pain of hunger and the prospect of our own deaths.

The Chinese officials listened to my story and for the first hour or so they did not interrupt. But when I told them about the food shortages, Fang Yuan rose from his chair and said in that slow pedantic way of his that the shortage of food was caused by the Soviets. He explained that China had incurred large debts with the Soviet Union, which had then demanded repayment in grain. Fang Yuan sat down again and I was allowed to continue. I told the officials about my disappointment when I was not released with the other prisoners in December 1962.

Often during those weeks I would be summoned from my cell without warning. Fang Yuan was quite gentle; he never lost his temper. But in the later stages the questions became more difficult. The officials wanted to know where I would have gone and whom I would have met if I had not been recaptured close to the Bhutanese border. These questions were all hypothetical, so I just reiterated that my only intention had been to live wherever the Dalai Lama was living. And then, just as abruptly, my interrogation came to an end.

I was not given any work, not that there was much work I could have done with my wrists and ankles in their shackles. The Chinese used several kinds of cuffs. Some were made out of heavy chunks of iron with only a short chain linking the two bracelets. Others were lighter, with a longer chain, but the bracelets had serrated edges. Sometimes, during an interrogation, the guard might press hard on the cuff and the sharp metal teeth would bite into the skin of the wrist.

There were two kinds of leg iron as well. One sort had a metal bar between the two ankle bands which made it almost impossible to walk. Prisoners in these leg irons waddled painfully around the compound, the iron cutting right to the bone. In summer the skin beneath the bands became tender and raw; the winter frosts would cause the skin to break up in fissures. I was kept in leg irons whose cuffs were linked by a short chain, just two rings long. I could move only by shuffling.

For six months I relied on my cellmates for everything. I could not even eat without their assistance. Everyone in the cell took it in turns to help me. They fed me and washed me and helped me over to the sanitary bucket. I still think of them now and of how much I should like to repay them; many are still in Tibet, though a few managed to escape to India. I remember how one prisoner would take a handful of *tsampa* and make it into dough. Then he would put the dough on the bed, next to my mouth, and I would take small bites from it. My discomfort was eased by the kindness of my fellow prisoners.

Chinese officials thought carefully about which sort of shackle they should use on which prisoner. Everything they did had some link to socialist ideals. Our imprisonment and the punishments and occasional rewards that were handed out to us all showed the power of the Communist Party. Every speech and question began with a eulogy to the Communist Party. For the Communists, physical confinement was a means of gaining control of our thoughts. Every meeting began with a lecture on the need for prisoners to reform their ideas and beliefs. They told us that we had to learn to cherish the Party in our hearts and minds. But the cuffs could not control the way I thought. My religious training brought me peace of mind. Physical restraints were only the outward sign of imprisonment; I still had the power to give my thoughts free rein.

One day I was approached by Yeshi Wangyal, our cell leader. Everyone called him Gyantse Pa-la, or father, because although he was only in his late forties Yeshi already behaved like an old man. He took his responsibilities seriously, always warning us not to get into trouble with the authorities and making sure that no one was listening to our conversations. Yeshi told me that he had just attended a meeting of all the cell leaders at which it had been announced that everyone involved in the escape would be subjected to a *thamzing*.

I had witnessed quite a few "struggle sessions" since the Chinese first invaded. My own family had been subjected to a *thamzing* on account of their class background. The Party claimed that these sessions allowed the people to vent their anger at landlords and other representatives of the exploiting class. The *thamzing* always started with a verbal condemnation and usually developed into beatings. Chinese officials watched the proceedings from a distance, as though they were street brawls. They hardly ever intervened in such violence because to them it demonstrated "the wrath of the serfs". This absolved the Party and its officials of all responsibility. If anyone was hurt, it was a consequence of the people's anger, not the Party's.

The villagers, the prisoners, the work units – we were all watched over by the Chinese cadres and anyone who did not participate in the *thamzing* with the required enthusiasm was sure to get a visit from Party officials, either that same evening or the next day. The official, with an expression of deep concern, would say that he had noticed you had not shown *nam-gyur yag-po*, a pleasing face. This meant that you were a marked man. At the next meeting you would be forced to pull some innocent person by the hair and shout abuse at them, and by that you would demonstrate your love for the Party and your support for the people. Almost all Tibetan high lamas and officials were subjected to this form of violence. The *thamzing* was, more than anything else, a display of the Party's power.

At Gyantse there was also a monthly meeting called "rewards and punishments", during which prisoners who had "reformed" were rewarded and those who had failed to reform were punished. The punishments mostly took the form of a *thamzing*. Gyantse Pa-la's warning helped prepare me for such punishment, though I was still apprehensive; no one ever knew quite what would happen in these meetings.

My turn came on a Monday morning. The Chinese officials were seated at a large table in the open yard. The compound was surrounded by soldiers, their guns fitted with bayonets, as well as by lines of warders. We were brought out into the yard and made to stand in rows while we waited for an announcement. My heart pounded. The gathering looked too ceremonial for a struggle session. Six months had passed since our escape and we had still not been sentenced. I thought I might be sentenced to death, since prisoners bound for execution were often shackled to stop them committing suicide.

A tall, unfamiliar official stood up and announced that this was to be a "reward and punishment" meeting. A Tibetan warden shouted; "The prisoners who escaped from Norbukhungtse, come forward!" I and my companions shuffled forward from the crowd, dust rising from our heels. We stood in front of the tall official. The other prisoners were instructed to sit down and we were made to turn and face them.

A young Tibetan interpreter stood up and denounced us. He said that we were reactionaries who had betrayed the motherland and opposed the people. The young man must have been from Gyantse, for he spoke the local dialect with a smattering of the new socialist jargon. He urged the other prisoners to expose our crimes and set themselves to punishing us for turning our backs on the people's government. The prisoners, like a chorus, began to shout, "Eradicate reactionaries! Eradicate reactionaries!" The voices of 2,000 Tibetan prisoners rang in our ears. When the shouting finally died down, a burly prisoner approached us, rolled up his sleeves and started to make a vigorous denunciation. I thought he was going to hit me.

"Why should you want to escape?" he asked. He said that under socialism prison was a place in which we could reform and educate ourselves. We had betrayed the Party and the country. Again he asked each of us, in turn, "Why should you want to escape?"

I had to decide whether to speak out or keep my mouth shut. I knew that all the prisoners supported me, despite the chorus of denunciations that now rose from the crowd. I realised that I could not remain silent. Here was my opportunity to discredit the Chinese and show my independence.

"The reason is obvious," I said, and began to list all my grievances, including the mass starvation of prisoners. The officials present were clearly uncomfortable, while the prisoners were secretly delighted by my defiance. They all knew why I had escaped. The burly prisoner looked startled by the response his question had provoked. The wardens instructed him to return to his seat.

97

Then the warders summoned another prisoner, called Thangtse Worpa. At the time of the Lhasa revolt, Thangtse had been a minor civil servant in the Gyantse district. He had been imprisoned because of his class background. He was determined to prove himself as useful as he could to the Chinese. In prison he had a reputation for beating other inmates, so I was frightened when he walked up to me. He praised the Party and socialism, then asked me, "Why should you have wanted to escape?"

"I escaped because I feared I would die of starvation," I replied.

Thangtse hit me hard on the left cheek and I fell to the ground. He put his hand on my neck and pushed me into the dirt. He said, "The earth is the Party and the blue sky is the people, and between the earth and the sky there is no escape for you."

Thangtse went up to each of the prisoners in turn, pulling their hair, spitting in their faces and ranting like a madman. A guard told him not to hit the prisoners, but this was just a show of benevolence intended to suggest the Party's magnanimity, for nothing that happened at those meetings was not part of the Party's strategy. If someone was beaten, they were beaten with the full authority of the Communist Party.

The *thamzing* came to an abrupt end and a senior officer stood up to read out our sentences. We were now described as the "big guilty" prisoners. The officer read out my sentence first: "Palden Gyatso from Panam County eight years, to be served consecutively, with a further three years of deprivation of all political rights." I did not know what to feel. I was glad that I was not going to be executed. But now I would have to serve a total of fifteen years in prison.

Others received similar sentences. The old man Gyalpo was already serving a twenty-year sentence and so his term was not increased. But his ankles were shackled in the heavy iron bands linked by a chain just two rings long. The officials announced that he was to remain in these shackles for four years.

I was determined that my capture should not diminish my resolve to escape again. The Chinese, jubilant after their victory in the Sino-Indian war, were being more boastful than ever, repeating over and over again their favourite expression: "Under the blue sky there is no escape from the Party." The prisoners were dejected, for our hopes of a quick liberation had vanished.

Fang Yuan came to talk to me a few days after my sentencing. He told me that the purpose of my imprisonment was to enable me to "reform" and become part of the "new society". I said nothing. He told me I ought to attend the education classes organised by the prison so I could see that the Communist Party was concerned only with the welfare of the people. But I knew what the Chinese meant by "reform". It meant accepting everything Chinese and denying every aspect of Tibetan life. I refused to give in. I had decided to refuse to co-operate with Chinese demands.

A few days later the warder, a tense, middle-aged Chinese man, came to see me. Prisoners generally did not have much contact with Chinese officials. We dealt mostly with Tibetans who were employed as inter-preters. This was the first time I had met a senior warder. He asked me, through an interpreter, if I intended to escape again and I said that I did not. "Do you have anything to say?" he asked.

I asked if my hands could be untied but my request was immediately rejected. The warder launched into a long speech about crimes against the people. He concluded by asking if I wanted to learn a new skill. I was young, he said, and should contribute to socialist construction. I did not reply. The warder scowled and turned to the interpreter. "Speak. Speak!" he said.

"I cannot even feed myself," I responded. "How am I supposed to learn anything when my hands and legs are bound like this?" The inter-preter translated for the warder, who lost his composure and told the guards to take me away.

Later I told my cellmates what had happened. They said that I was a fool not to accept the warder's offer. They all shook their heads, and Yeshi, our cell leader, asked me why I was making life so difficult for myself.

The following day two guards came in with the interpreter and told me that I'd been selected to train in the weaving of traditional woollen carpets. One of the guards took off my handcuffs and I felt that some part of my flesh was being lifted away, even though my hands remained in the same position. I tried to move them forward but nothing happened. I tried again, but my arms were stiff and would not come out from behind my back. Concentrating all my energy in my shoulders, I pushed my arms forward, though I was still unable to move my hands. A dreadful pain ran through my shoulders and down the length of my arms.

My heart raced as I confronted the thought that my hands were useless. The past seven months had been the worst period of my imprisonment, with my inability to carry out even the simplest of tasks and my complete dependence on my cellmates. I had been dreaming of the most commonplace actions: lifting a mug to my lips; untying my belt; running my fingers through my hair, which had now grown long, and scratching at the lice that had long since arrived there. The thought of losing my hands terrified me.

The prison official ordered one of my cellmates to rub my arms, but this only made the pain worse. I was taken to the dispensary, where a Chinese doctor gave me an injection and massaged my arms. It was nearly two weeks before I regained some of the use of my hands, and it was several months before they regained their agility and swiftness.

I was taught to weave by an old man called Rabsal Jhola. Rabsal was renowned throughout the Gyantse region as a master weaver. As soon as he saw my shackled feet, he told the guard, "He cannot work in leg irons." He pleaded that the chains be taken off, but the guard repeated that I was a "big guilty" prisoner and ignored his request.

The leg irons made it very hard to weave. Traditional Tibetan looms are constructed of wood and leaned against a wall. The weaver sits on the ground with his legs crossed. Of course, I could not cross my legs at all, so Rabsal and I had to devise a way for me to sit. Eventually we hit on the idea of digging a ditch two feet wide and three feet deep in front of the loom, so that I had somewhere to put my legs.

Weaving required dexterity and speed and I made slow progress. Tying knots caused me great pain, so feeble were my fingers. I hardly had the strength to wield the mallet that hammered the loose woollen thread into tight rows on the line. Rabsal was as calm and patient as could be. He never lost his temper at my clumsiness, but would just say, "Let's start again", and then show me how it was done.

By the end of 1963, life in the prison had settled into a routine. The Chinese had become more organised. After the war with India, our jailors had a renewed confidence and meetings became displays of arrogance and pride boosted by China's achievements. We were told again and again that the Tibetan refugees in India were all living as beggars and that sooner or later the Dalai Lama would be returned to China.

My life had fallen into a pattern of work and meetings and sleep. We were woken by a reveille when the sun rose and we rushed to get out of the cell, no matter how cold it was outside. That movement into the open air gave all of us a fleeting sense of freedom. And the fresh air would blow into the cell, which would by then be rank with the stench of the sanitary buckets.

Pairs of prisoners took it in turns to empty the buckets by pushing a pole through the handles and resting it on their shoulders. Perhaps the only bonus of being shackled was that I did not have to perform this task. All the nightsoil was tipped into a huge pool in the far corner of the prison and in the spring this manure was used as fertiliser on the fields. After the reveille, during the two hours before we were marched to work, labour reform prisoners would deliver two kettles of weak black tea.

Each prisoner received twenty-four *gya ma* of *tsampa* per month – about twenty-five pounds. The daily ration was distributed every evening and had to last the entire day. Prisoners who worked in the stone quarry received extra rations as their work was physically more demanding. After the Sino-Indian war there was a slight improvement in the food situation. Prisoners who had relatives nearby were allowed to receive food parcels once a month, although sometimes the guards kept these parcels for their own use.

At midday a bell rang for lunch and we returned to our cells. More black tea was brought in by the labour reform prisoners. The only good thing about the tea was that it was hot. A handful of tea-leaves had been added to the water to give it some colour, but it was completely tasteless. We had two precious hours to ourselves.

The prison officials took a break and slept during those two hours. We learned to concentrate all our thinking and relaxation into that brief span. I would sit at the end of the platform bed and recite prayers and texts from memory. Some prisoners went to sleep and others chatted about their past and exchanged stories about their families.

It was difficult to establish friendships in the cell because the authorities ensured that no one got the chance to know anyone else very well. All the prisoners changed cells every three months. This way there was no opportunity for conspiracy. New friendships were quickly broken up and different faces greeted you each morning. You never knew when you would see old friends again. Several criminal convicts were placed in the cells to serve as informers. They were vigilant and alert to any idle chat about socialism. Their surveillance was constant. If a prisoner made so much as a casual remark about prison food, this would be reported as a defamation of socialism.

We were supposed to work six days a week and have Sunday as a rest day, but this was never observed. Although there was no work on a Sunday, the day was taken up with meetings and study sessions. These meetings were traps. Supervising officials took a note of every comment we made and these notes were added to our personal files. The study sessions were no more or less than periods of indoctrination. We all preferred manual labour to these meetings.

In 1963 there was no electricity in the prison so our daily working routine was governed by the sun. Just before sunset a brilliant orange light suffused the prison. Guards would make sure we were all back in our cells. We'd climb into bed to the sound of the doors being bolted in distant cells, then the sound of steps approaching, the guard pulling our own door shut and the sound too of its bolt falling into place. The sunlight was shut out and the cell was dark. There was nothing to do but sleep and wait for the morning and the sound of the bolt sliding open again.

I liked my work. Weaving seemed leisurely compared to other tasks. Most prisoners were taken to work on construction sites. In the winter the looms were moved inside so that the weavers would be sheltered from the snow and icy wind. But in winter the iron bands around my ankles were like rings of ice glued on to my skin. I managed to spin some wool inside the bands to serve as a cushion.

In the middle of 1964 there were rumours that Gyantse prison was going to be disbanded and the prisoners moved to other parts of Tibet. One morning we were told to dismantle the looms because all the weavers were going to be transferred to Shigatse. The next day, just as unexpectedly, I was told to pack up my bedding and within an hour I was in the back of an army truck.

I glimpsed Gadong along the way. For more than three years my only view had been of the muddy wall that encircled the prison. Now I could see my old monastery and the strange wide prospect of mountains all the way to the horizon. Gadong stood as it had done for centuries. From a distance there was no indication of the sorrow that filled the valley. The absence of new prayer flags fluttering in the breeze over the monastery was the only sign that all might not be well.

In Gyantse prison I had received occasional news of my family. I knew that they were being subjected to beatings and had been deprived of all their property and possessions. My father and stepmother had been forced to move out of the family house and were assigned a small room which had previously been used as a store house. As former landlords, they had fared even worse than prisoners; the villagers and former tenants shunned them like lepers. In the new socialist society landlords were the lowest of the low. They could be beaten by anyone, especially those who had been labelled "serfs".

It was dark when we reached Shigatse. Several guards with torches led us into a large yard and told us we would have to spend the night in the open. The next morning we were moved into a room with no windows and a very low door. The floor was rough and uneven. There were no mats. The collection of rags I had for bedding had to serve as both mattress and blanket.

My job at the new prison was to set up a carpet factory. But soon after our arrival at Shigatse we realised that the timing of our transfer could not have been worse. In October 1964, the Chinese detonated their first atomic bomb. One morning all the prisoners were summoned to a meeting and the news was announced. The Chinese officials were jubilant and beaming with pride. One official, in a blue woollen suit with baggy trousers, stood up and declared that China was a great power and would never have to face humiliation at the hands of the imperialists. He denounced imperialist America and the Soviet revisionists, saying that, until now, they had been holding the world to ransom with their atomic capability.

I remember, a week later, sitting in the cell reading the *Tibet Daily*. The paper was required reading for all prisoners: during study sessions we would be made to discuss that day's editorial. I was struck by the bold headline, "The Panchen Clique". The word "clique" was used only as a term of abuse, applied specifically to those accused of organising groups with the aim of overthrowing the Communist Party. The article was denouncing the Panchen Rinpoche, accusing him of setting up a "black organisation" to oppose the dictatorship of the proletariat and separate Tibet from the motherland.

The article was particularly striking because I was living just below

1. Drepung monastery from the Kyichu river, 1939

2. The ruins of Drepung, from the slopes behind the monastery, 1986

3. Heads of Buddhas destroyed during the Cultural Revolution, Lhasa

4. Gyen Rigzin Tenpa, Palden's teacher at Drepung, whom he helped carry away from the monastery the day before it was shelled by the Chinese

5. Sangyip prison

6. Drapchi prison and surrounding work units, showing the greenhouses where the prisoners work, 1993

7. Lobsang Tenzin, a prisoner at Drapchi accused of murdering a Chinese policeman in 1988

8. Yulu Dawa Tsering, accused of "spreading counter-revolutionary propaganda" after talking to a foreigner. It was his arrest in 1987 that led to the biggest demonstration Lhasa had seen in ten years

9. Tanak Jigme Sangpo, the longest-serving prisoner in Tibet. He is due to be released in the year 2011 at the age of eighty-five

10. Palden with some of the torture instruments he smuggled out of
    Tibet, including handcuffs and thumbcuffs, serrated and hooked
    knives carried by the guards, an electric cattle prod and an electric
    shock gun with a capacity of 70,000 volts

11. Palden leading the annual demonstration commemorating the Tibetan uprising, London, March 1995

the residence of the Panchen Rinpoche. Our prison was what used to be the monastic granary below the Tashilhunpo monastery. I was bewildered. Why had the Panchen Rinpoche, who had been promoted as a "patriotic lama" and his monastery described as "the patriotic monastery", now been denounced so seriously? When, in 1960, all the monasteries had had their land confiscated, the Tashilhunpo estates had been left untouched.

One morning I looked out from the courtyard to see that the monastery was surrounded by soldiers. When we were told that there was to be no work we knew it could mean only one thing: a meeting. We gathered in the open yard and waited for the Chinese officers to arrive. They wasted no time in denouncing the Panchen Rinpoche. They declared that he had committed a treacherous crime and betrayed the Party's trust. An official ranted on about how the Panchen clique had severed its ties with the masses and now stood alongside the reactionary bandits of the "Dalai clique". At one point the Chinese officer even softened his voice and pretended that he was deeply hurt by the Panchen Rinpoche's actions. But still we did not know what the Panchen Rinpoche was supposed to have done.

My first thought was that he had escaped to India to join the Dalai Lama. The Chinese were calling the Dalai Lama and the Panchen Rinpoche "two slave owners supported by the Indian expansionists". It was only much later that the Chinese press mentioned the 70,000-character petition that the Panchen Rinpoche had sent to the Chinese leaders. The Chinese accused him of slandering the Party and the people's government. The campaign against him intensified. We learned that the Chinese had arrested many Tashilhunpo officials and were keeping them in Shigatse prison, but I did not see them.

These events worried me a great deal. The Dalai Lama had been chased out of his own country and we all looked to the Panchen Rinpoche as a figurehead inside Tibet. In the Panam area we had always felt a special devotion to the Panchen Rinpoche, even though, in the past, some

Tibetans had accused him of being pro-Chinese. His sudden fall made me very sad. We knew how the Chinese had treated other Tibetan leaders. The prison officials now announced that we must all re-evaluate our views about the Panchen Rinpoche and declare where we stood. In other words, we would soon be forced to denounce him.

My stay in Shigatse did not last long. One night I was woken by a torch shining in my face.

"Who is Palden Gyatso?" asked the figure behind the light.

"I am," I murmured drowsily.

He shone the light straight into my eyes and ordered me to roll up my bedding and come out of the cell. I had heard this before and knew that I was being moved again. I imagined I'd be sent to another work team or a different cell. The torch flickered over the bodies of the sleeping prisoners. The man called out the name of my friend Loden Kalsang. Loden woke up and gazed in my direction, as though to ask what was happening. He was given the same instructions. My leg irons rattled as I rolled up my bedding. I rolled up everything I owned into a neat bundle. In prison you learn to appreciate the importance of the smallest object and I ran my hand over the rough floor to make sure I had left nothing behind. I had still not seen the face of the man with the torch, but from his voice I knew him to be one of the Tibetan interpreters. Outside, he indicated where we should sit by pointing with the torch. We were brought some hot water and told to drink. As I sipped from the mug the interpreter told us we were being moved to Lhasa.

He said we were being moved because Drapchi prison was setting up a carpet-weaving unit and they needed us to teach other prisoners. This was the first time I'd been told where and why I was being transferred. The interpreter went on to say that we'd have to catch a public bus for Lhasa, leaving at dawn.

The best news was still to come. Four Chinese guards arrived, accompanied by an officer. The interpreter's demeanour changed immediately and he waited quietly to receive his orders. The Chinese officer said something to the interpreter, who nodded and, to my utter surprise, began to unlock and remove the leg irons from my ankles.

My heart lifted. Over the last two years the chains had become part of my body. I had got used to the way the length of chain restricted my movements and to the clanking of the chains against the stones in the courtyard. I had got used to the fact that I could not run as fast as the other prisoners in the morning rush to the latrine. Having been chained for so long, I had developed a way of walking which seemed natural and was at least comfortable.

Loden and I were ordered to pick up our baggage and were then marched to the bus terminal, with two guards in front of us and two behind. The officer and the Tibetan interpreter followed close behind the guards. It took us more than an hour to get there and the simple act of walking demanded all my concentration. I could not get used to walking without my chains. Any other prisoner would have been able to tell that my feet had been shackled for a long time just by looking at the way I walked.

A crowd of Tibetans and Chinese had gathered outside the bus terminal and onlookers identified us immediately as "big guilty" prisoners. We came to a halt several yards away from the other passengers, dropping our bundles on the floor and standing in the centre of a ring of soldiers. The officer disappeared for a while. He came back with some papers that we guessed to be our travel permits. He told us, through the interpreter, to be on our best behaviour. He opened a bag to reveal two sets of handcuffs. He told us that his instructions were to keep us shackled at all times, but that he had decided to spare us the embarrassment.

We climbed into the back of the bus with the guards and were joined by a dozen other passengers. We began the journey from Shigatse to Lhasa. The road was uneven and dusty. The dust blew through the windows of the bus and settled on our clothes and faces. The women covered their heads with scarves. When the road flattened out, one of the passengers brought out a basket full of biscuits and passed it around. When the basket came to me and Loden a young Tibetan woman who spoke Chinese asked a guard for permission. He waved his hand to indicate his approval, so I took a small biscuit. Loden did the same. The girl said, "Take more." I resisted the temptation and pushed the basket away. Then the girl took a handful of biscuits and placed them all in my lap and gave another handful to Loden. I was very moved by her thoughtfulness. It was the first time in four years I had eaten such delicacies. Prison taught you to be frugal with your food, so I saved the biscuits for later.

That evening, as the sun disappeared behind the range of mountains, we reached Yangpachen, the midpoint between Shigatse and Lhasa. I remembered passing through the town when I came to Lhasa for the second time. Trucks were pulled up in a long line at the roadside and the town was full of newly built Chinese houses. The whole area looked like a huge army camp.

We were led into a large mess hall, a pit-stop for all the truck drivers. Guards brought us a bowl of steaming noodles and I gulped them down, they were so good. Loden was just as engrossed in eating. The other Tibetan passengers saw the way we were devouring the noodles, as if we had never eaten food before, and later that night they gave us some more. These too I decided to save for later.

We spent the night in Yangpachen, then headed on for Lhasa at dawn the next day. The passengers were now allowed to talk to us and they asked us many questions. I wanted to ask them about what had been happening in the country. In prison, our only news of the outside world came from the Chinese and this was hardly reliable.

We arrived in Lhasa covered in dust. As we got down from the truck some of the passengers pressed Chinese money into my hand. I tried to give it back but they were already off the truck and disappearing into the crowds.

The terminal was bustling with people arriving from all parts of Tibet. It was clear to me that there had been a great deal of change during my years in prison. People looked different. They had taken to wearing Chinese clothing. Almost all the young people had discarded the traditional *chubas* and replaced them with the blue uniform of the proletariat. Men and women wore exactly the same clothes. At first I thought that they must all be in the army. It was only later that I discovered it was a fashion encouraged by the authorities.

We were met by a jeep and driven quickly through the city streets to Drapchi. This building had also changed. It looked more like a modern prison than an army camp. Loden looked apprehensive. I told him not to worry; we were bound to meet old friends from Drepung and anyway all we had to do was teach weaving.

In 1964 Drapchi was a model prison, the number one jail. The prisoners all wore smart uniforms. The prison had electric light. A naked light bulb hung from the ceiling of the cell. This was the first time I had been in a room with electric light. I stood there, wide-eyed, admiring the light. The other prisoners laughed and called me "the village man". The light was kept on all night.

Drapchi housed some of Tibet's most famous prisoners and dissidents. The prison was divided into five different brigades, or *ruka*. The fifth *ruka* housed all the former Tibetan government officials and high lamas, including Lobsang Tashi, the last prime minister of Tibet, and Lhalu, the former commander of the Tibetan army in eastern Tibet. The first *ruka* was for prisoners serving life sentences. The second was known as the *po ruka*, the grandfather *ruka*. The third was for women prisoners. I was kept in the fourth *ruka*.

Each brigade was further divided into *tsuks* made up of between twelve and sixteen prisoners. The *tsuk* referred to the cell where we slept and rested. Each *tsuk* had a *zuzhang*, or cell leader. The *zuzhang* was the most important person in the whole prison system.

The next day I was taken to a huge warehouse filled with wool. There were men carding the wool and men spinning it into threads. It looked like a factory rather than a prison. Loden and I were introduced as master weavers, so the other prisoners were respectful as we walked around the compound.

A few weeks later the authorities in Drapchi announced that the carpet factory would not, after all, be established. They said that the new prisoners who had just been brought to Drapchi would now be transferred again. There was a roll call and then everyone who had been brought to Drapchi to learn weaving was told to pack their bedding – all except Loden and I.

We had no idea what was going on. The atmosphere in the prison was fairly relaxed and there were no regular meetings. This suggested that officials were either busy or unsure of Party policy. It seemed that there were many administrative changes being made in the prison, but we had no idea what impact these would have on our uncertain future.

Chapter Seven

The Master Weaver

IN EARLY 1965 THE campaign against the Panchen Rinpoche intensified and rumours about his fate swept through the prison. Our brigade was taken to see an exhibition which, supposedly, contained the evidence that incriminated the Panchen Rinpoche and his accomplices. It was meant to show how he had organised a private army and amassed a personal fortune. I remember a black and white photograph accompanied by a caption that read, "Imperialist spy sent from India to establish secret contact with Panchen clique". I recognised the "spy" in the photograph. It was Tsewang Namgyal, a lean young man who had escaped to India with his mother in 1959 but had later been in Gyantse prison with me. Tsewang had returned to Shigatse the following year, after his mother's death, because it had been her last wish that he should visit Tashilhunpo to make an offering at the monastery where she used to pray. This was the only reason Tsewang had come back to Tibet. He'd been arrested and accused of spying. The photograph made me realise that the charges against the Panchen Rinpoche were pure fiction.

So now another of our leaders was being vilified. I was developing a sense of how the Chinese worked, the way they used people to serve their purposes. The Panchen Rinpoche had outlived his usefulness and had to be destroyed. It was no different in prison: prisoners were praised and rewarded for just as long as they served the authorities. And during struggle and study sessions, the Chinese pressed us to denounce one another so that we could be blamed if anything went wrong.

Prison life was becoming more organised and routine. Our rations were slightly improved: vegetables were added to our daily diet. And this period seemed to be more lenient and relaxed, with fewer denunciations and *thamzings*. Perhaps we were just getting used to it all. Perhaps we were now reconciled to our fate.

I had originally been sent to Drapchi as a master weaver. The authorities had piled up a huge quantity of wool. I'd given the carpenter designs for looms and people had been brought in from all parts of Tibet to set up a factory. Then the Party changed its mind. I was told that there was to be no carpet factory. When I asked friendly guards for an explanation, their reply was always, "It's the Party's policy." When you had been in prison for this long, you got used to performing meaningless tasks in a state of complete ignorance.

My own condition, however, had improved immensely. I was no longer shackled and had a great sense of movement. I was able to walk and run as freely as anyone else. Now that I no longer had chains around my ankles, I was able to sleep at night. I had never grown used to sleeping in chains. Every moment of the night was a search for comfort; each twist or turn of the body meant a stab of pain. Now the chains had gone. But since the plans for the carpet factory had come to nothing, my skills as a weaver were soon redundant. I worried that I might be sent to work in a construction camp, breaking stones.

One day I mentioned to an old monk from Drepung that I had not been assigned a job. He suggested that I join him in his work as a carpenter. The prison authorities were too busy to pay attention to minor goings-on like this. But my new job as a carpenter did not last long and I was told to train as a tailor. This was welcome news. I was relieved that once again I had been spared hard labour. My situation had not been better since I was first arrested.

Not that this was a cause of much joy. We could all see that the Chinese had established an iron grip on our country and there was no sign that things were going to improve. We noticed how confident the Chinese had become about their rule in Tibet. They boasted endlessly about the progress they had made and about how quickly the people's standard of living had risen. However, new prisoners brought us news of the great suffering of ordinary people.

One morning, walking to work, I saw a young woman approaching and recognised her immediately. It was Dolkar, the Lhasa girl who had interrogated me in Norbukhungtse. She wore a blue suit and her hair was bunched in two short plaits. She looked at me disapprovingly, without recognition. I remembered what she had said: "I would not hesitate to shoot you."

Dolkar was one of the senior guards in the women's brigade and in Drapchi everyone knew about her. The lay prisoners talked about how attractive she was. Dolkar was at the peak of her fame and power and everyone feared her. She was the darling of the Chinese, the model cadre. She had recently married a Chinese officer whom we nicknamed Tro Tro Lha Lo, because he spoke like a machine-gun, firing out his words in rapid succession. He was in charge of the construction brigade.

At the beginning of 1965, prisoners were asked for their criticisms. At first we were reluctant to speak, knowing that the authorities would make a note of everything we said and use it against us later. So most of us praised the Party as usual.

Only one Khampa man stood up and announced that he had a complaint. During a routine search of his cell, one of the guards had stolen a zhi, a precious stone prized by all Tibetans. We attributed various miraculous powers to such gems. The man said that it had been given to him by his mother and had belonged to his family for generations. He named Dolkar as the thief. The yard fell silent. We all turned to Tro Tro Lha Lo. His face was clenched like a fist.

The Khampa's courage amazed me. It was unheard of for a prisoner to make a complaint against an individual guard. But there was a reason for this Chinese leniency. To mark the occasion of the founding of the Autonomous Region of Tibet, which declared Tibet to be an integral part of China, the Chinese were launching a massive public celebration. Senior officials came to Lhasa from Beijing and a delegation came to the prison.

The authorities were keen to appease the prisoners and ensure that there was no trouble during the celebration. So they took the young Khampa's complaint seriously and his courage inspired others to speak out.

Almost all the complaints were against Dolkar. The women's section complained that she had been hoarding rations. Another unit complained that she had demanded an extra supply of fresh milk from the prison farm. The authorities acted swiftly. Dolkar was demoted and given the lowly task of supervising the prisoners who looked after the herd of prison cows.

A few days later her demeanour was completely different. She had lost all her composure and walked quickly to avoid looking any prisoner in the eye. She no longer strolled around the prison compounds with her old confidence. Even though I was glad she had been brought down to earth, I still felt a little sorry for her. But her eclipse would not last long.

Meanwhile, as always, our thoughts were with the Dalai Lama. We believed that as long as he was working for Tibet's freedom we still had a chance of regaining our independence. This hope was boosted when the official *Tibet Daily* reported, with great indignation, that the Dalai Lama was setting up an office in America.

America! This indication of American support for the Tibetan people was thrilling and we began to whisper the good news to one another, passing it throughout the prison. I remember hearing a prisoner called Tendar Nagbo ask Nyima Tenzin if he'd heard the good news. Nyima knew what Tendar was talking about and replied, "We just have to persevere a little longer. Now America, the most powerful nation in the world, is helping the Dalai Lama, it won't be long before we are free!"

This was dangerous talk and we knew it. One of the first things you learned in prison was to keep your thoughts to yourself. We learned techniques of camouflage so that we never betrayed elation or sadness. Such natural human feelings could not be expressed at will. You showed joy or anger only when the Party deemed it appropriate. We rarely confided our thoughts, even to our closest companions.

There were always a few prisoners who sought favour by reporting misdemeanours to the authorities, and Tendar and Nyima's conversation was duly reported. The news reached Dolkar.

It was exactly the chance she had been waiting for. She took the information about Tendar and Nyima to the authorities and they gave her permission to investigate. The next morning Dolkar burst into our cell and announced that we were all to remain in the compound. She was accompanied by three guards and a senior Chinese official, but there was no doubt as to who was in charge.

Prisoners from other units were also brought out into the yard. We were made to line up as if for roll call. Dolkar addressed us angrily: "There are people here who have been spreading counter-revolutionary propaganda. They have been giving prisoners empty hope." That term "empty hope" was one of the new phrases coined by the Communists. It was used frequently during meetings. It meant that it was hopeless to wait for Tibetan independence or the return of the Dalai Lama.

Dolkar strode back and forth in front of us, shouting out her denunciations. "The criminals pretend to have reformed," she said, "yet the reality is that they go on conspiring to oppose the Party and the people." She concluded by demanding that "the criminal" come forward and confess his crimes. She gazed expectantly at the ranks of prisoners standing before her.

We waited in silence. We had no idea what this meeting was about or which of us she meant by "the criminals". We never knew what would happen at these unscheduled meetings; sometimes they turned into executions. No one came forward. We stood there in silence. Watching prisoners shiver with fear seemed to give the authorities immense pleasure.

Dolkar decided to be more specific. "Yesterday," she said, "while visiting the dispensary, some prisoners took the opportunity to conspire and oppose the Party." There was an audible sigh of relief: most of us had not been to the dispensary that day. But Nyima Tenzin took a few meek steps forward. "I was at the dispensary yesterday," he said. That instant, two guards grabbed him and turned him to face the rest of us. "Do you confess?" Dolkar shouted at Nyima. I knew him to be strong-willed and not the sort of person who'd crumble at the slightest threat. He knew he must not confess until Dolkar revealed how much she actually knew. Dolkar looked pleased that she had succeeded in rooting out what she liked to call "evil reactionary bandits". But Nyima was shaking and on the point of tears.

Interrogations and *thamzings* were a test of nerves between the interrogator and prisoner. The interrogator's aim was to elicit a confession without revealing the prisoner's crime. "Confess!" was the watchword of these sessions. The prisoner would ask, "What have I done?" The interrogator would reply, "You have committed crimes and we have a mountain of evidence against you. You really should confess."

So then the prisoner would have to rack his brains and try to remember if he had inadvertently defamed or opposed the Party in any way. As almost any action could be construed as criminal, an experienced prisoner waited for clues as to what it was they were supposed to be confessing. But under pressure a prisoner could easily become confused. There were many cases of prisoners confessing to crimes they had not committed, or of prisoners making false accusations against other people in order to avoid beatings. So Nyima tried to stall, wanting to see just how much Dolkar knew and to find out just what it was he was supposed to have done. But the more he stalled, the angrier she became. "Confess! Confess!" she shouted, punching her fist in the air.

A Chinese officer, one of the senior Party officials in the prison, watched the whole performance. We found out later that a similar inquisition was being conducted with the construction brigade, where Tendar Nagbo worked. Tro Tro Lha Lo was in charge of that meeting. Tendar refused to admit to anything. But eventually Nyima gave in and confessed to speaking with Tendar.

Dolkar was triumphant. "The evil reactionaries Tendar and Nyima have conspired and spread counter-revolutionary propaganda," she declared. "They have praised the enemy of the motherland." Then Nyima was dragged away to confront Tendar, who was still refusing to confess.

The investigation went on for several days. We were all summoned to another meeting to denounce Tendar and Nyima. Then one evening there was a great commotion at lock-up time. A monk called Gedun Sonam was missing and the guards began to search for him. I heard jeeps roaring out of the prison gate. Soldiers were on full alert on the watchtowers. One of the guards even called out Sonam's name, saying it was lock-up time, as though the monk might momentarily have forgotten what time it was and where he was. I wondered whether Sonam had actually dared to escape. He was much older than me, a monk from Drepung who worked as a cook in our brigade kitchen. He was jovial and friendly and was known for his great learning.

The guards found him behind the kitchen compound. He had cut his own throat with a meat cleaver.

Gedun Sonam's suicide gave a new twist to Nyima and Tendar's case. The authorities announced that the events were connected, and that Tendar and Nyima were to blame for Sonam's death. They were sentenced to life imprisonment. A week later Nyima took his own life. Someone in his dormitory told me that he had found a strip of blunt metal, had gone quietly to bed and pulled the blanket over his head. When he failed to get up, the cell leader pulled back the blanket. It was covered in blood. Nyima had stabbed himself in the neck, making no sound which might have alerted those who slept next to him.

Many prisoners committed suicide. Some thought they were cowards; others that it was an act of courage. I dare not pass judgement. No one can understand the extreme despair that drives someone to take their own life. As a Buddhist monk I was brought up to regard human life as the most precious thing in the world, and I found strength in the desire to show my tormentors that they had not beaten me, that I still had the courage to live.

Tendar and Nyima's only crime was to imagine the prospect of liberation. The Communists were terrified of the people having such dreams. But the hope of liberation gave us prisoners the will to carry on. And that hope was given form in the freedom of the Dalai Lama.

The Chinese liked to begin meetings by telling us, "You must abandon empty hope." We were often called *a-yong go-khar*, which translates as "will it, white hair". This meant that we would wait for Tibetan independence until our hair turned white. To express hope of any kind was regarded as a serious crime.

After the suicides of Nyima and Gedun Sonam, Dolkar's reputation was restored and she was rewarded as a diligent defender of socialism. Once again she was put in charge of the women's brigade and could be seen striding around the prison compound as if it were her own personal fiefdom. I sensed that she was on the look-out for victims and we did all we could to avoid her.

However, it was almost impossible to stay out of trouble. What we assumed to be innocent behaviour might easily be considered by the authorities as a transgression of some unknown law. In October 1965, there was a celebration to mark the anniversary of the Communist Party's seizure of power in China. I had been sent to help in our brigade mess. I knew the cook from my Drepung days and I found him in a jolly mood, with a broad grin across his face. He told me that we were going to have steamed meat dumplings. "Aren't you excited?" he asked.

I responded by quoting a verse by the sixth Dalai Lama, who is regarded as Tibet's greatest romantic poet: "When you cannot have your beloved permanently, what is the use of a single day?"

I thought no more of this. But a few weeks later, in a regular assessment meeting, the cook was put under pressure. These meetings were held in all the dormitories to "expose criminals". We would sit in silence, hearts beating fast. We all lived in fear of being chosen as the meeting's victim.

I knew, of course, that I had committed no crimes. But each prisoner had to master the skill of making confessions which were pleasing to the Party. I used to rely on the technique of admitting to some minor transgression, wrapping this confession in a grand ideological explanation. So I might say that I had gone to the latrine frequently to avoid work, thus subverting socialism and hampering production. Then I would declare my desire to contribute to increased production. It was the moment we were asked to accuse and criticise others that caused us the most anxiety.

At this particular meeting the cook was ordered to criticise someone and he happened to criticise me. He transformed my casual remark in the kitchen into a defamation of socialism and a celebration of the old feudal society. My choice of verse was fashioned as an attempt to bring back the old feudal order.

I was made to stand up and a guard gazed at me with exaggerated astonishment. "You insolent reactionary," he said. "How dare you compare the conditions of the feudal age with those of the new society?" He then asked the assembled prisoners if they thought that conditions were better before the arrival of the Chinese. He announced that in the old society prisoners were never fed but were left to starve in dungeons, whereas in the new society even criminals who had pointed a gun at the Party were given the chance to reform.

I kept quiet. There was no point in trying to explain myself. Once accused there was no defence. I was instructed to examine my thoughts and conduct. "We will be watching you," the guard told me. "You must make a clean break with feudal sentiment and embrace the new society." And then for eighteen days I was interrogated about whether the old society was really better than the new socialist era.

I had been in prison for five years but I had still not got used to the prison regime. The loss of freedom is so tangible. My work in Drapchi was not physically demanding, but the fear of being criticised was a constant source of mental torment. To make things worse, I had no contact with my family. We were not allowed to write to each other, because any form of communication with the outside world immediately aroused suspicion.

At the same time, our families were being forced to denounce us. Any communication with a political prisoner was considered a criminal act. A Party official would visit the family and subject them to what was called "re-education". He would ask them if they stood with socialism and the working people or with "reactionaries who oppose the Party and split the unity of the motherland". Of course, there was only one answer to that question.

It was far safer for everyone to forget their loved ones. We all learned to live as though we were orphans, with no parents or brothers or sisters or even friends in the outside world. This was perhaps easier for me as a monk than it was for some other prisoners. I was used to being solitary. I had no strong ties, no memories of a wife or children tugging at my heart. There were many cases of wives remarrying in order to prove that they had completely severed ties with their reactionary husbands. The Party liked this sort of public declaration.

In February 1966 I was transferred once again to another prison. When we heard the order to pack our bags we all feared that we were about to be dispatched to Kongpo, in the south-east, near the Burmese border. Prisoners there lived in the middle of dense rain forest, so distant from Lhasa or any other centre of authority that guards administered beatings and other punishments at will.

A prisoner was never told why he had been transferred. This moving of prisoners was carried out not only for administrative reasons but with the specific aim of preventing them becoming a cohesive group. The Party saw conspiracies everywhere.

Every few months all prisoners had to move dormitories so that no one was in the same cell for long. If the authorities suspected that two prisoners were becoming friendly, they were immediately separated. Any good act of human kindness was frowned upon. A friendship was officially described as a "sugar-coated bullet", especially if it were between people from working-class and land-owning backgrounds. I remember that a former Tibetan aristocrat was immediately subjected to a *thamzing* when he gave a cigarette to a convict. This was described as an attempt to buy favour with the working class.

We were warned about the "sugar-coated bullets" fired by class enemies to thwart the socialist revolution. All prisoners learned to avoid unnecessary social contact. Convicts and political prisoners from poor backgrounds were instructed to assist the socialist revolution by exposing class enemies. Some of them took these instructions to heart.

I was moved many times, from cell to cell and sometimes to a different brigade. One cold February morning I was moved to Sangyip, a new prison named after a small village situated at the bottom of a narrow valley about fifteen miles north-west of Lhasa.

The valley's steep slopes protected Sangyip from the worst of the winds and it was to grow into a vast prison complex, with three separate jails as well as the training school of the People's Armed Police and the centre of administration for all the prisons in Tibet. But in 1966, when I was taken there, the Chinese had opened only two prisons: Outritu and Yitritu, meaning prisons number Five and One. I was sent to Prison Five, which was divided into five brigades. My brigade camped in the open and went to work wherever our labour was needed.

All the prisoners were housed in tents surrounded by thick scrolls of barbed wire. Guards patrolled the perimeter day and night. Each tent, which might contain up to fifteen prisoners, made a unit. My unit carried out odd jobs like painting, breaking stones and making bricks at the construction sites.

At night the temperature plunged below freezing and we huddled together for warmth. Often I could not sleep, so fierce were the blasts of wind against the tent. We woke each morning to find a thick frost stiffening the tarpaulin.

The Chinese were busy constructing the prison buildings which would soon dominate Sangyip. It was clear that they were preparing for the arrival of many more prisoners. I was initially given the job of reducing large boulders to rubble with a heavy hammer, though later I had the easier task of painting window-frames.

The weekly meetings, held in the tent, were a constant source of worry. After six years in prison it was a struggle to come up with new things to confess and the day before the meeting I'd have to think hard for some fault I could admit to. Usually I would fall back on a confession of laziness, and say that I'd been avoiding work, thus hampering socialist production. If I was lucky, the cell leaders would accept my confession and dismiss it with a reprimand. Sometimes they would keep harping on some minute transgression, accusing me of opposing the Party. There was no more serious crime.

In the spring of 1966 I sensed some change in the Party's policy. Every day, during our lunch break, there was a group reading of the *Tibet Daily*'s editorial and a discussion. Usually the discussion was a matter of denouncing the target of that particular editorial: imperialist America one day, Russian revisionists or Indian expansionists the next. We just followed whatever view was officially approved and expressed in the paper.

But that spring the editorials became much less clear-cut. They were full of vague denunciations of class enemies and revisionists. The Chinese officials were confused by the editorials as there were no clear guidelines as to whom the articles were attacking. Later, when I began to understand how the Communist Party operated, I realised that the lack of clarity in the *Tibet Daily*'s editorials was an indication of uncertainty or power struggles among the Party leaders. This confusion was the beginning of the Cultural Revolution.

One day in May we were ordered to stop work and dismantle our tents. We were bundled into trucks and taken back to Sangyip prison. Only three of the five brigades were housed permanently inside the prison, but that afternoon it was brimming with people. A Tibetan officer ordered us to pitch our tents right there in the open yard. Each unit raced to find a spot and soon the dirt of the yard was invisible beneath this new township of canvas.

May was an unusual time to hold such a gathering. Usually prisoners were gathered together only in winter, when the Chinese would hold a "reward and punishment" meeting that lasted for a whole month. My experience had shown that dramatic changes were normally the precursors of bad periods.

So it was hard to sleep soundly, with all the tents pitched close together and the fear of what lay in store. The next morning, at reveille, there was none of the usual rush. There were no guards chasing us out of the tents. Instead we just lolled about the yard. Even cell doors had been left ajar.

Then a group of officers marched into the yard and the leader of each brigade ran through a roll call. A senior Chinese officer took charge of the meeting. He said that Chairman Mao had personally instructed that every man, woman and child in China should take part in the Cultural Revolution and purge the Party of revisionists.

We were issued with a small booklet containing the "Sixteen Point Directive" by Chairman Mao. The Chinese officer warned us sternly that we were expected to memorise the points, make it clear where we stood and wage war against all enemies of the Party. I was amazed by the speed with which the authorities had produced the booklet and its Tibetan translation. The speed was an indication that the new campaign had to be taken seriously.

It was also announced that we were expected to give voice to our doubts and criticisms. Mao himself, apparently, had decreed that no one would be punished for expressing their views. The officer who told us this did so in a gentle melodic voice and appeared to be sincere. But I was not convinced. I kept thinking of the preamble that had become familiar from all my interrogations: *If you confess, you will be treated leniently.*

We were so desperate to speak out that this promise of leniency was enough to entice many prisoners to make complaints and give voice to feelings they had kept secret for many years. We had kept quiet about our lack of freedom, about intimidation in the weekly meetings, about the cruelty of cell leaders. Most of all we longed to be able to talk freely to each other without the fear that our words would be twisted into defamations of socialism or the Party. The promise of leniency was, of course, no more than a trap, a tactic the Chinese would later call "luring the snake out of its hole". That promise was the beginning of the Cultural Revolution, the revolution that for the next ten years would plunge Tibet into the deepest hell.

Chapter Eight

The Cultural Revolution

O NE MORNING THAT SUMMER I was sent out to paint a new house near Drapchi. I had not been painting long when I was distracted by a crowd of red flags approaching me, the flags flapping hard in the wind and the red colour bright against the clear blue sky. I heard the clashing of cymbals and drums beating. I heard slogans shouted over the noise of the cymbals and drums: "*Mao Wanzi! Mao Wanzi!*" This meant, "May Mao live for a thousand years.'

Looking at the crowd with their flags I imagined I was watching a group of children parading at a festival. None of the marchers looked a day older than fifteen. These same children would later be described as the vanguard of the Revolution. Even smaller children followed the marchers, clapping their hands with great enthusiasm. The marchers all wore red armbands to signify that they were Red Guards. They took no notice of the prisoners watching them pass.

That evening I learned that a similar group of youths had gone to the prison and presented a proclamation which demanded that all cadres engage in the Cultural Revolution and purge the Party of all reactionaries. The Red Guards were to create havoc in the coming years. Young people seized upon Mao's slogan "To rebel is good." Impressionable youths took to the streets, destroying anything that they thought was impeding the progress of the Revolution. There is one thing for which I owe the prison some thanks: it saved us, at least, from the brutality of the Red Guards.

Once, in Seitru, I saw Red Guards ransack an entire block of administrative offices. They made tall dunce's hats by rolling paper into cones, then placed them on the senior officers before tearing their clothes and chasing them out of the building. The officials were forced to line up in the small yard in front of the whitewashed building. It was strange to see them stooped so low, their hands resting on their knees. They shook with fear and the awkwardness of the posture. A Red Guard ordered them to bow.

At first I thought that these officials were getting what they deserved; they were getting a taste of their own medicine. This feeling of revenge ran contrary to my religious upbringing, but it is a powerful human impulse. Although prison officers and guards were at the very bottom of a long chain of command, it was their brute force that caused us pain. It was only natural for them to be the prime object of our anger. The Red Guards were spitting on them, accusing them of obstructing the Revolution by refusing to expose the enemies of the Party.

The following day the officials walked around the prison compound with stooped shoulders. They looked humbled and confused. As instructed by the Red Guards, prison officers held meetings at which they confessed their own lack of diligence in supporting the Revolution. Now they too had to undergo study sessions.

Our brigade was subjected to its own study session that began in mid-May 1966 and went on for a whole month. We had to study Mao's directives and follow the progress of the Revolution as reported in the *Tibet Daily*'s editorials. We were shown a film of Mao inspecting thousands of Red Guards in Tiananmen Square in Beijing.

Then it was announced that the Cultural Revolution was under the direct command of Chairman Mao and Lin Biao. I had never heard Lin's name before. He was described as the "number one follower of the beloved Chairman Mao". For the next two years no meeting would be complete without some mention of those two names.

We were told that the Cultural Revolution had been initiated by Chairman Mao in order to eradicate those factors which were hindering the progress of socialism and to eliminate those enemies of the Party who were trying to subvert the Revolution. We were told that we had to embrace the Revolution sincerely and reform our thoughts and actions. We were warned that if anyone strayed from the path of progress they would be exterminated like vermin.

I couldn't understand what all this had to do with Tibet.

One morning that summer we were told there would be no work that day. My heart sank; most of us preferred labour to the endless meetings. Work was actually a kind of escape from the duty of praising the Party and Chairman Mao. But that morning we stood in the yard while our prison officers and some other officials sat down on a raised platform. Our lanky prison leader, a Chinese man in his late forties, announced; "The old feudal society is dead. Socialism is the only path. You must reform yourselves and learn to love the Party and the masses." The first step, he said, was for us to abandon the "four olds": our old culture, customs, habits and thoughts. He brandished his fist and declared, "There is no escape from the iron fist of the proletariat!"

After a few more speeches in this vein the meeting was disbanded and we were told to return to our dormitories to discuss the issues raised. Our cell leader was already in the cell and he began to repeat what had been announced in the morning meeting. But, as he was speaking, we heard a loud commotion outside. We rushed to the door to find a huge pile of woollen blankets, books, shoes and clothes in the yard, with prisoners throwing their belongings on top of the pile.

They were abandoning the four olds. We were expected to destroy everything "old". The pile was lit and soon it was blazing like a pyre. We were encouraged to throw our belongings on to the fire. I had kept a full set of monk's robes which I had been using as an extra blanket. I threw the robes on to the fire. Other prisoners threw their most precious possessions, including religious books and objects, on to the fire. Thick clouds of black smoke rose up from the blaze.

A young guard marched into the dormitory, pointed to a pair of leather shoes and ordered that they be burned. "But they're new," said the bemused owner of the shoes. "They are made by Indian expansionists," replied the guard. Then the guard gazed at my small leather pouch, or *thang go*, and asked me, "Why are you clinging on to the old?" All Tibetan shepherds used a *thang go* to carry their *tsampa*. Pilgrims carried one tucked under their belts. You could also use a *thang go* as a bowl.

"It's an object favoured by the working class," I told the guard.

"It's a remnant of feudalism and we have no need for such things," he replied curtly. Then he added, "Thanks to the kindness of the Party, even prisoners can eat from 'modern' plates, a privilege that was previously available only to members of the exploitative class."

I went outside and tossed my feudal *thang go* on to the fire. I watched the leather crumble as the flames took hold and did not know whether to laugh or cry. Even a simple leather pouch was a target for our new rulers.

From now on all objects were classified as either "remnants of the old feudal society" or "new socialist objects". Some prisoners were forced to throw their traditional wooden bowls on to the fire. All our belongings were searched so that the guards could be sure we were not hiding anything. Anything maroon or yellow had to be destroyed, since these two colours represented religion. Or we could dye them red or dark green, the colour of the uniform of the People's Liberation Army. I chose to dye all my belongings. Others hurled theirs on to the fire to show their enthusiasm for the Revolution. The prison was in chaos.

A few days later I saw smoke drifting from the direction of Sera monastery, the third largest monastery in Tibet, a few miles east of our prison. For nearly a week I watched smoke rising from all points of the compass, an indication of the great frenzy of burning that was taking place, the destruction of books and robes and shoes and everything we held dear. Only when I was finally released from prison would I understand the full extent of the destruction of my country's heritage.

I remember walking from the main hall across the yard and seeing a charred page waft down to the ground like a leaf in autumn. I picked up the page and saw that it was one of the liturgical texts I had memorised as a novice. The blackened text crumbled in the palm of my hand. I began to weep, though quickly I wiped the tears away with my sleeve. I returned to the barracks to find a vast portrait of Mao hanging outside the building.

The campaign against the "four olds" induced something like a state of paralysis. I was unable to do or say anything without fear that I would be accused of holding on to the olds, on to my old thoughts or customs or culture or habits. Then it was announced that we had expunged the four olds and from now on had to adopt socialist customs and habits. We learned to speak and write differently, in a new socialist idiom that was appropriate to the new proletarian culture. And in order to survive we had to give at least the impression of compliance.

The daily meetings became increasingly intimidating. After work we would return to the barracks for the evening meal and this would be followed by a short study session during which we'd read Mao's "Little Red Book" or the editorials in the *Tibet Daily*. And once a week there was a special session of confessions and criticisms.

My earlier tactic of owning up to my own indolence and criticising other prisoners' laziness was no longer enough to satisfy the authorities. The cell leader was responsible for ensuring that we all criticised one another. I remember sitting on my bed, waiting for my turn, unable to think up a confession. Annoyed by my hesitation, the cell leader announced mockingly, "Palden is thoroughly reformed and thinks he should be released! Isn't that right?"

I knew he was provoking me and that it was best I should keep quiet. But the cell leader was relentless and I realised there was no escape for me. He was determined to force me to say something he could report as "anti-Party". Eventually he made a note that I had refused to confess and that I was arrogant because I believed I was a reformed person.

The following evening two prison leaders came to our dormitory. The older of the two sat by the door with a cigarette hanging from his lips, while the younger one walked the length of the cell and stood at the far end. I had a feeling they were here for me. The cell leader's note had been sent to the office. The other prisoners sat in silence, while the older guard approached me with his arms folded. "Some prisoners think they have become citizens of the new society," he said. "But guilty, reactionary prisoners cannot change overnight. They are like stones wrapped in cotton wool: soft on the outside but hard underneath." He turned and addressed me directly: "Palden, do you think we should let you out?" I did not answer. The guard smiled faintly, then said, "Those who refuse to confess are showing contempt towards socialism."

Suddenly he raised his voice, commanding me to stand in the middle of the room. He scolded me as if I were a child. "There is only one road left for you!" he shouted. He nodded to the cell leader, who raised his fist and shouted, "Eliminate reactionaries!" The other prisoners joined him like a chorus. The guard and the cell leader began to beat me. I cupped my hands in front of my face to protect myself. The beating seemed to go on for ever, but it could not have lasted for more than twenty minutes. After the guards had left, I crawled into bed and slept in spite of the pain. When I woke, I peeled off my shirt to inspect the bruises all over my shoulders and ribs. When I walked unsteadily to the latrine, the other prisoners busied themselves with this and that, so as to avoid meeting my eyes.

The Cultural Revolution lasted until the death of Chairman Mao ten years later. During that period I must have undergone thirty or forty of those beatings. No prisoner was exempt from *thamzing*. And because *thamzing* always involved other prisoners, the Party was absolved of any responsibility. We became puppets, unable to fend for ourselves. If the authorities had said that the sun rose in the west, we would not have argued.

Tibet was now divided into two opposing factions: Gyenlog, or rebel, and Nyamdrel, or alliance. Every office, work unit and family was divided along these lines, and very often members of the same family found themselves on different sides of the divide. Prison officers and guards were not immune from this factional struggle. Junior officials accused their superiors of being "power-holders" who had hindered the progress of the Revolution. *Tibet Daily* editorials urged the masses to weed out the agents of Liu Shaoqi, the former Vice-President of China who had now been identified as the leader of the capitalist infiltrators in the Party.

Such internal wranglings did not give us any peace. Meetings and punishments carried on as before. There was a steady stream of new prisoners, most of them young Tibetans and Chinese cadres. Many of these were former government or Party officials who had been accused of being agents of Liu and Deng in Tibet. By the summer of 1967, the struggle between the Gyenlog and Nyamdrel factions had brought the whole country to a halt. The army was the only institution still functioning, so the day-to-day administration of the prison was taken over by soldiers. We had to refer to these soldiers as "the defenders of the motherland".

The chaos of the situation was brought home to me one day as I walked to the communal kitchen. A group of Chinese prisoners was sitting down, enjoying the warmth of the sun. They were marked out as new arrivals by their clean outfits. One of them seemed familiar. He was smoking and talking with the others, but when I passed by he looked straight at me.

"Welcome, Cai Juzhang!" I said.

He jumped up and came forward to shake my hand, laughing heartily.

Cai had been the director of Norbukhungtse, where I had been imprisoned in 1960. He had never interrogated me but still I had got to know him well. He had a round, puffy face and wasn't a bad man, just short-tempered. He could snap very easily but would calm down almost as quickly and dismiss a prisoner without further ado. I was shocked to see him in prison, now a prisoner himself.

I was just as surprised to see Wangyal, a young Tibetan from Gyantse who had been Cai's personal translator. Wangyal had benefited from the Chinese rule in Tibet. He came from a poor family but had been sent to China by the Communists to complete his education. Now he looked confused and dejected. He recognised me but said nothing, perhaps because he was ashamed, or perhaps because he was afraid he would be accused of associating with a reactionary prisoner.

Cai remained in prison until 1976. Both he and Wangyal were accused of financial embezzlement, a false charge levelled at many officials.

The days passed slowly, with work the only distraction to keep our minds off the fear of being accused. The pressure to criticise and to confess was relentless. The result was an atmosphere of mutual surveillance. Hundreds of pairs of eyes observed your every gesture. Fear made us seem submissive and docile, though deep down I harboured a bitter loathing of the Chinese authorities and their petty cruelties.

Among the prisoners there evolved a mutual understanding and sympathy. We knew that we were all being forced to do the same things. So although a criticism was initially the cause of enmity, we soon learned to forgive each other for whatever accusations were made, and we bore no grudges.

You could not opt out. A refusal to join in with these sessions would be regarded as anti-socialist, tantamount to a revolt. During struggle sessions soldiers would make a note of everything you said. If they observed that your participation was not whole-hearted, they would accuse you of lacking revolutionary enthusiasm. You were expected to do harm to your fellow prisoners as if they were your worst enemies.

As a reactionary who belonged to the exploiting class, I was an easy target. In prison, as outside, the only beneficiaries of the Cultural Revolution were those classified as "poor peasants". Criminal convicts from a poor background were treated far more leniently and became cocky in their new-found status. We Tibetans called them "thick necks". Those "poor peasants" were said to have a clean political background: they were untarnished by the desire to restore feudal privileges. Criminals strode around the prison like the elect, and although they were not exempt from criticism themselves, you had to be very careful, because they could easily deflect any accusation by saying that it was an attempt to victimise the working class.

On both sides of the prison walls your worth was now dictated by your class background. If a criminal convict worked hard, criticised regularly and declared his enthusiasm for the class war, he might soon earn remission and be released.

By the end of 1967 the meetings had become litanies of petty accusations and admissions of trivial faults. The punishments were as cruel and violent as before. Even the way we sat was criticised. When we adopted the traditional cross-legged posture, which was supposed to emulate the Buddha in meditation, we were immediately accused of showing feudal respect to the Buddha. Instead we were forced to emulate PLA soldiers by squatting on the ground. I found squatting very uncomfortable and I'm sure that all Tibetan prisoners thought it was a stupid idea. The unfamiliar posture made our weak legs shake. After a few minutes I would have to get up, pretending I was fetching something.

In the spring of 1968 I was sent to work in a brick factory near the prison. Several months passed with neither criticisms nor beatings. Evenings were spent studying. This invariably meant reading Mao's "Little Red Book". One evening, as I was reading, two soldiers and a Tibetan official called Chung la, our brigade leader, came into our dormitory. Chung la had a dark complexion and quick temper.

One of the soldiers, a senior officer, began to speak. "The Party has been kind and patient," he said, with a note of exaggerated indignation. "The Party has given all reactionary criminals a chance to reform themselves, but still they oppose the people and the Party. These criminals are like butchers who have sheep's heads on display but only sell stringy goat meat."

He had a gift for melodrama, this soldier. But we knew that such a sudden outburst could mean only one thing: that one of us was to face the severest punishment. Even the cell leader was afraid. His failure to report the smallest violation could easily be regarded as an act of complicity. The senior officer glanced at the other soldier, who immediately called out, "Palden Gyatso." I froze.

All the faces around me relaxed as soon as my name was called. My cellmates sighed with relief. I had no idea what I was supposed to have done.

I stood up and walked to the middle of the room. The officer demanded my confession. He accused me of "firing missiles wrapped in wool".

"Confess! Confess!" he shouted. Some prisoners would have been so shaken that they blurted out their innermost secrets. I knew that I had to stay calm and keep quiet, waiting for the officer to reveal the nature of the charge. The soldiers were angered by my silence. The officer ordered the cell leader and another prisoner to take hold of my hands.

They pushed me down by the neck and began to twist my arms behind my back. "Bow your head!" the officer shouted. "You insolent reactionary!" A chorus of "Confess! Confess!" rose up from the prisoners around me. But still I kept silent. Two more people came into the cell, a prisoner and a guard. The cell leader pulled me up by the hair. He pointed to the prisoner who had just come in and asked me, "Do you recognise him?"

I recognised him. His name was Rigzin and he came from Lhasa. We were in the same brigade and I'd seen him quite a lot around the compound. He'd also been sent to work in the brick factory, but I couldn't understand what the connection between me and Rigzin could be. "Yes, I do know him," I said to my interrogator.

The cell leader pushed my head down and Rigzin was told to begin his condemnation. "Evil reactionaries like Palden," he said, "have never been reconciled to the defeat of feudalism. They dream in secret of resurrecting the corpse of feudalism." Then Rigzin revealed the crime I had apparently committed. He said that earlier that afternoon I had made the "ritual of water offering". This was a ritual performed by all Tibetans: you simply dip your finger into water and then sprinkle it into the air as an offering to the deities. I had not performed this ritual since the Cultural Revolution began, knowing full well the consequences in store for anyone caught doing such a thing.

"Do you admit to this?" the officer asked.

"I never made such an offering," I replied angrily.

The officer turned to Rigzin and told him to reveal the exact details of my crime. I couldn't believe my ears. Rigzin described how I'd dipped my hands into a stream and then tossed them in the air. I recalled the incident rather differently. After work, we walked back to the prison along a narrow, clear stream. I dropped my glove into the stream and bent down to retrieve it. I had cupped my hands to take a drink of the cool water. It was so refreshing that I splashed some water on my face. Then I shook the water off my hands to dry them.

Rigzin contorted this simple act into a religious ritual. The officer immediately ordered the other prisoners to subject me to a *thamzing*. My fellow prisoners rushed forwards and started to punch me on the back and sides. Some of them kicked me too. The cell leader wound an old, thick rope around my body, pinning my arms to my sides. I couldn't move. Blow after blow landed on my chest and arms and shoulders and on my ribs. The prisoners knew that if they didn't hit me hard they would themselves be guilty of hesitancy in support of socialism. I could not even raise my hands to protect my head.

I had watched prisoners die during a *thamzing*. An old, gentle man called Sholkhang Yonten, the thirteenth Dalai Lama's scribe, had refused to condemn His Holiness and was subjected to a beating. He fell unconscious and died on the way to hospital.

I would have welcomed a quick death. I told the guards to kill me. They were shocked by my audacity and replied with a blow to the side of the head and a kick in the ribs.

When the beating eventually came to an end the guards were panting like dogs. There was a stench of sweat. I fell to the floor. The cell leader untied the rope and with the rope gone I was able to breathe normally. As the guards were leaving the room, the officer looked back at me and said, "Don't think your case is finished. We'll go on investigating until you confess to your crime."

I crawled into bed. Gradually the pain subsided and I drifted into sleep. The next morning it was my turn to fetch the tea from the communal kitchen. My face was swollen and my ribs and arms were covered in bruises. All my cellmates could see that I was in serious pain. Each one of them would have been willing to take my place were it not for the fact that such a gesture would be characterised as "fraternising with a reactionary" or "showing sympathy for an anti-socialist criminal". So my fellow prisoners just watched as I struggled to lift the bucket and walk out into the courtyard.

Later, as usual, we were marched to the brick factory. The evidence of my ordeal was plain for all to see, but the other prisoners averted their eyes. I set to work as best I could, knowing that if I didn't work, things would get even worse. That afternoon I became increasingly anxious. I dreaded going back to the cell. When we marched back, the cell leader was already inside, waiting for us, smoking a cigarette. I began to climb on to my bed but the cell leader glared at me and asked, "What do you think you're doing?"

I said that I just wanted to lie down. The cell leader began to shout abuse at me. He called me *je-lu pa*, or "backward". Then the brigade leader Chung la came into the cell with the same two soldiers. He repeated the accusations of the previous day, asking me why I continued to make water offerings when I knew that such acts had been forbidden. I repeated my denials.

Again the cell leader was ordered to begin a *thamzing*. I lowered my head. The other prisoners began to punch me, denouncing me one by one. Some of them just grabbed my clothing and shook me, unable to bring themselves to hit one so vulnerable.

This went on every evening for thirteen days. I couldn't eat. Work was, strangely, my only respite. But when the evening whistle sounded and we lined up for the march back to the prison, my stomach tightened and my mind was full of fear and apprehension.

I remember that, at some time during my ordeal, yet another prisoner committed suicide. He was known as Mei Metok, a reference to the large moles on his face, and he'd been a monk at Namgyal monastery in Potala. Mei had been arrested in 1959 for taking part in the Lhasa uprising and at the time of his suicide he too had been the subject of a *thamzing*.

Mei worked with me in the brick factory. A dirt track led from the factory to the prison gate. Each day, marching to and from the factory, we walked alongside the track, through the dust thrown up by passing trucks. Mei marched three rows in front of me. One evening, returning to our cells, Mei broke out of the orderly line and threw himself beneath a truck that had just come in through the main gate. The truck stopped, but too late. I remember Mei's foot jerking violently, then resting motionless on the dirt track. I looked away. We were ordered to march on to the prison in quick step.

No one said anything about Mei's death. It was passed over as if it were an everyday occurrence, which in many ways I suppose it was. We were all too frightened to show how we really felt. Even our tears were secrets.

Our daily existence was so harrowing that we had learned to appear indifferent to beatings and torture. But I was beginning to feel the strain. The mental burden, the load of anxiety, that went with every new day was starting to crush me. I too considered following the example of Mei Metok. Back in the cell the *thamzing* began again, but the beating was less rigorous this time. Even Chung la seemed subdued.

For a fortnight I refused to make any confession. I stuck to my story. The officer at last gave up and said that my case would be dealt with during the annual assessment meeting. I think that my stubbornness won me the admiration of my cellmates.

The annual assessment meeting took place each winter. All the prisoners assembled and reports compiled by the brigade leaders were read out. Those "diligent" prisoners who had informed on others would usually be rewarded with a picture of Mao or a copy of his "Little Red Book". Prisoners who had apparently failed to "reform" themselves were rewarded with increased sentences. Each year a number of prisoners were sentenced to death for failing to reform.

We were woken one morning in November 1970 by the sound of the large metal gate grating on the ground. The gate was rarely opened. This was followed by the brigade leader's voice shouting at the guards, telling them to wake up the prisoners. The cell door was flung open and the guards rushed in, prodding us awake and out of our beds. We assembled in the yard. It was still dark outside, the sky a scattering of thousands upon thousands of stars. The icy wind cut into our faces. We heard the sound of trucks coming into the prison and our cell leader told us we were being taken back to Drapchi to attend the annual "reward and punishment" meeting. We knew this meant an execution.

It was still dark when we got to Drapchi. We jumped down from the trucks and guards instructed us to sit on the muddy ground. More trucks arrived and hundreds of prisoners disembarked. The residents of every prison around Lhasa had been summoned to this meeting. At dawn we were marched through into the prison courtyard. On the surface of the yard the numbers of each prison and brigade had been written in chalk.

An officer told us the three rules of the meeting: no talking, no sleeping, no visits to the latrine. We welcomed the warmth of the dawn sun. Officials from the judicial bureau emerged from their rooms and sat down on a long bench before us. One of them gave a signal and guards brought out those prisoners who were about to be executed. I was relieved that I had not been chosen and at the same time repelled by what was about to happen.

Armed guards dragged in the prisoners one by one, tightly bound and gagged with jute ropes. A large piece of wood hung from their necks filled with Chinese characters I could not understand. I guessed that they gave the names of the prisoners along with details of their supposed crimes. More and more prisoners were dragged out into the yard with these same wooden panels hanging from their necks. Soon there were more than fifty standing before us.

A guard signalled to the cell leaders and activists began to chant,

"Death to counter-revolutionaries!" Then a thousand voices joined in this shout of condemnation.

I recognised two prisoners from my brigade amongst those who were lined up for execution. I remembered how Dikhung Paldar and Lhabchug from Meldrogonkar had both been summoned two days previously. The rumour spread that they had in fact been released. There had been no indication at all that they were about to face execution. But here they were. It is hard to sit and watch someone you know in the moments before their death.

I heard my name being read out by an officer on the podium. I was ordered to come to the front and face the prisoners kneeling motionless, awaiting execution. One of them was grabbed by the hair, face pulled up to mine. She was an old woman, deep-wrinkled and toothless. Her face was swollen and bruised. She could hardly breathe. Even today the memory of her makes me shiver.

Two guards took hold of me and pushed my head down. The woman's name was read out, followed by a list of her "crimes": how she had opposed the motherland, engaged in counter-revolutionary activities and sought to overthrow the dictatorship of the proletariat. But I was not concentrating on her crimes, because her name alone had caused my heart to jump.

She was Kundaling Kusang la. I had heard that name many times before. Kundaling came from one of the great aristocratic families in Tibet and was widely admired for her bravery in standing up to the Chinese. She had organised and led the massive women's demonstration in Lhasa on 12 March 1959, and I had heard that during *thamzing* she had insisted on declaring that Tibet was an independent country. She was the heroine of the Tibetan uprising of 1959.

We stared at each other. Her eyes were red and misty and something in her face seemed to be asking for my prayers. It was winter but the sun shone brightly on the courtyard and the heat of it made me dizzy. I imagined an eagle high above us in the cloudless sky and it seemed to me that the bird was about to swoop down and scoop me up and carry me away from this place, away from the great imminence of death that was here.

I was startled by the presence of a soldier beside me. He placed his hands on my shoulders. My brigade leader appeared in front of me.

"Palden Gyatso," he said.

My throat was dry, but he did not expect a response. "Do you know," he went on, "that you are teetering on the brink of a cliff? You are *this* far —" the distance between his thumb and forefinger — "from these prisoners." He gestured to those awaiting execution. But I was so overwhelmed by fear and disgust that his threats hardly registered in my hearing.

The meeting dragged on and on. Readings of prisoners' case histories continued well into the afternoon. It was announced that the Party had decided to deprive these criminals of the right to live. In thunderous voice the audience demanded death for counter-revolutionaries and death for all enemies of the people. The prisoners were herded into the back of a truck. The truck drove slowly past each of the assembled brigades before coming to a halt at a trench five feet deep that had been dug by prisoners just outside the prison gate. The officers climbed on to the walkway on the prison wall to get a better view. Some of them watched through binoculars.

The prisoners were forced to kneel at the edge of the trench. Then they were shot by a firing squad. The force of the shots toppled their bodies into the trench. Soldiers took aim again and fired at close range into prisoners who had been only wounded in the first volley. Silence is more absolute than usual after a minute of such gunfire. Fifteen people were shot dead that day.

Their families would be informed of the execution by means of an invoice on which such expenses as the number of bullets fired and the length of jute rope used to bind the prisoner were itemised.

Death was our constant companion. It was also the ultimate expression of the Party's power. Prisoners confronted death in different ways. I remember, in the autumn of 1971, people being summoned one by one to a small office. The door of the office was left wide open and there was a large window through which you could observe everything that took place inside. An elderly monk called Jampa Choephel went in ahead of me.

Jampa was the abbot of the Shang Petok monastery and the great, learned monk of Ganden. He had a broad girth and a round face. No amount of beating or torture had been sufficient to make Jampa submit and renounce his religious vows. But no one could have predicted the way he reacted to the announcement of his death sentence. Jampa wailed for mercy. He prostrated himself before the Chinese officer, as monks used to do before their teacher or a high lama. He wept uncontrollably. Soldiers rushed forward and dragged him to a table. They placed his fingerprint on a document. Then, like a sack, he was tied up and thrown into the corner of the room.

A man called Pema Dhonden went in next. Pema used to be the chief steward of the regent Taktra, who had ruled Tibet during the Dalai Lama's minority, and he was well liked throughout the prison. Pema also had no idea that he faced a death sentence. He stood in front of the table and an officer announced that the Party had decided to take away his right to live. "*Thugche-che*," said Pema – "Thank you!" He sounded delighted. I was astonished and so were the Chinese officers. But we were even more surprised by what he said next. Pema recited an old Tibetan proverb, "*Du-po mi-tse tung-na ga, kyi-po mi-tse ring-na ga*" – "It is good to have a long happy life but even better to have a short unhappy one." Then, with the utmost assurance, Pema pressed his finger on the ink pad and rolled it firmly on the document.

Thinking back, it strikes me that Pema was a layman, with no training in meditation and Buddhist philosophy. How could he have faced death with such courage while a learned monk who had devoted his life to the contemplation of death and the belief that his physical being was nothing but an impermanent mass became so distraught, pleading for mercy?

Pema's response had rendered the power of the Chinese inert and trifling. His nonchalance made their cruelty meaningless.

Another prisoner was sentenced to death for accidentally defacing a portrait of Mao. His transgression was revealed during a weekly meeting. The cell leader presided, as usual. One prisoner accused another of harbouring a deep hatred for the Great Helmsman. The evidence cited was that someone had found a fingernail mark on his portrait of Mao. The precise dimensions of the mark were cited at the meeting. The authorities ordered the prisoner to tell them how the mark came to be on the portrait. The prisoner could not explain. He was sentenced to death.

During this period the Party launched campaigns in China that targeted Confucius and Lin Biao. In Tibet campaigns were aimed at the Dalai Lama and the Panchen Rinpoche. We all knew that the Chinese wanted us to denounce His Holiness as the number one enemy of the Party and the new socialist society. We tended to get round this by denouncing the Tibetan aristocracy instead. The cadres kept repeating the question: *Who is the source of all misery in Tibet?*

One day a prisoner called Thupten Kunga stood up during a meeting. Thupten was serving a twenty-year sentence for taking part in the 1959 revolt. Very calmly, he made the statement the rest of us had been trying so carefully to avoid. "The Dalai Lama," he said, "is the source of all misery in Tibet." We could not believe he was saying this. "The Dalai Lama," Thupten continued, "is the slave-master who betrayed the motherland. We must expose the crimes of the Dalai Lama."

Kunga's prison term was reduced by seven years and he was later appointed cell leader.

By the end of 1970, most of the factional wrangling had come to an end. The army was now firmly in charge. All the monasteries and temples were closed or had been destroyed. The people of Tibet now lived in communes. These were described as "the highest stage of development".

Chapter Nine
Reform through Labour

B Y THE END OF 1970 I had been in prison for ten years. I had begun to believe that I would not live to see my own freedom. I was very weak, both mentally and physically, and constantly short of breath. I sought permission from the brigade leader to visit the prison dispensary but the request was dismissed.

Two hundred of us were sent to work on a hydroelectricity construction site in Tolung, to the south of Lhasa. We were told that the hydroelectric plant was a sign of Tibet's development into a modern society. We dug channels to divert water from the river and we worked so hard that we completed a week's work in just three days. Senior officials from the electricity office congratulated us, rewarding each of us with a bar of soap and a towel. We put so much into our work because it was a sort of escape from the mental burden we all carried. It gave us relief.

When I returned to Sangyip my health had got even worse. Permission to attend the clinic was again refused. The guards said that my illness was just a trick to avoid work. I was sent to work in a quarry, one of the hardest jobs of all. One day I fainted.

I came round in the local dispensary. The room was spotless and the smell of antiseptic chemicals was overwhelming. A doctor told me I was in hospital. "Why didn't you come to the clinic before?" he asked. I told him that the brigade leader had refused to give me permission. The doctor was furious. He told me I was very sick and that I needed to be transferred to a larger hospital. So I was taken back to Drapchi.

For the first time in my life I was given a thorough medical check-up. A young Chinese doctor called Wang examined me. He spoke some Tibetan. He kept saying, "*Yag-po min-do*" – "It's no good." I kept quiet.

When the examination was over he summoned a young Tibetan nurse to translate the medical terms. He told me that I had a heart problem, but the details of his diagnosis were lost in translation.

It was strange to be sleeping in a bed of my own, away from the crush of the cells. The clean white cotton sheets were an unbelievable luxury. I was given clean new clothes. I was fed three meals a day, with snacks as well. In the mornings we were given proper Tibetan buttered tea and often there was rice and even vegetables.

Wang was genuinely concerned for his patients' wellbeing, but the Party worked through the medical staff too. Wang had been given my file and knew my case history, and he would often ask me why I persisted with my reactionary beliefs. He advised me to embrace socialism. He told me that socialism meant progress throughout the world.

Softened by the gentle attention of doctors and nurses, many prisoners divulged secrets they had kept for years. I was determined not to fall into that trap. Even so, one day I was caught off guard and tricked into making a "slanderous" remark about socialism. The authorities placed a trusted observer in every cell, work unit and hospital ward, so that they were always informed about everything that was going on among the prisoners. These observers, or stool pigeons, were usually criminal convicts from "clean" class backgrounds, with instructions to report everything they heard and saw to the authorities. Stool pigeons were also encouraged to criticise individuals directly.

The day after I was transferred to the hospital I became aware that there was an informer on the ward. A young man from Nagchu in north-eastern Tibet had been moved in next to me. He did not seem very ill. He introduced himself and announced with surprising nonchalance that he had murdered his wife. He added that his class background was "poor nomad". This meant that he had benefited considerably from the Chinese occupation. Everyone called him Mardho, or Red, on account of his revolutionary leanings.

I was wary of Mardho. I took that mention of his class background to be a warning. But I was determined not to give him the chance to provoke me. He nagged me constantly. One day I lost my self-control when he demanded my new pyjamas, which were tucked beneath my pillow.

"As a poor nomad, you have been granted everything by the Party," I shouted. "But I am a member of the exploiting class and everything has been taken away from me."

Mardho looked delighted. I could see how my rash words would be twisted and embellished until they demonstrated my profound opposition to socialism. Sure enough, the brigade leader soon came to my bed and lectured me about "reactionaries who were not reconciled to the defeat of feudalism".

For the next two weeks I was subjected to a *thamzing* and told to confess my crimes. Instead of the usual pounding of fists I was assailed by a barrage of verbal abuse. My fellow sick prisoners did their best to make their outrage seem genuine. They all made the mandatory denunciations. I confessed. Mardho looked very smug, thrilled that he had done his duty and exposed a reactionary.

Once my recovery was under way I was given some light work in the hospital, either cleaning or making bandages and cotton buds. I was still feeling short of breath and had developed a severe pain in my chest. I was discharged at the beginning of 1971 and taken back to Sangyip prison. I was allocated to cell number one, well known as the toughest cell of all.

After three days of dispensation from work I was once again marched out to a quarry, where I joined hundreds of other prisoners breaking boulders into neat square blocks. At first I had the task of shaping the blocks, but soon I was made to carry boulders on my bare back 100 yards from the quarry to the building site.

On my second day at the quarry I saw a young man lying motionless on his back with a huge stone pressing down on his chest. There was no end to the cruelty of the guards and officials. A month later the cell leader Wangyal cracked open a prisoner's head with an iron rod.

The skin grew hard and calloused on my fingers and palms. Some prisoners made hand-pads out of discarded shoe soles and I too began collecting as many soles as I could. I collected six soles and sewed them together with wire. The pad protected my hand from the sharp edges of the stones and became one of my most prized possessions.

That September I noticed two soldiers removing portraits of Lin Biao, whom the Party's National Congress had named as the chosen successor to Chairman Mao. For nearly five years, morning and evening, we had had to chant, "Long live Lin Biao." The removal of the pictures suggested that something serious had happened.

A few days later we were summoned to a meeting. The director of the prison announced that Lin Biao had attempted to assassinate Mao. The attempt had failed and the plane on which Lin had fled with his co-conspirators had crashed, killing everyone on board. The Chinese officers appeared bewildered by these events.

So now there was a new campaign aimed at discrediting Lin Biao. We studied the *Tibet Daily* and made the appropriate denunciations. Such denunciations were now second nature to all of us. All references to Lin Biao were quickly erased from Party literature. Murals and paintings were altered or destroyed. Pages on which his name appeared were torn from books without ceremony.

At another meeting, a young Tibetan official called Tenpa announced that Henry Kissinger was visiting China. The name meant nothing to me. Tenpa explained who Kissinger was and told us that the relationship between the United States and China was becoming much stronger. A few months later we were told that President Nixon would be visiting China.

Nixon's visit was seen as a victory for China and the proletarian Revolution. We felt nothing but disappointment. Since 1960 we had hoped that the Americans would liberate our country. In Drapchi in 1961 I had heard that a Tibetan army had been formed in India and that they were being trained by Americans. The prisoner who told me this had himself been flown to America for training and then been parachuted back into Tibet.

Our expectations gained strength from the vehemence of China's denunciations of the United States. The Americans were described as reactionaries bent on world domination. They were regarded as China's foremost enemy. We had spent meeting after meeting denouncing American imperialism. So it was very depressing to hear that the United States had now bowed to China. The Chinese liked to say that the east wind had prevailed over the west wind.

We were forced to listen to interminable victory speeches. We were told that we had hoped in vain for assistance from American imperialists and that they could be of no more help to us than our gods. We were shown newsreel footage of the welcoming ceremony that had greeted Nixon in Beijing. The prison tannoy blared out nothing but the Sino-American friendship for several weeks. We were told that the American president had come to Beijing like a dog with its tail between its legs. And the following year China became a member of the United Nations. It seemed that all prospects of Tibet's liberation were fading.

Our only comfort was that the Dalai Lama was still free in India.

It seemed more unlikely than ever that I would be released. Nor was release necessarily something to be wished for. I learned of the death of a master craftsman called Dram la, who made bronze ritual objects. Dram la had been arrested in 1960 and imprisoned for ten years. When he returned to his village in 1970 the welcoming ceremony that greeted him was in fact a *thamzing*. All the villagers, including his own family, had gathered to bear witness against him. They denounced him as a class enemy and reactionary. After a few days of "freedom", Dram la killed himself.

The authorities told us this story as a warning. They said that we had to reform ourselves completely if we were to escape the anger of the masses. They said that the Tibetan people were fired up with revolutionary enthusiasm and looked to Chairman Mao as their guiding light. The Chinese were implying that there was no difference between prison and what lay outside the walls.

* * *

In 1975 my fifteen-year sentence should have been coming to an end. On the morning of 24 December I was told that I was not required to go to work but should instead report to the main administrative block. I knew that this did not mean release, only another transfer. A few other prisoners were waiting outside the office and they too knew better than to expect happy reunions with families and friends. When formal sentences expired, prisoners were often sent to labour reform camps, another kind of prison.

A Tibetan man stepped from the office and read out my name. The director of the prison and the brigade leader were both waiting inside. They tried to create an atmosphere of excitement and encouraged me to think that I was going to be released. Then the brigade leader told me I was going to Nyethang Zhuanwa Chang.

"Zhuanwa Chang!" I exclaimed, almost laughingly. It was notorious as a place of hard labour. Guards even used to threaten us by saying we'd be sent to Zhuanwa Chang. The labour camp was situated about fifteen miles from Lhasa, at the edge of Tibet's mightiest river, the Tsangpo. It contained one of the largest factories in the whole country and produced a vast quantity of tiles and bricks. It was just the sort of destination I had expected.

When I went to pack my belongings I found a receipt for some items that had been confiscated in 1960. I took the receipt to the office. After about twenty minutes a guard emerged with a bundle. I looked through the bundle and soon realised that my watch was missing. I went back inside and told the Chinese officer, showing him my receipt.

I was told to wait outside. After several minutes the brigade leader emerged. He told me my watch had been destroyed.

"But the owner is alive," I said.

Only the belongings of dead prisoners were destroyed. The official went back into the office and I heard some argument going on there. A Tibetan officer came out and asked to see my receipt.

"It's a gold Rolex," I said. "It's the best watch in the world. I have heard that it goes on working even if you put it in a fire or under ice."

"How can we find the watch if we don't have any details?" the officer asked.

"You must have the original of this receipt in my file," I replied.

We went back into the office. The guard showed the receipt to the *juizhang*, the prison director.

"We will refund your watch," he said calmly.

I wasn't satisfied by this. I told him that it was very expensive.

"There is an official exchange rate for gold," he answered.

I was beginning to enjoy myself.

"But my brother did not buy the watch at the official rate. And anyway, I would rather have my watch than the money."

I pretended to be upset, accusing them of theft and breaching prison regulations. Years of *thamzing* had taught me that the best way to attack was to question an official's loyalty to the Party and his ideological position.

"Chairman Mao taught the PLA to observe certain rules of conduct which forbade the soldiers from taking so much as a pin from the people," I said. "Only a reactionary soldier would actually *steal* from a prisoner."

Finally the prison director said that the matter would be investigated and that the watch would be sent to me in Nyethang Zhuanwa Chang. He told me that the tractor was waiting, so I gathered up my bundle and ran out to it, exhilarated by my encounter with the officials and flushed with a sense of triumph. The tractor pulled out of Sangyip and headed for Lhasa.

It took us about three hours to reach the tile factory. I rode in the trailer with two other prisoners, a Chinese man who had been an accountant and a former monk from Shigatse. We passed right by Potala Palace, the first time I had seen that magnificent place since 1964.

The factory's office was a new building with a tin roof. Two officers, one Tibetan, one Chinese, were sitting behind a desk inside. The Tibetan, Trinlay, was scrutinising my file. The Chinese officer just looked at us, drawing heavily on his cigarette. Trinlay did all the talking. He asked me my name and other details and checked them against what was written in the file.

"You are no longer a prisoner," he told me.

My lack of response was a clear indication that I did not agree with his assessment. Trinlay was not concerned. He gave me a pair of gloves and a white cotton mask like that worn by a surgeon. He told me about my work in the factory and briefed me on my rights and duties as a *ley-mi*: a "reform through labour" prisoner.

Ley-mi were not allowed to travel outside the immediate district. We were not allowed to visit Lhasa. We could shop at the co-operative store, though only with permission from our brigade leader and in the company of another *ley-mi*, each acting as the other's guarantor.

The barracks were no different from those in a prison. They had mud walls and uneven muddy floors. In the corners you could see the glimmer of iced-over puddles. Portraits of Marx, Engels, Stalin and Mao hung on all the walls. There was a wooden hook for clothing and one long raised platform to serve as a bed for all the *ley-mi*. Five bundles of bedding indicated that I was to share the room with five others.

It was late afternoon and everyone was at work. I fell asleep for a few hours, only to be woken by the stamping of feet and the sound of voices. The other prisoners were surprised to find this new face. They smiled at me and we exchanged greetings. We asked each other question upon question. Two of them were former monks from Drepung, so we had a lot of friends in common. I felt at home among them.

The atmosphere here was much more relaxed than it had been in prison. There were still study sessions and *thamzing*, but people were more open; they spoke more freely. The two monks took me under their wing, teaching me all about the life of a *ley-mi*.

Each morning every single *ley-mi* rose before dawn and walked out in the dark with a large basket on his back. We were each required to collect one basket full of dung and human excrement to be used as manure. There was fierce competition to get your hands on the stuff. Every morning 200 prisoners raided the nearby hills in search of their quota of manure.

One prisoner, called Tseten Wangchuk, had refused to go and collect his share. When all the baskets were weighed, Tseten just stood there holding his empty basket, insisting that there was no more shit around. He was immediately subjected to a *thamzing*.

As the former estate manager for an aristocratic family, he was labelled "a representative of the exploiting class". He also had a quick tongue and always answered back. His former estate was only half a mile from Nyethang and the peasants there mocked him as he searched for manure in the fields. One day Tseten responded to their taunts by saying, "What a wonderful time this is that we live in. We collect shit as if it were precious cake." This was reported to the authorities. Tseten was again subjected to a *thamzing* for defaming socialism.

The following morning Tseten refused to get up. His fellow prisoners pleaded with him but he wouldn't budge. The brigade leader arrived with several guards and reprimanded him. Tseten told them that he had roamed all over the hills and could not find any shit. The brigade leader said that he should be more diligent and start searching by the roads.

"I didn't know trucks could shit," replied Tseten. "Socialist trucks must be far superior to capitalist trucks."

Work was cancelled that day. All the *ley-mi* and all the inhabitants of surrounding communes were summoned to a meeting. The peasants from Tseten's former estates were told to denounce him. The prisoners had to criticise him too. He was harangued and beaten. And then he was executed.

After I had collected my quota of manure I would be marched into the factory and instructed to mix mud until it was smooth enough to be made into tiles. I had to bake the tiles in the kiln. It was hard to breathe, the dust was so thick. I was paid a modest wage for my work, which I was allowed to put towards a monthly ration of grain. I was also allowed to purchase thirteen yards of cloth and eleven pounds of sugar per year. Our pay levels were determined by our political backgrounds, so of course my wages were among the lowest.

At mealtimes we lined up at a hatch in the main hall and food would be passed out to us. We had to say how many buns we wanted and a guard would put crosses by our names, one cross for each bun. Beside our name was written the maximum amount of grain we were entitled to. If we had consumed our quota for the month, we would not be given any more. Every month the guards calculated the total number of buns consumed and this would be subtracted from our entitlement. The authorities would also deduct payments for electricity, water, salt, tea, vegetables and cooking fuel from our basic pay.

The labour camp was designed to be self-financing, the cost of administering the camp met by deductions from the prisoners' wages. It cost the state almost nothing to run an extensive network of labour camps.

The authorities kept to the motto, "Consume less, produce more." Instead of different uniforms for winter and summer we now received only one padded uniform which we had to wear all year round. My shoes were in tatters and my uniform was soon held together only by patches.

The whole of Tibet was now organised into communes. All private property had been confiscated and redistributed. Agricultural production had gone into rapid decline and people were getting by on meagre rations. The entire country had been turned into a prison. No one could travel or purchase anything without a permit.

Meanwhile, the labour camps served two purposes: to isolate class enemies and to provide cheap labour. We were told that the only way to escape was by enthusiasm in labour and diligence in reform. Just as in prison, we were made to attend weekly meetings at which we had to criticise ourselves and our friends. Like everyone else, I was subjected to many criticisms and I made many criticisms.

I never got used to the pain that the denunciation of a friend could cause. But we had to learn how to forget the endless forced betrayals. The camaraderie among the prisoners was genuine and unmistakable, and we all tried to avoid making accusations that might lead to an increased sentence or execution. However, there were always a few prisoners ready to prove their loyalty to the Party by their accusations, regardless of the consequences. We called these people *hurtson-chen*, the diligent ones.

Not long after my arrival at Nyethang, a prisoner called Pasang committed suicide after three weeks of the most severe *thamzing*. He was well liked by all of us. Another prisoner, called Sonam Palden, was always looking for the chance to show how keenly he embraced the new society. Sonam found out that Pasang had managed to hide a small badge with a picture of the Dalai Lama and during one of the weekly meetings he stood up to expose Pasang's secret. After he was found dead, the authorities announced that Pasang had taken his own life because he could not adjust to the new socialist society.

Chapter Ten
Death of the Helmsman

THE LABOUR CAMP WAS a half-way house between prison and the new socialist society. In theory, these reform camps were re-education centres, but in practice they simply provided the Party with pools of cheap labour. They functioned as a kind of quarantine, keeping our dangerous ideas of Tibetan freedom and independence away from the rest of society. Prisoners transferred to a labour camp knew it was more than likely they would die there.

The regime in Nyethang Zhuanwa Chang was not very different from that in a proper prison. The Chinese senior officer, a vicious man with a foul temper, was always referred to by his official title: *Changzhang*, the director of the factory. He ran the tile factory as if it were his own private kingdom and even the guards were terrified of him. He had a Tibetan assistant called Wangdu, who was short and stout and sympathetic to our situation.

The absence of guards patrolling the compound day and night gave the impression that our barracks were no different from any other large dormitory building near a factory. But we were *ley-mi*, not free men. The lack of sentries did not mean we were not under surveillance. The Party had discovered a more effective means of observation.

We were divided into two categories, the capped and the uncapped. The capped were political prisoners, those of us labelled "reactionaries". The uncapped were the criminal convicts. This was the basis of a system of mutual surveillance: it was obligatory for the uncapped to watch over those with caps. The authorities were again using the idea of class struggle as a way of creating conflict and distrust among prisoners. Those prisoners without caps were told that they were defenders of socialism and the Revolution.

So they strode about the camp, relishing the power they had over us. They reported the slightest misdemeanour to the central office. In return, they were promised a quick "merger" into the new society.

Soon after I was transferred to the camp, I was sitting outside the mess hall during the midday break when a group of children appeared at the main gate, urging one another to go into the compound. Eventually they did come in and, to my astonishment, one of them approached me and started to beg for food. He said that his family had not eaten for days.

The Party had told us that hunger and food shortages were things of the past. But the faces of these children were faces I'd seen in Tolung prison during the worst years of my life: horribly bloated and the skin turned a pale, sickly green. They could hardly open their eyes. They had no shoes and their clothes were all in tatters. Even beggars in the old "feudal" society were better off than this; at least they walked on a full stomach.

I wondered if they'd been neglected because they were the children of former landlords. I knew that the families of the "reactionary" class were severely discriminated against and treated no better than farm animals. So I asked the children what their class backgrounds were. This had become the overriding issue. Your class background was clearly written on your ration card, identity certificate and medical card.

The children told me that they were from the "poor peasant" class. This surprised me, as the Party had told us that "poor peasants" were benefiting from the socialist Revolution. But the children told me that all the nearby communes were facing food shortages. Some of their families had been forced to eat grass. They would boil the grass until it formed a thick, still-indigestible broth. I gave some of my buns to the children and they soon became regular visitors to the camp mess.

The whole of Tibet had now been brought to what the Party called "the highest stage of Communist development". The Nyethang region was divided into twelve huge communes or brigades. Now all property and livestock were supposed to be held in common ownership and people were paid according to a complicated system of work points.

But more and more people came to beg at the camp. I began to make a note of which communes they were coming from and it became apparent that the whole of Nyethang faced the same food shortage. When adults came to beg, I asked them to explain the reasons for such a famine. They told me that it was not the result of any natural disaster.

The shortage of food was caused by the fact that people had to surrender most of what they earned in the form of a "voluntary" contribution to the government. People were already obliged to pay a wide range of taxes and the communes' administrations were under pressure to report higher production figures and send even more to the government.

In order to extract maximum yields, the Party created fierce competition between the peasants. They were told that their contribution expressed the extent of their love for the motherland, the Party and Chairman Mao. Under such an edict, no one wanted to appear idle. There was a similar rivalry between the communes, with each one wanting to show that it was making the greatest contribution to socialist construction. This led to the falsification of production figures and a subsequent rise in taxes. In the end, the poor farmers went hungry.

In the "new socialist society", people were finding themselves forced to eat the husks that were, in the "old feudal society", fit only for the animals. Everyone knew that the situation was appalling, yet no single official would dare question the wisdom of the Party and its leader. The labour camps were a permanent reminder of what happened to those who opposed the Party.

Those young, emaciated children bore witness to the suffering of the entire country. At least, as prisoners, we *expected* to be treated badly, but ordinary people had no such consolation; they were supposed to be the beneficiaries of the great proletarian Revolution. The whole apparatus of oppression was apparently created to free poor farmers and nomads from the servitude of the feudal society, but the past twenty years had brought them nothing but misery.

When the district office found out that labour reform prisoners had been giving food to the farmers, a complaint was made to the prison authority. I was named as one of the principal culprits, guilty of encouraging the capitalist practice of begging. I was summoned to the director's office and asked to explain my actions. Then, to my surprise, the complaint was dismissed. There was some rivalry between our work unit and the commune outside and it seemed that the camp officials were rather pleased that we had made the commune look so bad.

In the spring of 1976 I finally heard news of my family in Panam. I was told I had a visitor, my first since I had become a prisoner. I was perplexed, and eager to see who it might be. When I got outside, I saw a chubby young woman wearing a blue headscarf, patched up trousers and a green padded cotton jacket. She had a cracked face and watery eyes. She carried a thermos and a small basket.

I apologised for not recognising her and asked who she was.

"I am Nangma Mingke," she said.

I was not familiar with that name.

"You may have confused me with someone else," I said. "I am Palden Gyatso, a monk from Drepung."

She began to explain that she was the daughter of my father's cook. It was over fifteen years since I'd left Panam, and there was no way I could have recognised her. I asked her how she had known where to find me. She told me that she'd seen me working at the factory.

Mingke had just moved to the Nyethang area. She and her husband were working on a road that was being built close to the labour camp. She told me that my father had died in 1965. As a former landlord, he was repeatedly denounced by the villagers and subjected to many *thamzings*. My oldest brother, for whom I had the deepest admiration, had been killed during a *thamzing* in 1968. My family became one of the Red

Guards' favourite targets. Every member of the family was subjected to public beatings, sometimes individually and sometimes all together. My stepmother had been left paralysed by a particularly brutal struggle session.

I couldn't sleep that night, my mind full of the faces of my family and thoughts of the pain they must have suffered. I had known that all those regarded as feudal landlords had been targeted by the Red Guards, but this foreknowledge was no comfort to me.

Mingke used her class background to her advantage. As a former servant she was regarded as "clean" and could come and go without impediment. She became a regular visitor and always brought what little food she had to share with me. One day her husband brought me a brand-new quilt, which must have cost them dearly.

Their visits and kindness were like a balm, something to warm me in the bleak winter. I was dejected and lonely, but Mingke brought me memories of happier times. As a worker she was allowed to return home to her family in Panam, and through Mingke my family learned that I was alive.

By early 1976, China's premier, Zhou Enlai, and the founder of the PLA, Zhu De, had both died. Their deaths were widely reported in the press and mourning ceremonies were held in the camp. Officials tried to create a mournful atmosphere; *hurtson-chens* acted as though they'd lost a close relative. The authorities used such occasions to assess your attitude to the Party, so it was important to act rueful and distraught.

A month after Zhu De's death I read in the *Tibet Daily* that China had been struck by a huge earthquake. The Chinese were right to suspect that I had not left behind my feudal ideas, for I thought immediately that the earthquake and the pair of deaths were auguries of events to come. My superstitions were further aroused when, some time in August, I saw a comet blazing in the night sky.

Tibetans consider comets to be portents. I went straight to my dormitory, wanting to ask if anyone else had seen the comet. But then

I checked myself, realising that such a question would simply result in my being accused of encouraging superstition and spreading rumours.

I had read in the paper of a "rain of rocks" somewhere in China – which I suppose meant meteorites. The next morning, unable to keep my sighting to myself, I asked a monk named Tashi Lather if he had seen the comet. He nodded, but was too scared to talk about it openly.

News of the comet spread quickly through the camp. Everyone remembered that Tibet had been struck by an earthquake just before the Chinese invasion in October 1950 and that a comet had been sighted then too. Despite nearly twenty years of repression and Chinese indoctrination, the appearance of the comet swiftly rekindled our traditional beliefs.

I was convinced that these manifestations indicated that Mao was nearing his death. We all knew that Mao was old and ailing, though of course none of us would have talked about this openly. On 9 September 1976, my suspicions proved to be correct: Mao died in Beijing. I remember the moment I learned of his death as if it were yesterday. For years the Chinese had sought to convince us that Mao was superhuman, some sort of immortal being, though now he had gone the way of all living things.

I had just finished work and was waiting in the line outside the mess with my mug in my hand. The loudspeaker mounted on a high pole in the middle of the compound emitted a loud crackle. We paid little attention to whatever rubbish blared out of the tannoy and the prisoners waiting in the queue just went on chatting. Anyway, announcements were always made in Chinese first, so the majority of us who spoke no Chinese never bothered to listen to the first part of any broadcast.

Then the voice of another speaker, a Tibetan, came over the tannoy. "From the radio station of the People's Central Government," he began, his voice quivering. He sounded choked with emotion and kept stumbling over the beginning of the announcement, stopping and then starting again. Someone near me asked, "What's the matter with him?" The speaker took another deep breath and launched into the customary invocation of the Great Helmsman and all the other superlatives that always preceded Mao's name. Then he said, "The Red Sun of our Hearts, the people's beloved Chairman Mao, is no more with us."

The announcement left all of us in a daze. Was Mao really dead? It must be true, for no one would dare play such a trick. Back in the dormitory, as the news began to sink in, I was filled with a sense of elation. I could have jumped up and broken into song right there! Mao had been my tormentor and my adversary. For almost twenty years I had had to recite his name every morning and night. Even when I could not open my jaws wide enough to take a sip of water from a mug, I was forced to make the familiar invocation, "*Mao Zedong Wanzi*." I had kept his "Little Red Book" with me at all times and I'd even made a red bag just big enough to hold the book, because I knew that for some prisoners spoiling the book had meant the death sentence.

Mao's name was written all over my suffering and all over the deaths of thousands of prisoners. Mao's name linked us all. I could not help but see his death as a break in the chain of suffering.

I'm sure this is what the others felt too, though of course such emotions had to be kept hidden from view. I adopted a pensive look and pretended to be deep in thought. I had no way of knowing whether life would now improve, but one thing was certain: it could not remain the same. I had visions of the Dalai Lama returning to Tibet, but then these would be dispelled by the thought that someone even worse than Mao might come to power. So there was joy, but fear too. The great tyrant was dead, but who would now fill his throne?

The next day we were summoned to another meeting. All the prison officials were wearing black armbands and some had white paper flowers protruding from their jacket pockets. An official announced, "Our Beloved Leader, the Brightest Sun in Our Heart and Our Guide, the Great Chairman Mao, has died." Mourning music sounded from the loudspeaker.

Some of the prisoners burst into tears and wept loudly. I heard one prisoner wailing, "Chairman Mao is kinder than my parents." The other prisoners stood to sullen attention. We'd been warned that we were required to adopt the "correct attitude" during this sad occasion. I had become an accomplished actor. I wore a mournful expression and kept quiet. Soon prisoners were weeping or even pretending to faint; this was what the Chinese meant by the "correct attitude". Up on the stage, the officials were sobbing uncontrollably.

Two guards appeared, carrying a sack full of black armbands. These were distributed to all the prisoners except for those of us labelled "political prisoners". The privilege of mourning was reserved for the criminals. We "reactionaries" were not fit to mourn the death of Mao. One prisoner from my unit pulled on his armband with unmistakable pride. He raised his arm towards me and gave me a wink, like a little child showing off his sweets. The following day all the uncapped prisoners were driven to Lhasa to attend a massive rally to mourn the death of that Great Helmsman.

Mao's death in fact resulted in a more relaxed policy in the camp. The endless cycle of meetings came to an end. In 1978 we were told to burn Mao's "Little Red Book". That was an extraordinary feeling, burning the book that had been such an integral part of our lives for nearly twenty years. We were also allowed to drop the morning ritual that invoked Chairman Mao.

Life improved rapidly. I was asked to start weaving and producing carpets. The camp kept a flock of sheep, but in the past wool had been either sold to the camp co-operative or left neglected in a corner. There was a huge store of wool to work with and I welcomed the chance to escape from the tile factory.

The problem was that I was the only prisoner who knew anything at all about weaving. So I had to do everything myself, including spinning the wool into threads and then dyeing it. It was tedious work, but at least I could work alone. I was no longer under the surveillance of my co-workers.

The newspapers were full of stories about the Gang of Four,

particularly Mao's widow, Jiang Qing. The Gang were accused of trying to take control of the Party following Mao's death and blamed for the violence of the Cultural Revolution. The Party was now promising to rectify the mistakes of the past decade and we soon felt the benefit of this in the camp. Our prisoner's allowance was increased and we were even paid a hardship allowance called "the wind and sun".

In the winter of 1977 all capped prisoners were summoned to a meeting, at which we were again questioned about our roles in the 1959 uprising. I repeated my story. Some prisoners denied, foolishly, that they had even been present at the revolt. We were not told why we were being questioned again after all this time.

A few days later, during the morning roll call, my name was read out along with those of three other prisoners. We were told we were going to Lhasa. We drove to a large military camp on the edge of the city and joined hundreds of prisoners from other labour camps all gathered in a spacious hall. The hall was decorated as for a banquet and along one wall there was a line of tables laid out with dishes of food. I had never seen so much food. Friendly soldiers served us tea, treating us like visiting dignitaries. I saw many familiar faces from Drapchi, Seitru and Orithridu, and we greeted one another warmly. We all suspected that we might just be on the point of freedom.

A senior Tibetan Party official named Wangchuk walked into the hall and began to address us. "Comrades and friends," he said. Comrades and friends! I could not believe it. Wangchuk extolled the virtue of the Party and said that what had happened to Tibet in the last twenty years had been an aberration and should not be held against the Party. He blamed everything on the Gang of Four. Then, in a soft, clear voice, he announced that all political labels and caps would now be removed.

Wangchuk went on to say that, under the leadership of Chairman Hua Guofeng, we were at the dawn of a new era and that we should now all contribute to the building of a socialist Tibet. We were used to this sort of talk. I was sitting next to an old monk from Drepung called Choephel Tharchin, a wise old man with a long grey beard such as those I remembered from the images on the monastery walls that were said to represent longevity.

"What will you do?" I asked him.

"I would like to go back to the monastery," Choephel replied, and this made me think that I should like to return to Drepung.

We were told to submit our requests in writing the following day. The officials said that we would be allowed to return home, though Wangyal quickly added that many of us were well educated and literate and should therefore think of contributing to the new socialist construction.

The meeting lasted for three days. We all slept in the hall and each morning soldiers brought us tea. I heard someone remark that we were like lambs being fattened up before they were taken to the butcher's. On the third morning, I was told that my request had been accepted and that I could have a residence permit to stay at the monastery. I was jubilant and waved my paper in the air. I discovered that out of 200 former monks in the hall, only three of us had applied to return to our monasteries. The others had simply not believed that their request would be granted and had instead applied to be teachers, believing that this gave them a better chance of being sent home. But as soon as they found out that our requests had been granted, they all changed their minds and pestered the unlucky officer whose task it was to distribute the permits. He couldn't change anything. This was still the Communist Party and once a decision had been made by a senior officer, no one dared question it or waver from putting it into effect.

I went back to Nyethang full of excitement at the prospect of my release. Some of the other prisoners came up to congratulate me on my good fortune; others had letters for me to take to their families. I expected to be released immediately, but nothing happened until a few days later, when an army jeep drove into the camp and I was summoned to the office along with the two other monks, Choephel Tharchin and

Thupten Dhundup. Tharchin emerged after a few minutes, grinning wildly and waving his hands in the air. He was free.

It was my turn to go into the office. The brigade leader was sitting behind the desk, his eyes scanning a thick file. He acknowledged my presence by coughing. As politely as I could, I said, "I was due to return to the monastery."

The camp opposed my request on the grounds that I was an essential worker. As part of the Party's new economic policy, the camp was to expand its carpet production. Since I was the only prisoner who could teach the necessary weaving skills, I had to remain. My protests fell on deaf ears. The only consolation was that I was now free to travel to Lhasa at weekends.

It was at about this time that Lobsang Wangchuk arrived at the camp. I had first encountered him at Drapchi in early 1964 and I was now to learn to revere him as a mentor and friend. Everyone in the prison referred to him simply as *Gyen*, teacher. I remember how once, in Drapchi, Gyen Lobsang stood up at a meeting and announced, with much courage, that he had written a prayer beseeching the protecting deity to avert natural disasters in Tibet, something that the Chinese had said amounted to "spreading reactionary rumours".

Gyen was tall by Tibetan standards, with a lean, sensitive face, a pencil-line moustache and a natural humility that belied his great strength and learning. He had first been arrested in 1960 for his involvement in the previous year's uprising. Since 1970 he had been a *ley-mi*, a worker in a labour reform camp.

I asked the brigade leader if I could have a man to help me spin the wool. The official told me to select one from a group of men working in a nearby field and I chose Gyen Lobsang Wangchuk. I thought that weaving might be more manageable work for an old man, as Gyen was by this time sixty-four years old, skinny and frail.

We started to work together in August 1978, just the two of us in a room, me in one corner weaving and Gyen nearby spinning wool. Most of the prisoners were enthusiastic about the changes taking place and I asked Gyen what he thought about them.

"It's just a new pair of shoes walking on the same old road," he said.

Over the following days I began to see what he meant. I realised that there were two fundamental issues on which the Communist Party would not be moved. The first was the question of Tibetan independence; the second the question of religious freedom. But people all around us seemed to be forgetting the past in a hurry. Nothing had really changed for us. We were still prisoners, still subject to every whim and fancy of the prison officials and warders. Just because the Party had decreed that a new era had dawned was no reason for celebration.

Talking with Gyen as he spun wool into thread for me to weave, I began to look at my captivity in a different light. My confinement was only a smaller version of the imprisonment of the whole of Tibet. Thousands of prisoners, innocent of all crimes, had been tortured and starved. Our country had been occupied and we, its inhabitants, placed in prisons. How could we call ourselves free? I began to despise the Communist Party even more than I had before. The Party claimed to be serving poor people even as it sent thousands to their deaths. It had no regard for human life.

One cold February morning in 1979, all the *ley-mi* were again summoned to a meeting. This time we were told to speak out and make all our criticisms known without fear. These meetings were usually held when there was some kind of power struggle going on among the most senior Party officials. Criticisms were harvested from prisoners and the populace and then used as evidence against the present holders of power.

The meeting was dominated by sycophants making lengthy speeches about the new era, full of praise for the Communist Party. This made me angry. I thought we should use this opportunity to voice our grievances and let the officials know how much we had suffered. When I went back to work, Gyen was already sitting on the floor, surrounded by heaps of spun wool. He looked at me and asked, "Have they forgotten, in just a few days, what they endured for twenty years?"

Gyen suggested that we should write down our opinions and submit them as a petition. We could start by saying that we'd wanted to speak during the meeting but had not had the chance. I agreed immediately and for the next two days Gyen set about writing a long petition, stopping now and again to read bits out to me. As I listened, I was amazed at his knowledge, and his composition read beautifully.

He wrote the petition in a crumpled notebook, starting with quotations from the Dalai Lama's "Prayer for Universal Truth". Each section opened with four verses taken from the prayer. The first part of the petition detailed the suffering endured by the Tibetan people in recent years. The second section described Tibet's 2,700-year history and declared that Tibet was an independent nation.

The Tibetan New Year was approaching and all the guards and officers were in a festive mood. For the first time, the Chinese were allowing people to celebrate the New Year. I suggested to Gyen that this might be a good time to hand over the petition. He agreed and immediately took it to the office. The guards had no time to listen to him; they merely instructed him to leave the petition on the table. But as he was leaving the office, Gyen turned back to the guards and asked, "Can the people read this document?"

"Yes," replied the officer, without even looking up.

Gyen had been allowed to visit his relatives in Lhasa for the 1979 New Year. He got up before dawn and set off towards the centre of Lhasa, carrying with him the nineteen pages of our petition, which we'd signed "Labour Reform Prisoners Palden Gyatso and Lobsang Wangchuk". Gyen pasted all nineteen pages on to the wall of the Tibetan Medical Institute in Lhasa. This was the first wall poster to appear in Lhasa after the death of Mao.

Back in Nyethang, Gyen told me that throngs of people had crowded round to read the petition as soon as he had finished pasting it up. Other prisoners told me that the petition had caused quite a stir in Lhasa. It took the police ten days to start interrogating us. First they summoned Gyen, then, after an hour, a Tibetan guard called Pasang came for me.

We were interrogated but no charges were made. Gyen and I insisted that we had obtained permission from the officer in charge. We had even left a copy of the petition at the office! The authorities were trying to convince us that better times had really arrived and were keen to show leniency wherever possible. So, rather than punish us, they simply transferred Gyen to a new work unit and told the other prisoners to keep an eye on us both. From then on we had to meet in secret.

In September 1979 a group of senior Party officials visited the camp and announced that for the next two weeks no one would be allowed to visit Lhasa. Soon we learned that a delegation of Tibetan exiles, sent by the Dalai Lama, was on its way to the capital. Clearly, the authorities wanted to prevent us meeting them. Later I would learn that the delegation had asked to see Gyen Lobsang Wangchuk.

Fearing that the Chinese would try to convince the delegation that the Tibetan people were happy under the new regime, we decided to put up more posters, urging the people to rise and fight for their freedom. I wrote a number of posters demanding independence and the eviction of the Chinese from the Land of Snows. I showed them to Gyen and he seemed pleased. He said that he too would write some posters.

That day, alone in his room, Gyen began work on a large poster, but he was spotted by Rongpa, one of the prison's most notorious informers and sycophants. Rongpa rushed to the warder's office to report what he had seen and added that I'd been seen visiting Gyen that morning.

Pasang, a Tibetan guard, came to fetch me from the weaving room. "Why did you visit Lobsang Wangchuk this morning?" he asked.

"I went to give back a book," I replied.

Pasang scowled and walked me briskly to Gyen's dormitory. Gyen was standing in the middle of the room with his hands raised above his head.

His unfinished poster was spread out on the floor and beside it was a crumpled piece of paper on which he had made notes of all the slogans he wanted to include. Several guards were rummaging through his belongings.

"Are you involved in this?" one of them asked me.

"I was at work. This has nothing to do with me," I replied, thinking about the posters I'd hidden.

Gyen tried to protect me by saying, "Palden has nothing to do with this."

"Why were the two of you meeting this morning?" asked Pasang.

"He came to return my book," said Gyen.

My heart pounded.

On 1 October another prisoner, called Samten, who would later escape to Nepal, smuggled my posters out of the camp and pasted them up in Lhasa. The following day, two police jeeps arrived at the camp and Gyen and I were both summoned to the main office.

"Did either of you go to Lhasa yesterday?" asked a young Tibetan officer.

"The brigade leader can confirm that we never left the camp," said Gyen in his gentle voice.

They couldn't link us with the posters in Lhasa.

Despite the fact that Gyen had been caught red-handed, the authorities took no further action. Gyen was transferred from Nyethang to work at the Tibetan Medical Institute, where he was asked to collect and edit ancient Tibetan medical texts that had been largely destroyed during the Cultural Revolution. My request for a transfer to Drepung was again rejected, on the grounds that I was an essential skilled worker.

I would discover later that the Chinese had in fact placed both of us under surveillance, suspecting that we were part of a larger underground organisation known as Tag Drug, the Tiger Cubs. The Chinese wanted to capture as many members of the organisation as they could. Three prisoners were assigned to watch my every move. The Chinese were biding their time, gathering evidence, hoping for a bigger catch.

For more than six months I had no contact with Gyen and concentrated on my work in Nyethang. After a while, the prisoners assigned to keep an eye on me began to get bored and became careless. It wasn't until 1981 that the authorities actually made their move, arresting Gyen in Lhasa and sentencing him to another term of imprisonment at Gutsa prison. This was very sad news, as Gyen was one of the few sources of inspiration we had left. He wrote to me, urging me to continue with my work, saying that we should never give up our fight for freedom and independence. A few weeks later, I went to Lhasa and managed to paste up a poster informing people of Gyen's arrest and demanding his release.

I think that many Tibetans now had a false sense of security. Many of the friends and relatives who had disappeared since 1960 were now beginning to return home and it seemed that no more arrests were taking place. I wanted to show people that arrests were still being made, even if the Public Security Bureau now knew better than to abduct people in broad daylight. On one of my posters I wrote an account of life in a labour reform camp that ended with the declaration, "There are still prisons." The Chinese authorities refused to admit that the labour reform camps were prisons. Our official documents contained no reference to time we may have spent in such camps. Gyen Lobsang Wangchuk, for example, had been formally "released" in 1970, but he spent the next ten years confined to a labour reform camp.

Other prisoners warned me that my activities would only bring back the bad old days. They wanted me to desist, saying that conditions were much easier now and rules more relaxed. They seemed to live in a kind of self-induced amnesia; no one, understandably, wanted to be reminded of the horrors they'd lived through. It was easier to accept the Party's maxim, "The past is past."

The Party wanted us to forget what it was like to starve. They wanted us to forget the taste of watery broth, the weight of leg irons and the pain of beatings. These were "things of the past", never to be repeated. In 1980 Hu Yaobang, the new Communist Party Secretary, came to Lhasa to make a public apology to the Tibetan people. The guards distributed copies of the *Tibet Daily* so that we could all read the transcript of Hu's promise of greater freedom and, specifically, the restoration of religious freedom.

Yet still I woke up every morning to find myself in a prison. The Nyethang labour reform camp still held over 200 prisoners, even though all of us had already served our formal sentences. Still we went out of the camp every morning with our baskets to gather excrement and dung. Still we were made to attend study sessions, which now consisted of endless repetitions of the Party's promise of a new era.

In February 1982 I decided to put up another poster in Lhasa. It was a cold morning and I wrapped up warm in a *chuba*. We were now at least allowed to wear traditional Tibetan clothing again. I walked quickly and got to the city before the sun was up. I made my way to the Barkor, the inner circle surrounding the Jokhang, Tibet's holiest temple, and was surprised to find so many people making their morning circum-ambulation of the temple. People from other parts of Tibet had at last been permitted to travel to Lhasa on pilgrimage.

So the centre of the capital thronged with pilgrims muttering prayers under their breath. There were far too many witnesses here for me to put up my poster. I had no idea how people would react. I walked on to the main government offices, where all was quiet. No sentries were guarding the military office, so I decided, there and then, to paste up the poster on its wall.

My poster urged the Tibetan people to wake up and fight their oppressors. I said that we were living in the throat of a wolf and it was only a matter of time before the wolf swallowed us down. I told people that the reforms and the policy of liberalisation were no more than window-dressing. I wrote that as soon as Mao's successor, Deng Xiaoping, had secured his grip on the country, he too would use his power to suppress the Tibetan people.

I got back to Nyethang just as the cocks were beginning to crow. The authorities had not noticed my absence. I saw the smoke coming from the mess hall and went straight in to collect my tea. Two years would pass before the Chinese discovered that I was responsible for the posters.

In September 1982 Hu Yaobang was re-elected Secretary of the Communist Party of China. Hu was famous for being behind the policy of liberalisation and I remember reading in the *Tibet Daily* that the Dalai Lama himself had sent a telegram congratulating him on his appointment. This seemed to be an encouraging sign. Hu had promised to withdraw a large proportion of the Chinese forces from Tibet and we saw the immediate effects of this in our own camp. The Chinese *Changzhang* was recalled to China and his Tibetan assistant, Wangyal, was promoted to leader of the labour camp.

One morning that winter, walking towards the mess hall to collect my tea, I saw a group of prisoners crowded round a poster. Curious, I went over to join them and was surprised to read an announcement from the Party's Central Committtee. All labour reform camps had been disbanded! The camp authority now had no power to keep us here and prisoners started to demand immediate release.

Most of the *ley-mi* were allowed to go, until by the end of that year only ten of us were left in the camp. We were given the same reason as before: skilled workers were needed to complete essential jobs in the camp. It wasn't until the spring of 1983 that I was allowed to leave the camp.

I'd been wondering if I should go back to Panam or Drepung. I knew it would be easier to get a residency permit for Panam, but I was not sure I had the heart to go back there. The previous year I'd had a visit from my brother's son. He turned up unexpectedly, barefoot, dressed only in rags. He told me that my sisters were no longer on speaking terms with my stepmother. During the Cultural Revolution my sisters had denounced my father and watched as Chinese soldiers beat him to death. My stepmother would never forgive them.

I learned too that my brother's murderers were still free men, and that some of them had even become important local cadres. The monastery at Gadong had been completely destroyed. Did I really have the strength to go back to such ruins?

Chapter Eleven
Among the Ruins

THE BUS DROPPED ME off at the bottom of the hill and I set off up the slope to Drepung. But the monastery had lost its dazzle in the thirty years since I first set eyes on it, after that long trek from Panam. I remembered whitewashed walls shimmering in the thin air of these high mountains. I remembered the glitter of the gilded roof. But that had all gone. It was hard to believe that the Drepung now ahead of me had once been a thriving city with a population of more than 6,000 monks. The walls were muddy and scarred. They were naked and crumbling, like some disfigured being.

I closed my eyes and rested against a boulder. When I opened them again, it was as though I had travelled in time. A group of Khampas was walking slowly towards me. The men wore *chubas* and their hair was plaited with bright red silk tassels. The women were festooned in fine jewellery and huge balls of amber. The shoes they all wore, identical blue canvas slippers with rubber soles, were the only indication of period, the scene's single reminder of the presence of the Chinese.

These happy pilgrims grinned as they walked by me, swaying from side to side. I joined them and we walked up to the ruined monastery together. We stood at the threshold, looking in on the open courtyard surrounded by more crumbling walls. The pilgrims shook their heads in disbelief and fell to the ground.

I raised my hands high above my head and prostrated three times, the first time in over fifteen years that I was able to do this without glancing nervously over my shoulder. But the dereliction all around me brought tears to my eyes and I walked slowly among the ruins, trying to work out the former layout of the great monastery. I tried to locate my first *shag*, but there was nothing left standing.

I came across another group of former monks wandering through the ruins doing just the same as me, putting the monastery back together in their heads. An elderly monk looked directly at me.

"Which *dratsang* did you belong to?" he asked.

"Loseling," I replied joyfully, and the old monk made a circle in the air in front of him to indicate that Loseling had once been here. We were standing in the Loseling *choe-ra*, the open cloister that had served as our debating ground.

We stood in the cloister exchanging stories about friends and the places we'd been imprisoned. They asked me if I was coming back here. I said that I had permission from the labour reform authorities, on condition that the monastery was willing to accept me back.

They directed me to the office of the Democratic Management Committee of Drepung Monastery. This office had been set up by the Religious Affairs Bureau and all the remaining temples were administered from here. The officials were supposed to have been elected by monks, but I soon found out that the names of the candidates were provided by the Party and we were simply expected to vote for one of them.

Right at the back of the monastery there were a few buildings left standing, their colour faded and their walls daubed with revolutionary slogans written in red Chinese characters. I went through a large gate into a cloister paved with stone slabs. In one corner a group of women were busy doing their washing.

One of the women in a red headscarf pointed me towards a red door. This was the office of the DMC. Inside, I was greeted by an ex-monk called Jinpa Lhentsog, a frail-looking man with a dark complexion and a rather sickly appearance. In fact, Jinpa was a man of great energy and ability who, contrary to his reputation for being a puppet of the Chinese, had actually defended the monastery from marauding Red Guards. Jinpa was responsible for saving whatever was left of Drepung. He was the *zhuren*, or chairman, of the DMC. I told him that I wished to move to the monastery.

"Which prison?" he asked, even though I had not said anything about being in prison. He knew that almost all the former monks had been imprisoned by the Chinese.

I gave him a brief account of my life in various prisons and told him that I was a weaver and carpenter. Jinpa's expression changed as soon as I told him I could weave carpets. He loved the idea of the weaving.

"You can teach the women how to weave," he said.

This puzzled me. Wasn't Drepung a monastery? Soon it became apparent that Drepung was now more like a village. All the monks were married. They said that they'd been forced to take a wife during the Cultural Revolution to show their revolutionary enthusiasm and prove that they were not *je-lu pa*, or backward. Jinpa himself was married with two children.

The DMC readily agreed to take me back and in May 1983 I moved to Drepung. The *zhuren* told me to choose any room I wanted and I decided upon a small *shag* with two rooms and a wonderful view over the Lhasa valley. I had very few possessions – just my bedding and two old *chubas*. For years I'd dressed in prison uniforms. I had no cooking utensils, but while I was in Nyethang I'd bought two large Chinese thermoses.

As the labour reform camps were disbanded all over Tibet, there was a sudden influx of elderly monks returning to the monastery. The monastic authorities were keen to accept them all back, as there was a desperate need for their skills. I was assigned to the restoration of many of the damaged murals in the remaining temples.

This new monastic life was something of a farce. None of us wore traditional robes. People used to call Drepung "the drama school", because the monks were always changing their costumes, but now we had to wear workers' blue uniforms and were allowed to meet only to perform our prayers three times a month. The monastery was really run just like another commune, with everyone receiving work points and with rations distributed accordingly. Yet still it felt wonderful to be back at the monastery, no matter how strange these changes were for all of us.

One day, as I was showing a group of young monks how to memorise long texts, I was told that a group of police and cadres from the Religious Affairs Bureau had arrived at Drepung. A few days earlier we'd heard that there had been some trouble at Ganden monastery, so I assumed that the authorities were just taking precautions. I thought no more of it.

For several days the cadres and the police in their smart new blue and white uniforms patrolled the monastery. I was concerned by the way they had commandeered a large quarter to be what looked like a permanent office. Police jeeps came and went all day long.

One evening there was a knock on my door. I was sitting on my bed reciting some prayers and a young monk poked his head round the door curtain.

"Are you asleep?" he asked.

"Come in," I told him.

"Kusho Palden la," the monk whispered, "the police are asking questions about you. You need to be careful." Then he left me to my prayers.

I was in my room again the following evening when I heard more jeeps approaching the monastery. There were hundreds of stray dogs in the monastery, most of them chased there from Lhasa as part of the city government's clean-up operation to prepare the city for foreign tourists, and that evening they all began barking excitedly. I wondered what could possibly have got them so disturbed. Then I heard footsteps on my roof — not a dog's but human footsteps. I kept still, alert to every sound. A few minutes passed and then there was a knock on my door.

"It's not locked," I called out.

The room was pitch dark.

"Where's the light?" someone asked.

I told him where the light was and as the light went on in the front room of the *shag*, the muzzle of a rifle appeared through the thick woollen door curtains. I sat up in bed, not knowing what was going on. Then the curtains were pulled aside and two young Chinese policemen rushed through into my bedroom, pointing their guns at me.

The two policemen were followed by about fifteen others who'd all been waiting outside. The front room of the *shag* was full of people. They were led by a senior Chinese officer with a large, puffy face. He stood still for a while, taking in his surroundings. Jinpa Lhentsog, the head of the monastery, stood beside him. Then, through a Tibetan interpreter, the Chinese officer asked me abruptly, "Who are you? What is your name?"

"Palden Gyatso," I replied calmly. I thought it better that I remained seated on my bed.

The Chinese officer took a piece of paper from his pocket and read from it in Chinese. The Tibetan interpreter then translated: "By order of judge Thupten Tsundro of the High Court in Lhasa, we have come to arrest you." No charges were mentioned. The police told me to stand up and, as I did so, everyone else in the room had to shuffle backwards to make space for me. A policeman placed my wrists in handcuffs, a brand-new style made of light steel that glistened in the dim light of the room, and I felt once again the cold rings of metal against my skin.

The police began searching my room. I'd bought a large piece of white cotton material to cover the ceiling and prevent dust from falling on to the floor. A policeman ripped it down and all its gathered dust filled up the room like smoke. The policemen found a pile of religious texts and threw them out into the middle of the room. My heart sank when I saw a piece of paper slip out from one of the books. It was the tracing paper I'd used on my poster and the headings were still clearly visible. The policemen were delighted. Here was their first piece of evidence.

Two policemen were examining my thermoses. In one of these, between the glass flask and the metal casing, I had hidden a Tibetan flag and a number of writings by the Dalai Lama. The policeman emptied the water from the thermos and began to shake it. His colleague held the thermos by the end and unscrewed the metal casing from the flask. The flag and the pieces of paper fell to the floor. The policemen were overjoyed.

The senior Chinese officer tapped me on the shoulder and asked me, in perfect Tibetan, "Palden Gyatso, do you not recognise your crimes?" He pointed to the evidence on the floor. "These are your crimes. Have we not hit the target? *Sa gung-treng tang, nam gung-treng tang*." "The Party rules the earth and sky": I had heard those words when I was first arrested in 1960 and remembered the beating I had been given at Norbukhungtse.

I noticed that Jinpa Lhentsog was trembling. He knew the authorities would ask him why I'd been given a residence permit for the monastery. Migmar, the junior secretary of the DMC, was also nervous, but he began to denounce me as "a wolf in sheep's clothing".

"There is no need to throw stones at a drowning dog," I said to him.

The Chinese officer signalled that I should be taken out. I was pushed down the stairs at gunpoint, then out into the yard and into the back of a jeep. Two guards got in beside me. There were police all over the place. We drove down into Lhasa, then changed direction repeatedly before heading for Old Seitru, a former prison that had housed all the senior Tibetan figures, including the last prime minister, Lobsang Tashi.

Seitru was now being used as a detention centre: prisoners were held here indefinitely while waiting for the court to pronounce a formal sentence. A number of guards were expecting us, and I recognised one of them as Zuzhang Dhargyal, a tall Tibetan brigade leader. Four young Chinese guards stood nearby carrying a three-foot-long electric baton. Dhargyal opened the door of the jeep and pulled me out by the shoulders. It was dark and some time after midnight.

I was led through a series of doors, through a small, cold room and then out into an open yard surrounded by prison dormitories. I was taken to brigade number six. The guards removed my handcuffs, then threw me into a cell along with a bundle of bedding they'd brought from my *shag*. The door slammed shut behind me.

It was at that moment that the reality of my arrest sank in and, standing in the cell alone, I had the feeling that I would be in prison for a very long time. As far as the Party was concerned, I had failed to reform; I had veered from the true path of socialism. The cell was bare but for a single straw mat on the cement floor. The floor had been painted green and polished so thoroughly that I could see my reflection in it. I had been out of prison for three months and eighteen days, but now I was in a cell again.

My new cell was more sophisticated than any I had previously experienced. There was a smell of fresh paint. Opposite the door there was a small window, impassable for its thick iron bars and wire netting. There was a tiny peephole in the new steel door and at the foot of the door there was a hatch, bolted on the outside.

I spread my bedding on the straw mat and tried to sleep. Soon I heard the engines of more jeeps and the sound of chains dragging across the ground. Four of us were arrested that night.

The morning reveille was sounded by a new electric bell fixed just outside the cell. No one came to open the door, but after a while the hatch opened and a hand pushed a mug of hot tea through into the cell. Several hours passed before I heard the door being unbolted. It was Zuzhang Dhargyal. He ordered me out of the cell and took me to another room, where a photographer took a shot of me from the front and two shots in profile. I thought of the hundreds of photographs with black crosses brushed on to them that I'd seen over the years: photographs of condemned prisoners facing execution.

The next day I was taken into an interrogation room – another cold, forbidding place with the same smell of fresh paint, the same harsh cement floor and walls, so unlike the walls of traditional Tibetan homes, which were made of yellowish mud bricks that filled the room with the distinct odour of earth.

Zuzhang Dhargyal leaned towards me. "Think carefully," he said. "Make a full confession."

Two Chinese officers and an interpreter sat behind a long line of tables. The older of the two had a distinguished look to him and my first thought was that he was not likely to start beating me. It was always hard to attribute much humanity to the Chinese officers. They were figures of authority and repression and our contact with them was always at one remove, since the interpreter always had to intercede between us. The presence of the interpreter seemed to block the emotional interaction between prisoner and official. The prisoner's relationship was with the interpreter, not the interrogator.

I sat on a wooden chair and one of the officials, via the interpreter, invited me to confess. I said nothing. There was a long pause.

"Why do you think you have been arrested?"

"I don't know why I have been arrested." Twenty years of interrogations had made me wise to all their tricks. I was determined not to divulge any information before I knew what I was actually being charged with. I was asked to tell them my life story from the age of eight.

"I was a labour reform prisoner at Nyethang Zhuanwa Chang from 1975 onwards and before that I was at Sangyip," I began. Then I paused. "There is no need for me to tell you my life story," I went on. "I have repeated this many times since 1960. If you're really interested, then you can read my file."

The interrogators did not react, though I was convinced I was about to be beaten. Instead, I was told I could go and warned that I should "think carefully". But I had my reasons for not talking. I had to find out how much they knew. Did they know, for example, about the report on conditions in Tibet that I'd written in Nyethang and that Samten had smuggled out of the camp and passed on to the Dalai Lama? We had all signed our names on that document. I had to find out if I had been arrested in connection with the report.

The interrogation continued over several days. Still I refused to make a confession. The Chinese officials did not lose their composure and never administered the beating I feared. One morning, expecting to be taken to the interrogation room, I was told instead that some relatives had come to see me.

"Do you have any relations called Lobsang and Dolma?" asked Dhargyal.

I nodded.

Dhargyal led me into another room, where Lobsang, my older brother's son, and his sister Dolma were waiting. It was Lobsang who'd come to see me at Nyethang in 1981. He'd put on his best clothes and his face was gleaming with oil. On a table before them was a thermos, a basket of biscuits and a piece of Tibetan hard cheese. Dolma poured tea and pushed a cup towards me.

Lobsang told me that they were now in Lhasa, where he was making a good living as a tailor. My stepmother was there with them too, but she was very ill. Lobsang wanted me to know that the police had been questioning them.

"*Pon-po la* said they would release you if you made a sincere confession," he said.

I said nothing.

"Please, Palden," he went on, "confess for our sake."

Then both Lobsang and Dolma began to cry. I told them not to worry and asked them to take good care of my stepmother. Then Dhargyal took me back to my cell.

The next time I was taken to the interrogation room, I couldn't get the image of Lobsang and Dolma in tears out of my head and I told the officials that I was ready to speak. The youngest Chinese officer poured me some tea from a thermos and offered me some biscuits. I began telling the story of my life from the age of eight onwards and the officers did not interrupt me.

When I finished my story, the senior officer leaned forwards and asked, "What do you think you are in prison for?"

"Have I been arrested because of the evidence found in my room in

Drepung?" I asked. I didn't want to give anything away before I had an idea of what the officials actually knew.

"So you do recognise your crime?" said the senior officer.

I was relieved. He knew about the poster, but he clearly did not know about the reports Samten had smuggled out to the Dalai Lama. I admitted that I had put up the poster and this prompted a further torrent of questions: who gave me the paper, the pen, the gum and so on? They were trying to find out if I had acted alone or with accomplices and I kept repeating that no one else had been involved.

My answers did not satisfy the officials. The next day I was asked to list the names of everyone I'd had contact with over the previous year. How could I now avoid implicating friends? Instead of providing the officials with such a list, I decided to tell them the name of my "accomplice". I said that the flag and the writings found hidden in my thermos had been given to me by an elderly monk called Lobsang Gelek, whom secretly I knew had died on the night of my arrest.

"Where is Lobsang Gelek?" asked the interrogator.

"He's in Nyethang," I replied.

They noted down his name and other details and at last they looked pleased with what I'd told them. I had been questioned every day for eleven days.

My strategy worked. A few days later a Chinese officer told me that they had detained Lobsang Gelek and he had made a full confession. Of course, this made me laugh. I knew that the Chinese could not afford to lose face. But I remained bewildered as to how I had avoided being beaten. Were my interrogators just unusually kind-hearted? Later I would learn that it had been announced that I was to be executed, along with the others arrested at Drepung that night. My relatives had gone to light butter lamps in the Jokhang, the main temple at the centre of Lhasa. I was to learn that Tibetans in New Delhi had demonstrated outside the Chinese Embassy, demanding my release, and that this was all that had saved us from our death sentences.

* * *

The interrogation came to an end at the beginning of 1984. Four high-ranking officers in the dark blue uniforms of the judicial office read out a list of the charges against me and asked me if they were correct. I nodded and placed my fingerprint on the document. Previously, prisoners had simply been handed a piece of paper informing them of their sentences. During the Cultural Revolution, Tibetans had been thrown into prison without even the preamble of an interrogation. But now, in this "new era", the authorities had established something approaching a judicial system.

So one morning I was pushed into another jeep and driven to a courtroom in Lhasa. I'd been in prison for over twenty years but this was my first experience of an actual trial. I had no idea what to expect. The judge was a chubby Tibetan called Dorje, and he briskly introduced all the officials in the court. An old man called Phurbu was brought forward as my defender. Then the judge asked me if I had anything to say. I looked towards Phurbu, thinking that he might have some suggestion, but he just sat motionless, facing the judge.

"Do you have anything to say?" repeated Dorje.

"I don't know my defender or any of the people bringing evidence against me," I replied. The judge seemed to ignore me and immediately ordered that the proceedings should begin. A young Tibetan officer stood up and read out the charges. He mentioned all the items discovered in my room, as well as the fact that I had confessed to putting up posters. The judge then gave me another chance to speak and I launched into a speech about how the claims made by the Chinese about progress in Tibet were entirely false. I said that the people of Tibet had not been freed from serfdom, as the Chinese were fond of announcing. I told the court about the condition of the villagers in Nyethang, and the great problem of food shortages there.

The judge let me finish, then gave a disapproving smile and said, "A blind man will see only darkness. A reactionary will see only darkness in the great socialist motherland."

On 29 April 1984 I was sentenced to a further eight years in prison. I was fifty-one years old and had spent most of my adult life in Chinese prisons, in my own country.

My new home was to be Orithridu prison. I was issued a set of summer and winter uniforms and told that these must last three years. I was assigned to a brigade consisting mainly of old people and we were given slightly easier work, such as tending the vegetable garden or helping in the prison kitchen. Meetings had lost their former rigour and we no longer had to pretend we cherished the Party and its leader. But we still had to attend regular study sessions at which we would read and discuss articles in the *Tibet Daily*.

I remember a strange encounter in September of that year. I was summoned to a room in the main office block and told to sit down at a table covered with fine cloth. There were a thermos, two expensive mugs, a plate of biscuits and a glossy calendar on the wall showing lots of modern Chinese buildings. After a while I was joined by a young Chinese man wearing a tie and carrying an elegant leather bag. His interpreter poured us tea and offered us biscuits.

"How are they treating you?" he asked. He told me that he had come from Beijing and needed to know if the prison officials had treated me well or if I needed a medical check-up. His concern seemed genuine.

At the time I was bewildered by such treatment, but I know now that I had been adopted as a prisoner of conscience by an Amnesty International group in Italy and that this visit was a direct result of the letters they had been writing to the Chinese government and the authorities in Lhasa.

But it did not take long for the guards to revert to their usual cruelty. One day I complained to the cook, Dawa, that the tea they were serving was cold. A short while later, Dawa came to my dormitory with a guard called Jampa, whom we all knew as "Grandfather" because of his white hair. Jampa asked who had complained and I said that it was me. Then he said that he wanted to test whether the tea was still cold and emptied a thermos full of scalding water all over the bare skin of my right arm.

The other prisoners backed away as Jampa came towards me waving his electric baton. The pain of the burn was excruciating. Then the guard began to prod me repeatedly with the baton, sending electric shocks through my shoulders and chest. The cook looked on, enjoying this demonstration of power, and Jampa stared at the other prisoners, as if to say, "Who's next?"

The pain was too much and I let out a scream. Other prison officers rushed into the dormitory to see what was going on and I shouted, *"Go-treng tang gyi-mi se-gyi du"* – "The Party is killing a prisoner." A senior Chinese officer motioned everyone away and began to scold Jampa and the cook. I was taken to the dispensary, where a young nurse dressed the burns on my arm.

The Communist Party had changed its tactics. Previously, confession and criticism meetings had been held with the intention of reforming us and converting us to socialism. Now, however, the Party had realised that political prisoners would not reform just because the Party told them to. We were labelled "the unreformable" and treated accordingly. The only way to make us submit was to keep us in isolation and cause us as much pain as possible.

Beatings were routine in Orithridu. The guards were armed as if for battle. They had a pistol and two knives sheathed in their belts and often two kinds of electric batons: a short, foot-long prod with a shiny plastic handle and a longer baton they could wield like a sword. They wore armour too, sometimes so much armour that they had difficulty walking. The guards did not hesitate to use their new weapons on us "unreformable" prisoners.

Chapter Twelve

A New Generation of Splittists

O N 28 SEPTEMBER 1987 the *Tibet Daily* ran a report on a demonstration in Lhasa. Twenty-one monks from Drepung had demanded independence and freedom for Tibet. I was amazed, for this was the first time I'd seen such a report in an official paper. The article may have been tucked away on page four, the page usually reserved for international news, but the paper normally confined itself to news that glorified the Party. The reporter dismissed the demonstration as the work of "a handful of splittists", "splittists" being the new term for Tibetan nationalists, since the Chinese regarded the idea of Tibet's freedom as "splitting" the motherland.

This was thrilling news. The demonstration was the first serious public protest since 1959. The paper listed the names and ages of the twenty-one monks and I was struck by how young they were. They had not even been born when I was first arrested. They had been what the Communists liked to call "nurtured in the bosom of the Party" and yet here they were shouting slogans demanding Tibetan independence.

For a political prisoner, there is nothing more heartening than learning that people outside share your beliefs and aspirations. I knew now that our struggle would continue through the voices of these young protesters.

The prison authorities, of course, immediately held a meeting at which we were required to denounce the demonstration. We had to read long articles in the *Tibet Daily* which condemned the protesters as misguided youths.

In the weeks that followed, we began to receive news that the authorities had been arresting scores of people in Lhasa. I was passed messages from the outside asking for news of missing people, giving the name of someone who had disappeared and asking if they had been detained in the prison. We had a network of contacts that enabled us both to let people know who was in the prison and to receive news about what was going on outside.

The demonstration of September 1987 inspired others to march on to the streets of Lhasa. The monks from Ganden monastery, the second largest in Tibet and once home to more than 5,000 monks, staged their own demonstration. The monastery had come under particularly ferocious assault during the Cultural Revolution and I remember passing by just after my release from Nyethang. It had been razed to the ground, with not a single building left standing.

There followed more protests by monks and nuns, and later the young people of Lhasa organised demonstrations too. As a result, the political prisoners in my prison (there were only five of us; most of the inmates were criminal convicts) came under increased surveillance. We were constantly being questioned about events outside. Whenever there was any disturbance anywhere in Tibet, we were summoned to a special meeting and asked to give our opinion on the matter. I would simply reply, "I am a prisoner and have no connection with the demonstrations outside."

That winter, I heard that Geshe Lobsang Wangchuk had died aged seventy-five, having spent much of his adult life in the Communist prison system. The Chinese would say that he died of old age, but I insist that he was murdered. The authorities treated him with special brutality. Even at the age of seventy-five, his hands and feet had been shackled and he'd been forced to do hard labour. One day after returning from work, he'd been accused of laziness and malingering. He'd been chained to an iron bar and beaten unconscious by a guard called Paljor, at whose hand I was myself to suffer also. Lobsang must have suffered internal injuries. He was rushed to hospital, but there was nothing they could do. The authorities then asked one of his relatives to nurse him and released him into their care, but he died the next day. Thus the authorities were able to deny all responsibility for the death of one of the finest men I have ever known.

Over the next two years, the demonstrations multiplied. Each successive protest triggered a larger uprising. I remember in March 1989 I was working in the prison's apple orchard. The older prisoners had been assigned to work in the orchard, which had become one of prison's main sources of income. It was hot and humid in the huge plastic greenhouses that housed the apple trees. I was preoccupied with tending the trees when I heard loud singing coming from the direction of the main gate.

I went outside. A long line of prisoners was being marched back into the prison. I was puzzled. It was only midday, so why had they been brought back so early? They looked happy enough and the way they were singing certainly did not suggest anxiety. I went back into the greenhouse. Suddenly, two guards came in and told us to return to our dormitory. On the way there, I noticed that there were armed guards on the roof and in the watchtowers.

I asked my cellmates what was happening.

"There's trouble in Lhasa," one of them answered.

I knew this could mean only another demonstration. We all lay in our beds, waiting for further news.

Next morning there was an unusually large number of guards in the yard. They had set up a big machine-gun on one of the walls, with ammunition belts piled in a heap beside it. I realised that what was going on in Lhasa must really be serious.

After the morning roll call we were told that there would be no work details that day. The guards brought us board games and playing cards. This created an almost festive mood, with everyone forming groups and sitting down wherever they could find a space in the yard. We all knew that the prison authorities were terrified that we too might stage a demonstration.

That afternoon I caught the attention of a young nurse who worked in the dispensary and had always been friendly to me. As she was walking across the yard, I called out to her and asked her to take a look at my shoulder. I took my coat off and raised my shoulder towards her, whispering, "What is happening in Lhasa?" She pretended to examine my shoulder and answered, "The people are rioting in the Barkor and the police cannot control the city." She told me that the demonstration had been going on for three days.

I saw black smoke drifting from the direction of Lhasa. Suddenly it was announced that four of the brigades, including mine, were to be transferred to another prison. We were told to pack our belongings and get ready to move. We had less than an hour, but I had got used to these sudden changes. It was one of the rules of prison life that things could happen without the slightest warning.

We were hurried by guards out of the dormitory, carrying our bundles on our backs, and ordered to clamber into a row of covered trucks that had just arrived in the yard, engines roaring. There was a lot of shoving and jostling as we all squeezed into the backs of the trucks. We had no idea where we were going.

Then, just as suddenly as our departure had been announced, the trucks came to a halt at the main gate and we were ordered to get out. We were marched back to the dormitory. It was pure chaos. I had been rushing around all day and my limbs were weary, so I just climbed into bed, wrapped myself in an old blanket and pondered on the day's events. I was desperate to know what was happening outside.

The next day the prison officials wanted to keep us isolated. We were not marched out to work. Incredible though it may seem, the authorities actually preferred to keep us busy by entertaining us! They even brought out a large video screen and began showing popular films from Hong Kong. A huge crowd of prisoners gathered to watch the films, though I never liked them.

That evening I heard another fleet of trucks arriving in the yard and peered through the window to see what was happening. The searchlight was on in the outer compound and I could see the trucks backing up to the buildings of brigades one and two. Then, beneath the trucks, I could just make out the feet of new prisoners being walked slowly into the barracks. I imagined that the feet belonged to the protesters in Lhasa.

The new prisoners were shouting defiantly. Trucks were unloading prisoners at the dormitory of the women's brigade as well and the women too were shouting slogans of defiance. We crowded at the window, full of apprehension. Then the shouting turned to wailing. The guards must have burst into the dormitory and started to beat the prisoners. The prison filled with the sounds of wailing and breaking glass, and when I went to the latrine the following morning I saw all the broken windows and broken glass scattered across the yard. The new prisoners must have fought back.

We were confined to our dormitory that day. From the window I watched the guards put out desks in the yards and interrogating officers come out to sit at the desks with notebooks and pens. I watched young boys, not even old enough, as Tibetans used to say, to wipe their own noses, emerge from the barracks and line up at the desks. Young girls emerged from the women's dormitory, their hair tied back in bright ribbons and looking like dolls. One of the girls sauntered across the yard with her hands in her pockets, as if heading for a sweet shop. They were fearless, without the slightest sign of anxiety.

The realisation that there was a new spirit of resistance among the people of Tibet cheered me greatly. These young protesters were living proof that even the brutality of the Cultural Revolution and three decades of indoctrination had not persuaded the youth of Tibet to follow the Party. On the contrary, it seemed that the spirit of nationalism was as fervent as ever.

Later I would ask some of these young prisoners if they had learned Chinese at school. One boy looked at me in disbelief and asked me scornfully why anyone should learn the language of the oppressor. Many of the young monks and nuns said that they had joined monasteries rather than go to local schools, because they had no desire to learn anything the Chinese had to teach them.

The Communists saw this uprising of young people as a rejection of the Party. They believed that young Tibetans were simply not aware of the bad old days when Tibet was ruled by feudal landlords and the masses lived in abject poverty. So the Party organised study sessions to teach these young rebels about the past. Things did not go quite according to plan. When Party officials said how grateful young people should be for the "golden age" in which they now lived, the Tibetans answered back with stories of the starvation and beatings suffered by their parents during the Cultural Revolution. The authorities had no way of countering that, other than by saying that it was all the work of the Gang of Four.

It was strange seeing all these young boys and girls. I was reminded of my own early years in prison. The new prisoners faced exactly the same problems we had faced. They had no mugs, no bedding, no plates or spoons. The older prisoners began to hand over all their spare mugs and blankets.

The action of these young protesters stirred something in all of us and I noticed a new atmosphere of camaraderie and defiance in the prison. Even the criminal convicts were moved by their courage and began to fend for them and advise them on how to deal with interrogations. These people were all under twenty. They had not even been born when the Chinese first entered Tibet. They had been raised under the Red Flag, yet they had discarded Communism and demanded "*Bo Rangtsen*" – "Freedom for Tibet."

We tried to help the young protesters as much as possible. The arrival of these politically aware young men and women had an extremely good influence on the many juvenile criminal convicts in the camp. One young criminal called Pemba was so stirred by the courage of the protesters that he came to see me, saying that he wished to contribute to the struggle for Tibetan independence. Pemba looked about sixteen, with a thin, pale face. I worried at first that the prison authorities might be using him to trap me, for criminal convicts were often used to keep an eye on political prisoners and we were all wary of mixing with them. But Pemba was pleasant enough and every day, after work, he would sit waiting for me outside our dormitory. He was illiterate and I told him that the first thing he should do was learn to read and write. I even began to teach him myself, but I was still careful not to discuss anything political with him, in case it could be used against me later. That was how cautious you had to be.

One day a guard found the words "*Bo Rangtsen*" scrawled on the wall of the latrine. The offending graffiti was photographed and the authorities announced that this was a serious counter-revolutionary crime. They were alarmed by the audacity of the new prisoners and saw this incident as a dangerous precedent. Determined to stamp out any sign of resistance, the guards began examining people's handwriting to find out who was responsible for the slogan. Every prisoner was asked the names of everyone they'd seen going to the latrine the day the slogan was discovered.

One prisoner reported that he'd seen Pemba coming out of the toilet and had noticed that his hands were covered in charcoal dust. Pemba was quickly arrested, shackled and thrown into solitary confinement. "Solitary" was a specially constructed room so small that you could stretch out your arms and touch both sides with ease. It was cold, with no bedding or blankets. There was no window and a prisoner was held there in complete darkness. When I saw the young boy being led away, I was frightened that he would be sentenced to execution.

The whole of Tibet was now under martial law and the authorities were demanding the toughest punishments for any infringement. The intensity of Chinese condemnation of the demonstrations was, as always, a sign of international support for the Tibetan cause and so, paradoxically, was a source of great encouragement to us. The recent surge of protests across the country, and particularly in Lhasa, had indeed caught international attention.

But this was not good news for a suspect like Pemba. Since he was a criminal convict and had never shown any interest in politics before, the authorities soon concluded that he must have been paid or influenced by one of the political prisoners. They learned that he had visited my dormitory several times and that I had loaned him some books. Suspicion soon fell on me. I would hear later that Pemba was beaten and tortured for several days, but that he had refused to implicate me, insisting that he had acted alone. I never saw him again.

The situation in the prison was very tense after Pemba's arrest and I was not really surprised when I was summoned from the dormitory by the chief officer of Orithridu. I had never made a secret of my delight at the recent uprisings in Lhasa and had openly congratulated the young political prisoners who had come pouring into the prison in the aftermath of the demonstrations. It was hardly surprising that the authorities should think I was a bad influence. I was taken to the main office on the other side of the courtyard.

"You have to go," an officer told me.

"Where?" I asked.

"You have to go up," said the officer.

When Tibetans don't want to specify a particular place, they just say up or down.

"You mean you weren't informed this morning?" asked the officer's Chinese superior.

"No."

"You are being moved to Drapchi."

Back to Drapchi! The number one prison in the whole of Tibet and the place that had been my home between 1964 and 1975. Once again I rolled up my bedding, packed my belongings into a bundle and climbed into a waiting jeep. The driver was Tibetan, a woman who had once asked me to teach her daughter to read.

"What happened?" she whispered when no one was looking. But then a guard and a senior Tibetan officer got into the jeep, the officer with a thick file under his arm. I knew this was my case file, containing all my details from 1960 onwards. The jeep headed off down the track out of the prison, sending up a trail of dust in its wake.

We drove in silence to Drapchi, where, after my luggage, such as it was, had been thoroughly searched, I was taken to dormitory number seven. It was a familiar sight: sparsely decorated, with everyone's belongings neatly rolled on their beds – not separate, individual beds, but one raised platform on which everyone had to find their space. The prisoners were still out at work, except for one man who was resting on the bed when I came in.

He got up and introduced himself as Yeshe. He poured me some tea from a thermos and we chatted for a while. Yeshe was a monk too, from Lokha region, just south of Lhasa. He was suffering from tuberculosis. He told me that there were seven of us in the dormitory.

Suddenly the door burst open and a Tibetan guard ordered me to go with him. He took me to an interrogation room, where I was met by one of the old guards, whom I immediately recognised. It was Paljor, the guard I held responsible for the death of my friend and mentor Lobsang Wangchuk. In the old days we called Paljor "the light hand", because he never hesitated to raise his hand in order to beat prisoners. He was tall and smoked constantly. His fingers were stained yellow from the cigarettes and his eyes were watery. He was sitting down behind a table. The two Chinese guards who had searched my luggage stood beside the door.

Paljor was pretending to read my case file, but as soon as I came in he put the file down on the table, stood up and walked towards me, shouting, "Rascal!" This was followed by a stream of abuse. I had no idea what was going to happen. The interrogation room reminded me of the shrine rooms dedicated to wrathful deities. An array of batons hung on the wall. A bunch of shining steel handcuffs dangled from a hook. Paljor took down a long baton and walked around me, waving it in the air.

"You've been thrown in prison three times and still you have failed to reform," he said.

He began questioning me about my past offences, even though he must have known all about my case history from my file.

"How old are you?" he asked.

"Sixty."

"No! You are fifty-nine!" Paljor was clearly trying to provoke me.

"I was born in the year of the monkey, and that makes me sixty."

Paljor had moved back to the rack of batons. He selected a shorter one, about a foot long, and pushed it into an electric socket to recharge it. Sparks shot out and there was a crackling sound.

"Why are you here?" continued Paljor.

"Because I put up posters in Lhasa calling for Tibetan independence."

"So you still want Rangtsen?" he asked, still trying to provoke me.

Paljor did not wait for me to answer. He pulled the electric baton from the socket and began to poke at me with this new toy. My whole body flinched at each electric shock. Then, shouting obscenities, he thrust the baton into my mouth, took it out, then rammed it in again. Paljor went back to the wall and selected a longer baton. I felt as though my body were being torn apart. I remember dimly that one of the guards put his fingers in my mouth to pull out my tongue and prevent me from choking. And I remember too that one of the Chinese guards ran out of the room in disgust.

I can remember as if it were yesterday the way the shocks made my body vibrate. The shock seemed to hold you in its grip, like a furious shiver. I passed out and when I woke I found myself lying in a pool of vomit and urine. I had no idea how long I had been there. My mouth was swollen and I could hardly move my jaw. With great pain, I spat something out. It was three of my own teeth. It would be several weeks before I could eat solid food again. In due course, all my other teeth fell out too.

I was taken back to the dormitory. Yeshe was there.

"Who did this?" he asked me.

"Paljor," I mumbled, as Yeshe helped me on to the bed.

The past few years had been comparatively easy for me, with no meetings or *thamzing*. On the whole, the regime in prison had been quite relaxed. So Paljor's brutality came as a shock and a reminder of the nightmarish years of the Cultural Revolution. I suspect that the beating was ordered by some higher authority keen to teach me a lesson, angry that I had been so enthusiastic about the blossoming of opposition to Chinese rule.

I heard the unmistakable clanking of chains dragging across hard ground and the voices of the prisoners returning to the dormitory after work. One of them, a strong-looking man in his early twenties called Lobsang Tenzin, came straight over to me and asked, "Kusho la, have they caused you much pain?" I couldn't reply. I raised my hands over my face.

Lobsang had taken part in a demonstration in Lhasa on 5 March 1988, during which a young policeman had died after falling from a window. The Chinese accused Lobsang of murdering the policeman. There was no evidence that Lobsang was responsible for his death. The demonstrators had run into a building close to the Jokhang, the temple at the centre of Lhasa. They were followed by the police and in the ensuing scuffle the unlucky policeman had fallen from the window. Lobsang was arrested and given a death sentence, suspended for two years. When I arrived in Drapchi in October 1990 those two years were almost up. But he showed no sign of fear. In fact, he was exuberant.

There was a special brigade for political prisoners in Drapchi, so I found myself sharing a dormitory with kindred spirits. All of the seven prisoners in the dormitory had either taken part in demonstrations or written posters demanding independence. This was some comfort to me, though the pain from Paljor's assault was searing. I could hardly open my mouth. The brigade's cook, a former monk, brought melted butter and told me to drink it. Tibetans attribute the most miraculous properties to butter. It warmed me and helped to soothe my stomach.

My request to see a doctor was turned down and the very next morning I was assigned to work in the kitchen. This was a cushy job. We sat around a huge pile of vegetables, sorting the rotten leaves and roots from the edible parts and throwing the latter into a cauldron. Other prisoners asked me who had done it and I told them it was Paljor. They shook their heads when they heard the name.

Political prisoners made up Drapchi's fifth brigade, which was divided into eight *tsuk* or dormitories. I was in *tsuk* number seven. I got on well with all my fellow inmates. The oldest was a seventy-five-year-old monk called Hor Lharken. Then there was a boy called Sonam Topgyal, who must have been about eighteen. Sonam was a gifted artist and painted portraits of other prisoners. Dawa, another young prisoner, had put up a poster in his village denouncing Chinese rule in Tibet as colonialism. Lobsang Kalsang, a young monk from Drepung, had been one of the leaders of the first demonstration on 27 September 1987. Yulu Dawa Tsering, Lobsang Tenzin and I made up the full complement of seven.

I took great comfort from the company of these brave, like-minded people. There was a buoyancy and sense of excitement in our brigade such as I had never experienced before. In the past, prisoners had lived in constant fear of denunciation by their fellow inmates, but the new generation of political prisoners was not so easily intimidated by the threat of violence. People were ready to answer back.

Our dormitory was the hub of the brigade's activity. One of the prisoners had smuggled a small radio into the prison and every evening Lobsang Dorje would listen to the BBC's Chinese-language broadcast and another prisoner called Ngawang Lobsang, who understood some English, would press his ear to the radio so that he could listen to the World Service news. This way, we often heard about the Dalai Lama's travels abroad.

We began to find ways of smuggling information out of the prison. We wrote reports on prison conditions and made lists of the prisoners. As people often had no idea who exactly had been arrested, it was important that we should keep the people of Lhasa informed, so that they in turn could inform the relatives of the prisoners. Later, these lists were smuggled out of Tibet and passed on to human rights organisations. Tourists were surprised to find complete strangers thrusting pieces of crumpled paper at them, with instructions that they should deliver them to the United Nations and their own governments.

It was in Drapchi that I met Yulu Dawa Tsering, a gentle, cautious man and a great listener. Yulu, one of the renowned incarnate lamas from Ganden monastery, had been in prison from 1960 to 1979 and had been rearrested in 1987. I had heard about Yulu's case on the Chinese television news, but now he told me the story himself with a certain bewilderment. He had gone to a friend's house for dinner and while there had met a monk he had known many years before, a monk who had fled from Tibet in 1959 and settled in Italy. The monk had returned to Tibet with an Italian friend and Yulu had joined them for dinner. During the course of the meal, Yulu happened to remark that Tibet's problems could be solved only if the country regained its independence.

Their conversation somehow reached the ears of the Chinese Security Bureau, which promptly arrested Yulu and his host, Thupten Tsering, and charged them with "spreading counter-revolutionary propaganda". A simple conversation had been elevated into an international conspiracy! The purpose of the gathering, according to the Security Bureau, was "to win the support of foreign countries".

Soon after Yulu's conviction, the monks of Ganden monastery had demonstrated in Lhasa to demand his release. It was this protest that led to the biggest demonstration Lhasa had ever seen and that forced the Chinese to declare martial law across Tibet.

Every prisoner in the seventh brigade had his own story of hardship and torture, but we kept our spirits up. The Chinese continued to arrest large numbers of people and soon there were hundreds of political prisoners in Drapchi, most of them young monks. The Chinese called them "the Dalai Lama's running dogs". This was meant to be a derogatory label, but we were all rather proud of this title, because to us the Dalai Lama still represented freedom.

We were not deterred by the beatings and continued to organise protests in the prison. We told the younger prisoners that they mustn't let the guards see that they were frightened, because fear was what gave the guards power. And thirty years in prison had taught me that you should never beg for mercy, because mercy was not what you'd get.

In the winter of 1990 the antagonism between the authorities and political prisoners developed into open conflict. I remember how cold it was that winter and think now how lucky I was not to have been assigned to outside work. I was working mainly in the humid, claustrophobic greenhouses. Insecticide sprayed over the saplings and mature trees left an unbearable stench in the closed, hot domes.

On 15 December we organised the first ever demonstration *inside* Drapchi prison. We were spurred into action by what had happened to the youngest of the political prisoners, a boy called Lhakpa Tsering. Lhakpa was serving a three-year sentence for forming a pro-independence group called Singi Tsogpa (the Snow Lion Organisation) in his school, Lhasa Middle School Number One. He was very popular among all the prisoners and Lobsang Tenzin treated him as his younger brother.

Lhakpa had been savagely beaten at Gutsa detention centre when he was first arrested, and he'd been badly beaten as soon as he arrived at Drapchi by a guard called Pema Rigzin, whose name was a byword for brutality. We could all see that these beatings had caused serious internal injuries. Lhakpa had difficulty walking and his whole body was bent over like an old man's. I can remember him complaining again and again about a pain in his stomach. We gave him some Tibetan medicine and Lobsang advised him to visit the dispensary.

But Lhakpa had repeatedly been sent away by the doctors, who had reported him to the authorities as a malingerer. One night we were woken by the sound of groaning coming from the next-door dormitory. People began to call out, "Lhakpa! Lhakpa!" They began to shout louder and louder, but there was no sign of movement from the guards' quarter. Prisoners in the other dormitories began to join in calling for help. Soon all the dormitories were shouting the same words in unison, like a chant: "*Nga-tso mi shi-gi-du*" – "Our people are dying."

A prisoner shouted that the guards were coming and the chanting ended abruptly. I recognised the voice of the *duizhang*, the brigade leader, shouting abuse and reprimands.

"Where is the sick prisoner?" he demanded.

"Dormitory number eight," the prisoners shouted back.

That night, Lhakpa was moved to the dispensary. The brigade leader made some threat about how he would be dealing with this in the morning. Sure enough, the following day, it was announced that brigade five would have to attend a meeting. We were walked out into the yard, surrounded by armed guards. Another group of guards carrying long electric batons stood even closer to us. The *duizhang* demanded to know the meaning of the night's activity.

We paid little attention to him, for in the far corner of the prison compound we could see the three-wheeler prison ambulance driving out of the main gate. I knew they were taking Lhakpa to hospital.

That evening I learned that he had been taken to the police hospital in Lhasa. But that same evening, Lhakpa came back to the prison. The doctors had not found any serious injuries. During the night his condition deteriorated and he was once more driven off in the three-wheeler ambulance. This time, Lhakpa died on his way to hospital.

The first I knew about any of this was in the morning, after breakfast, when a criminal convict who worked in the dispensary came into our dormitory and broke the news to Lobsang Tenzin. Lobsang stood there, frozen, as tears welled up and rolled down his cheeks. We all looked at each other, wondering what we should do.

News of Lhakpa's death spread quickly among the political prisoners. We never planned it out loud and I'm still not completely sure how it happened, but something that had never taken place in the history of China and Tibet was now about to take place here, in Drapchi. Looking back, I don't know how we dared to do what we did.

Lobsang Tenzin picked up the white sheet that covered his mattress and tore it in half. On one half he wrote, in beautiful Tibetan lettering, "We mourn the death of Lhakpa Tsering." On the other half he wrote, "We demand improvements to the conditions of political prisoners." Then we held the sheets up like banners and marched slowly behind them into the courtyard.

Word spread like wildfire that *tsuk* number seven was staging a demonstration. There were ten of us in the dormitory by this time, and we were all in complete agreement. Nothing was going to stop us. Lobsang Tenzin and Pema walked in front, carrying the first banner. They were followed by Kalsang Tsering and Gaden Gyathar carrying the second banner. When we stepped out into the courtyard, we were exhilarated to find all the other prisoners in our brigade lining up behind us in four columns. In all my years in prison I had never witnessed such defiance and we were all dizzy with our own daring and courage.

There must have been over 150 prisoners in our brigade and they all joined the demonstration, all except for one man whose sentence was due to expire in a few weeks. We marched like soldiers, in a column so neat you'd have guessed we'd rehearsed the whole thing. We made our way towards the main office building. This stood less than 100 yards from our dormitory, but that distance seemed like miles, such was the courage required to cover it.

The ninety minutes between breakfast and the start of work were usually a private time for prisoners, a period during which the guards left us to our own devices. So all our preparations had gone unnoticed and there were no guards watching as we made our way across the yard. When we reached the main administrative building, there was one young Chinese guard waiting outside the office. His face went bright red and he was obviously frightened. The march came to a halt just a few steps away from him.

"Is it true that Lhakpa Tsering is dead?" asked Lobsang Tenzin in Chinese.

The guard must have said yes, but I couldn't follow the Chinese words they exchanged. The young guard then ran into the office, slamming the door behind him. Still there was no sign of soldiers. We waited in the cold morning air in the open yard. It was the middle of December but I could hardly feel the cold; the excitement was keeping us warm. Suddenly a small gate was flung open and guards rushed to take up positions all around us, some of them armed and some of them brandishing the long electric batons. On a wall in the distance, I could see them setting up a Bren gun.

I was standing quite near a prisoner called Bagdro, a young monk serving a three-year sentence for his involvement in the death of a policeman in March 1988. Bagdro had been severely tortured during his interrogation and his nerves had still not recovered. All of a sudden he got up and began yelling and making violent gestures at the guards. I knew how dangerous this was. It would be seen as provocation. Some of the older prisoners grabbed hold of him and held him firmly in the midst of the column of marchers.

The *yuanzhang*, the head of Drapchi prison, walked slowly towards us in his long blue woollen coat. He was accompanied by the Chinese doctor who ran the dispensary, and by the *kezhang*, the director of prisons, one of the highest-ranking Tibetan officials. They were surrounded by guards and other officials.

"*Gan shen ma?*" shouted the *yuanzhang*. "What are you doing?"

Lobsang Tenzin said something to him in Chinese.

"A prisoner died last night," said the *kezhang*. "What is his name?"

Everyone began to shout, "Lhakpa, Lhakpa."

"Who is your leader?" asked the *kezhang*.

We told him that we did not have a leader.

The Tibetan *kezhang* walked calmly towards the first protesters and asked us all to voice our grievances. Lobsang Tenzin gave a detailed account of what had happened to Lhakpa, particularly the beating he had received at the hands of the notorious guard Pema Rigzin. Then Lobsang demanded that Lhakpa's case be investigated and that all the guards and medical officers involved in his death be punished. Another demonstrator demanded that a post-mortem be carried out and that a representative of the prisoners be present. All the prisoners at the front of the column spoke out, listing their grievances. Many of them referred to beatings administered by Pema Rigzin. His name came up again and again.

Soon it was my turn. As I began to speak, I noticed one of the guards whispering something to the *kezhang*. We older prisoners were always regarded as troublemakers and treated with disdain. I spoke about Lhakpa, insisting that it was no good pretending the boy had died of natural causes. I affirmed that he had died from beatings and medical negligence. The *kezhang* began to show signs of irritation and the doctor also looked uncomfortable. I went on, describing the treatment I'd received at the hands of Paljor. His name too came up again and again.

The *kezhang* was a shrewd man. He knew that the only way to defuse the situation was to let every one of us have a chance to speak. The prisoners soon calmed down, our initial anger subdued by the fact that we had been allowed, for the first time, to speak freely. The *kezhang* promised that Lhakpa's case would be thoroughly investigated and that all those who had been negligent would be punished. He announced that all our complaints about beatings and torture would also be investigated. We felt much better, happy that we had accomplished our objectives. The Tibetan guards approached the older prisoners, urging us to go back to our dormitories.

By now the sun had risen right above our heads and it was a warm day. We headed back to our dormitories. Since our *tsuk* had been the main organiser of the demonstration, we expected some sort of retribution from the guards and the great euphoria of defiance was starting to disappear.

Lobsang Tenzin took off the badge of His Holiness the Dalai Lama he had pinned to his uniform. Lobsang's two years had now expired and after today's incident he could be certain that he would be executed.

"I don't have long to live," he said, handing me the badge he had worn so proudly.

We all cast down our eyes. The clinking of Lobsang's shackles was the only sound.

For a few days, the authorities acted as though nothing had happened. We were angry that nothing was said about the post-mortem or about punishing Pema Rigzin and the others involved, but the behaviour of the guards and medical staff had definitely changed. They seemed to be treating us with more respect.

The day on which we'd demonstrated was also the day criminal convicts were allowed visitors. These visitors ensured that news of our protest spread quickly beyond the prison walls. The response of the people of Lhasa was wonderful. The following week, when our relatives came to visit us, they brought vast quantities of food contributed by the general public so that political prisoners should not have to rely on the meagre prison rations. However, when the prison authorities found out about this, they imposed strict quotas limiting the amount of food each political prisoner was allowed to receive.

Four or five days later, all the prisoners were called to a meeting in the yard. An official read out a list of names and we were separated into groups of between ten and fifteen people. I was in the first group with

Lobsang Tenzin and Yulu. We were told to change cells, with our group instructed to move to *tsuk* number one. This reshuffle made little difference: I was still with my friends. Yulu was appointed *zuzhang*, or cell leader. Formerly, the *zuzhang* had always been someone with a "clean" political background, but now the authorities were more interested in appointing someone who had influence over the prisoners.

It wasn't long before we were summoned from our new dormitory to an interrogation room. The authorities knew that our resolve was strong, so they chose to question us one by one. A guard fetched me while I was dozing during the afternoon rest. My interrogator was a Tibetan called Jampa Kalsang and his questions were predictable: why had we demonstrated, whose idea was it?

I repeated the story of Lhakpa's death and described again my own experiences. I opened my mouth wide and pointed to my swollen and still-discoloured gums and tongue.

"For an old man, you got a fat mouth," Kalsang told me. "I know your type!"

I knew what he meant by this. He had concluded that I was one of the "unreformables" and the only way to deal with unreformables was brute force.

I took every opportunity to complain about Paljor. All the prisoners, guards and officials knew about him and my public complaints must have been a source of considerable embarrassment to that vicious man. I remember one afternoon I was secretly performing a religious ritual, prostrating myself on the floor of the dormitory. I remember hearing the creak of the door, and turning round to see Paljor disappearing, closing the door behind him. He had been watching me.

The authorities reneged on all their promises. A month after our demonstration it was announced that Lhakpa had died of appendicitis and that no one was responsible for his death. Neither Pema Rigzin nor Paljor was punished for his brutal treatment of prisoners. As far as I know, they are both still working in Drapchi.

I know now why so many guards could act without fear of punishment. Many of them were related to other senior officers in the prison system. Paljor's wife was the daughter of Pasang *shuji*, the political commissar of Drapchi prison and the prison's highest-ranking Communist Party official. Paljor's brother-in-law was a high-ranking officer called Phuntsog, who worked in the prison's judicial section. Guards like Paljor were well protected.

The authorities then announced that all our sentences would be increased by five or six years. This caused great resentment. The atmosphere grew tense once again, with many prisoners talking openly about another protest. Realising that they were about to have a riot on their hands, the authorities quickly abandoned these extended sentences.

In the spring of 1991 we received news that a foreign delegation was to be brought in to inspect Drapchi prison. The sudden improvement in prison conditions was a clear sign that the arrival of the delegation was imminent. In April the kitchen suddenly filled with a wide variety of fruits and vegetables. Chunks of meat and fat appeared in our diet. For a week the criminal convicts were assigned to the task of making the prison look beautiful. All the buildings were given a fresh coat of paint. All the prisoners were given new uniforms.

Once again our dormitory became the centre of activity. Lobsang Tenzin said how important it was that we should make contact with the foreign visitors. We decided to organise a petition in which we would describe the reality of prison life and detail the use of torture instruments. We would tell the story of Lhakpa's death. Lobsang agreed to write the first draft.

Our main problem was keeping the whole plan secret from one member of the dormitory, Hor Lharken, not because he was an informer but because he was particularly excitable. We knew that Hor Lharken would not be able to keep such a project to himself. So, because he was illiterate, we began to communicate only in writing. We all made notes of the points we wanted Lobsang to include in the petition and he soon came up with a first draft. The petition did not contain endless complaints about rations or living conditions. Lhakpa's case and the treatment of political prisoners were what really mattered.

We listed the names of all the prisoners who had been tortured. We described what had happened to a group of nuns in Gutsa. They had been raped, in a way: guards had pushed electric batons into them. We ended the petition with a letter of appeal addressed to the American president. But how were we to get the petition into the hands of the foreign delegation?

We thought that the delegation would be shown only the section of the prison that housed the criminal convicts and might perhaps be taken to the dispensary. Lobsang Tenzin said that he would find some way of handing over the petition, adding that he was already sentenced to death and there was nothing further the authorities could do to him. We all knew how resourceful Lobsang was and we accepted his proposal that he should hand over the letter.

One day, when we returned from work for our lunch break, a criminal convict came to tell us that a visitor had arrived. I would learn later that this visitor was James Lilley, who was then serving as American Ambassador to China. The guard on duty in our brigade that day was an easygoing retired Tibetan official and Lobsang asked his permission to visit the dispensary, saying that two Chinese prisoners needed to see the doctor. The guard consented. As they were about to leave, another prisoner, Tenpa Wangdrak, also asked if he could visit the doctor. All of them were led through the gate of our compound into the open yard.

Lobsang, Tenpa and the others were walking across the yard towards the dispensary when the visiting delegation emerged from the main office. Lobsang's group were quickly pushed into a nearby kitchen. The visitors and the accompanying Chinese journalists walked on a little and came to a halt near the kitchen door. James Lilley had asked to see Yulu

Dawa Tsering, whose case had been widely reported in the international press and who had been adopted by Amnesty International as a prisoner of conscience. Yulu was brought out to meet James Lilley and they talked briefly through an interpreter.

This chance meeting was Lobsang's opportunity to hand over the petition. All he had to do was walk out of the kitchen and approach the delegation. He was on the point of doing this when Tenpa Wangdrak said that *he* wanted to hand over the petition. Lobsang refused.

"Don't you trust me?" Tenpa asked.

Lobsang relented. He did not want Tenpa to feel that he was not trusted. So Tenpa, a rather clumsy, abrupt sort of man, emerged from the kitchen and rushed towards James Lilley. He thrust the petition into the ambassador's hand. But Lilley was startled and before he knew what was happening a Chinese girl had snatched the petition from his hand.

I was working in the greenhouse at the time but the petition was all I could think about. I was confident that Lobsang would find a way of handing over the document, but when I returned to the dormitory I found him sitting on the edge of the bed looking dejected.

"We couldn't hand it over," he said.

My spirits dropped. But as Lobsang described exactly what had happened I became less worried. An important foreign visitor had witnessed the whole thing and would surely demand an explanation. I was sure that our efforts had not been in vain. The others, however, were worried that our petition was now in the hands of the Chinese. Lobsang Tenzin said that the authorities would identify his handwriting and that he would then insist he had acted alone.

Tenpa Wangdrak was distraught. We tried to console him but did not have much success. The atmosphere in the dormitory was made even worse when Hor discovered that we had planned all this without telling him. It was some comfort that Yulu Dawa Tsering had met with James Lilley. He told us that he had raised all our grievances with the ambassador.

The Chinese authorities were furious. Our audacity had embarrassed them in front of this important foreign delegation. We were certain they would seek the maximum penalty, but for several days the incident was not even mentioned. I suspected that they were waiting for instructions from higher authorities, or that James Lilley was still in Lhasa. Lobsang was convinced he would now be executed, but he was calm in the face of death. He had no regrets. We could not face the thought of losing him with such equanimity.

I know now that James Lilley had requested that the Chinese authorities suspend the death sentence on Lobsang Tenzin. But at the time these were anxious, anxious days.

Tenpa Wangdrak and I were working on repairing the narrow canal that ran along the edge of the greenhouse and I asked him if he was ready for interrogation. He said that nothing would happen. His confidence surprised me, for I knew that there was no way the authorities would simply forget the whole incident. Sure enough, a guard came to summon him shortly after our conversation.

At midday we stopped work and were marched back to the dormitory for our lunch break. I washed my hands and face at the tap in the yard, then went into my cell. A group of prisoners was standing at the door. They didn't say anything. Lobsang Tenzin and Tengpa Wangdrak's bedding was missing, leaving patches of bare cement where they had slept. Some other prisoners arrived and told us that the door to the *jin bi* – the isolation unit – was bolted and that someone had seen prisoners being led in.

We all felt helpless. What could we do to diminish their suffering? We bribed a guard to supply Lobsang and Tengpa with extra rations and we sent Yulu and a prisoner called Ngawang Phulchung to urge the authorities to release them. But their requests were ignored. The mood in the prison became gloomy once again. All our efforts to force the Chinese authorities to make changes had been in vain. Many looked to us older prisoners for leadership. The new generation of political prisoners seemed to be expecting us to tell them exactly what to do. Some of these young prisoners were talking openly about going on hunger strike. "Are we just going to leave our people in the *jin bi*?" they asked me. I did not know how to answer them.

Back in the dormitory, three of the most senior prisoners, including Yulu, who as an incarnate lama commanded much respect, were taking their afternoon rest. I told them that the younger prisoners were waiting for their advice. I mentioned the talk about hunger strikes, hinting that if these elders were to give their approval, then the younger prisoners were certain to rise up.

"I can't shoulder such responsibility," said Yulu.

It was obvious to me that he felt the consequences of such actions would be grave indeed.

Lobsang Tenzin and Tenpa Wangdrak had been in solitary confinement for nearly three weeks. Tenpa had initially declared that he would go on hunger strike, but had got so weak that he had agreed to accept food again. I was confident that Lobsang would manage all right. Despite his age, he was mentally tough and, with the threat of execution hanging over him, he feared nothing.

One morning in late April 1991 a prisoner whispered that he had seen the door of the *jin bi* ajar. My first reaction was to think that they'd been freed and after work I hurried back to the brigade, hoping to see them. But there was no sign of our two friends. We were all puzzled by their absence. Their bedding was missing. The next morning I discovered that two other prisoners had been summoned and that their bedding too had gone.

I joined a group of young prisoners outside the door of our brigade office. Angry and tense, they were all shouting questions at the guards. "Where are our people?" they asked. The guards stood firm and tried to dismiss them, but no one moved.

"It's not your concern," the guards shouted back.

"Where are our people?" the prisoners asked again.

This went on for several minutes. More and more prisoners joined the crowd, demanding an answer from the guards. The guards, who were by now looking extremely worried, rushed into the office to call for help.

All the political prisoners had now gathered outside the office and we waited quietly for some response. Suddenly the main gate into our yard was flung open and a group of Chinese soldiers, armed with rifles, took up a position. The two representatives of the Communist Party in Drapchi, a Tibetan woman called Pasang and a tall Chinese officer, walked towards us from the protection of the group of soldiers.

"What's going on?" Pasang asked.

"Where are our people?" we all shouted back.

We got no answer. Two police officers had taken out their pistols. One brandished his gun in the air and ordered us to sit down on the dusty ground of the yard. The tall Chinese officer was shouting at us and pointing his pistol threateningly at each of us, one by one. I couldn't follow what he was saying, but all the prisoners in front of me began to stand up. So I too jumped to my feet. Then, without warning, the Chinese officer hit a young monk called Ngawang Rigzin on the side of the face with his pistol. The gun flew out of his hand.

I would discover later exactly what had happened. We had all stood up just after the Chinese officer had threatened to shoot anyone who dared stand up to speak. We had stood up spontaneously, as one single body. We stood there in a swirl of dust kicked up from the yard.

Then the soldiers came rushing in. Some of them carried guns fixed with bayonets; others carried the long electric batons. They seemed to be targeting the younger prisoners. A boy called Phurbu who was standing at the front of the crowd turned to run from the charge, but a soldier thrust his bayonet into the back of his head. I saw blood spurt from the wound and Phurbu falling to the ground. I was left dazed by what I was witnessing, but then I felt the butt of a rifle landing on my back and fell, gasping for breath.

All around me prisoners were running from the Chinese soldiers. The older Tibetan guards tried to intervene by standing between us and the soldiers. One of the old guards begged us to run to our cells and stay there. "Please, ask for mercy," he told us desperately, "or you will all be killed." Many of the prisoners had managed to get back to the dormitories, but I could see a number of young prisoners lying on the ground being beaten by soldiers.

We started to shout, "Murder! Murder!" But the soldiers went on regardless, charging into the cells and dragging out all the younger prisoners. I was terrified. I thought we were all going to be massacred that day. I saw more officials arriving in jeeps. And then the soldiers were ordered to withdraw.

I had made my way back into the dormitory, feeling the pain not just on my back but on my legs too from repeated blows with rifle butts. I saw soldiers come through the gate into our compound and empty sacks full of handcuffs and shackles outside the dormitory. Then guards began to drag individuals from the cells. It was clear that they had been instructed to target the younger prisoners.

The first prisoner they dragged out was Ngawang Phulchung, who was serving nineteen years for organising the first demonstration in 1987. Ngawang looked tired and dishevelled. He had been the most vocal of all of us in asking questions about the whereabouts of Lobsang Tenzin and Tenpa. The guards shackled his legs and hands and led him off to an interrogation room. From the dormitory, I could see two women doctors waiting outside the interrogation room into which Ngawang had just disappeared. They carried a medical box and a steel tray with a line of syringes. I shut my eyes and began to recite the prayer, "*Om mani pad mai hum*".

Twenty minutes later, Ngawang was brought out. He looked like a rag doll, his face all puffed up and hardly recognisable for all its bruises. He was thrown into the *jin bi*. One by one, the younger prisoners were shackled, taken to the interrogation room, beaten and thrown into solitary confinement. There were not enough isolation units to hold them all, so some were simply left chained up outside.

The authorities decided that brutality was the only way to react to our rebelliousness. Guards began to use violence to punish the slightest infringement. But the prisoners were unyielding. They said openly that they would prefer to die than submit to the Chinese. It was a battle of wills. For those who use brute force, there is nothing more insulting than a victim's refusal to acknowledge their power. The human body can bear immeasurable pain and yet recover. Wounds can heal. But once your spirit is broken, everything falls apart. So we did not allow ourselves to feel dejected. We drew strength from our convictions and, above all, from our belief that we were fighting for justice and for the freedom of our country.

Chapter Thirteen
Confronting the Enemy

AT THE NEXT MORNING'S roll call we were a sorry sight. Some prisoners were covered in bandages and some had their arms in slings. Prisoners held on to their cellmates for support. Many of the younger inmates had shackles on their wrists and ankles.

Security was tightened considerably after the protest. Many more soldiers were positioned outside and we were kept under constant watch. Armed soldiers even stood by us while we got on with our work. But our defiance had created a euphoric atmosphere in the prison. Even the criminal convicts supported us surreptitiously by smuggling news and medicines into our cells.

The authorities announced that points would be deducted from our annual assessment award, which meant that most of our sentences would be increased by several years. The officials expected us to appeal for a reduction in our sentences, but we had already decided to stay firm. We raised no objection to these further punishments. We wanted to show that we were no longer afraid of prison and were perfectly prepared to face the consequences of our actions. We had to let the authorities know that they could no longer intimidate us.

They took no further action. The Chinese were planning a massive celebration to mark the fortieth anniversary of the "Seventeen Point Agreement", which the Tibetan government was forced to sign in the aftermath of the invasion in 1950. They announced that many important figures from Beijing would be visiting Tibet for the celebration and they were clearly concerned not to provoke us into another protest at such a sensitive time.

So I went back to work tending the apple orchard in the greenhouse and cultivating the vegetable garden. The work was pretty easy, but the greenhouses and vegetable gardens had become important sources of revenue for the Chinese. The authorities had even decided to expand and build a further fifty-five greenhouses in Drapchi. They imposed a system of quotas, by which each greenhouse was required to produce a certain quantity of fruit and vegetables every year.

A few weeks after our demonstration, we learned that Lobsang Tenzin, Tenpa and the two others had all been sent to Kongpo prison in southern Tibet. Lobsang particularly had been a source of great inspiration and courage, and all the prisoners in our brigade missed him dearly. After another month, we received a message from him saying that he had arrived safely in Kongpo and that we shouldn't worry.

That summer we were allowed to watch television coverage of sports events in China. I was not familiar with world sporting events, but the younger prisoners told me that China was playing football in the qualifying matches for the Asian Games, which were to be held in Beijing in the autumn. These younger prisoners loved football. They knew all the teams and could talk at great length about all the players.

The Chinese were keen for us to watch these matches as a sign of the progress and prosperity of China. But we managed to turn the occasion into an opportunity to show our resistance once more. My initial lack of interest in the games turned quickly into enthusiasm, because we would all sit in the hall and cheer and clap as loudly as we could whenever China lost. When one of China's opponents scored a goal, we would celebrate with thunderous applause. Even the criminal convicts joined with us and cheered whenever China lost a game.

That evening it appeared that the authorities had been alarmed by our jeering and feared another riot. A line of soldiers surrounded the hall. More prison guards stood by the doors carrying electric batons. And in the morning we were again reprimanded by an angry guard.

We learned later that the guards had been hard on the criminal convicts who had joined us in jeering the Chinese national team. They were told not to make mistakes, but to be patriotic and support the unity of the motherland. We didn't want there to be any animosity between us and the criminal convicts, so we stopped jeering during the football matches. The last thing we wanted was dissension among the prisoners.

The bond among the political prisoners was as strong as ever. There was no secret organisation and there were no clandestine meetings at which we would plan our protests and defiance, yet we were still able to act as one. Our small individual concerns took second place to the struggle for the freedom of our country. Only in captivity have I experienced such complete solidarity.

The Communist Party devised various means to break up this unity of purpose. I remember the occasion on which they instigated a system of points and rewards. If prisoners performed certain tasks and conducted themselves well, they would be awarded a certain number of points. These points would then be added up during the annual assessment meeting and rewards handed out to whichever prisoners had accumulated the most. The top prize was a reduced sentence.

This was certainly an attractive inducement, but we all saw it for what it was: an attempt to make us competitive, to pit us against each other and force us to conform to the prison regime. So we ignored the rules for acquiring points. I threw away the booklet about the scheme without even opening it. We refused to have anything to do with it. Needless to say, none of the political prisoners earned any points.

In fact, we continued to defy the authorities at every chance we got. In December 1991 a delegation from the Swiss government came to visit Drapchi. A sudden improvement in our rations and a rush to make the prison look beautiful alerted us to some imminent visit, just as they had done before James Lilley's arrival. We were locked in our compound while the delegation was given a tour of the criminal section of the prison.

Somehow, a political prisoner called Tanak Jigme Sangpo, a sixty-six-year-old monk with a distinguished lean face and a long white beard, had managed to mingle with the criminal convicts and get himself into their compound. When the delegation strolled into the yard, Tanak began shouting, in English, "Free Tibet! Free Tibet!" Tanak had learned this English phrase especially for the occasion. The authorities told the Swiss delegation that he was mad.

Tanak's sentence was promptly increased by eight years. He was first arrested in 1983 and sentenced to fifteen years' imprisonment for spreading "counter-revolutionary propaganda" and "criticising the leadership of his country". In 1988 his sentence had been extended by five years for shouting pro-independence slogans. With these additional eight years, Tanak is now due for release on 3 September 2011, aged eighty-five. After the incident with the Swiss, Tanak told me he had no regrets and would do it again as soon as he got the chance.

About thirty of the political prisoners in Drapchi were women and twenty-seven of these were nuns. Between them they had staged many demonstrations in Lhasa, calling for Tibetan independence. One of the lay women, a teacher called Dawa Dolma, was charged with teaching a "reactionary song". She had merely taught her students to sing the Tibetan national anthem and for this she had received a three-year sentence.

During interrogations, many of the nuns had been stripped naked and made to stand still while guards paraded before them, brandishing their electric batons in a lewd, provocative manner. The nuns' resilience seems awesome to me when I think of the humiliations and terrible beatings they received.

The women were kept in brigade three, along with the female criminal convicts. It occurs to me now that they may have felt that since our brigade had organised a series of protests, it was now their turn to do something. Their opportunity came in the spring of 1992. A week before the Tibetan New Year the authorities announced that we were not allowed to decorate our dormitories or wear new clothes. It was customary in Tibet to wear new clothes on the first day of the new year and considered inauspicious not to do so.

In previous years we had been allowed to celebrate the new year in the traditional way, and had even been given a three-day holiday. This year we were still given the three-day holiday, but with it came these prohibitions against our traditional celebrations. We could not understand what was going on.

We decided to ignore the prohibitions and celebrate the new year as usual. The nuns did just the same, decorating their dormitory with presents sent by relatives. And, on the first day of the new year, they discarded their baggy khaki uniforms and put on brand-new sets of clothes.

We wore new clothes too and for three days there were no morning roll calls or marches to work. Prisoners sat about in the yard playing cards and board games. We moved about the yard as the sun travelled, settling down again according to the movement of the light and shade. Since I was not that fond of games and since monks weren't allowed to gamble, I spent quite a lot of time sitting in the dormitory reading and reciting prayers.

On the second day of the holiday, Yulu Rinpoche came back from a stroll around the yard looking perplexed.

"Soldiers are going into brigade number two," he said, pouring me a mug of tea.

"They must be drunk again," I said casually.

Brigade number two was part of the criminal section. Days would pass before we had any indication that there had in fact been a riot in the women's dormitory.

The leader of the women's brigade, a severe Tibetan woman in her fifties who was notorious for her harshness and as vigilant as an eagle, had marched into the women's dormitory on the first day of the new year and demanded that the nuns remove the decorations and change back into their drab prison uniforms. When the women refused, the brigade leader called the guards, who promptly burst into the dormitory and beat the prisoners savagely. Two young nuns and the teacher, Dawa Dolma, were identified as the leaders of the protest and thrown into the isolation unit.

On the second day of the holiday, the nuns began shouting demands that their friends be released. The guards went into the dormitory for a second time and once again beat the women senseless with their favourite weapon, the electric baton. Criminal convicts in the second brigade saw what was happening through the dormitory window and began shouting, "Murder! Murder!" I am sure that those shouts saved the nuns' lives.

The authorities were quick to blame the protest on a group of older prisoners. In an attempt to eliminate their influence, the Chinese built new barracks and moved all the younger prisoners there. I was kept in the old compound, along with nine others. I think the Chinese suspected us of being the inspiration behind all the protests.

So we were kept isolated in our compound. All normal prison routines were suspended. There were no roll calls and we were not even marched out to work. We quickly became very bored and Yulu requested that we be allowed to work. His request was turned down. It seemed that the authorities were trying to oppress us through sheer indolence. Work at least gave a prisoner some sense of normality and it was certainly the best way to pass the time. Those summer days were long and hot. It seemed an age before the sun finally set over the mighty Himalayas.

My term was due to come to an end soon, but I did not let myself dwell on that. We all knew how easily the authorities could find some pretext for detaining a prisoner further. I passed that summer of 1992 reading and reciting from memory many of the devotional prayers I had learned as a novice. I spent the days in the dormitory, avoiding the surveillance of the guards outside. I began to prostrate myself every day, working up through fifty prostrations a day to about 200. Tibetans believe prostrations are a means of sustaining both mental and physical discipline. I hoped that once I was released I would be able to devote all my time to religious practice and believed that these prostrations were good preparation for a spiritual life in a monastery again.

I was interrogated repeatedly as the summer ended. The authorities wanted to know what I intended to do after my release.

"I am a monk and my place is in a monastery," I told them.

I was sure I would not be allowed to return to Drepung this time. The Chinese were already forcing the monastery to expel all the monks who had at any time been involved in political protest. When I was asked if I would continue to protest and put up posters, I replied with a quotation from Mao's "Little Red Book": "Wherever there is oppression, there will be resistance." This so angered the guard that he promptly walked out.

I couldn't believe these interviews. The authorities were still trying to convince me that Chinese rule in Tibet had brought great benefits to the people. They still wanted me to be grateful to the Party for allowing me the chance to reform. I just repeated all the stories of the suffering undergone by the Tibetan people. Paljor was present at one of these interviews and I told the officials what he had done to me. I opened my mouth wide to show them my bare gums. Paljor's beating had left me with only three teeth.

"This only happened once," the guard said.

I had received news from friends that the situation outside was dangerous and that Drepung was not accepting any former political prisoners. My friends advised me to leave Tibet. They told me that if I remained in the country I would be kept under constant surveillance and that anyone seen with me would immediately come under suspicion.

I began to hatch a plan of escape. It is hard for me to talk about the events that followed, for many of the people who helped me are still living in the shadow of the Chinese army and police. Though I am now free to write about my experiences, I know how careful I must be to avoid betraying trusted friends to the Public Security Bureau.

All I can say is that about a month before the date of my release, I contacted friends outside the prison and told them I wished to flee to India. I wanted to use my freedom to continue our struggle for independence; I wanted to devote more time to my religious practices; and I wanted, above all, to see His Holiness the Dalai Lama, the incarnation of the Buddha of Compassion.

My desire to get to India was given special urgency by the publication of the Chinese government's "White Paper on Human Rights in China", which was distributed throughout the prison. It claimed, incredibly, that there were no political prisoners in Tibet and that no prisoners had been tortured. The document described Drapchi as "a new type of socialist prison, where the prisoners are regarded as human beings . . . and where they receive fully humane treatment".

This gave me the idea of gathering evidence so that I could show the world something of what had been happening in Tibet. Friends told me that I was well qualified for this task, having been in prison for so long. They agreed that since the Chinese were being so selective about what they showed to foreign delegations, the existence of a living witness, free to speak openly, was crucial.

But it was a daunting task. How was I to escape from Tibet? There was no way I'd be given a travel permit and I knew I'd be kept under surveillance day and night. Anyone I spoke to would immediately be brought in for interrogation by the police. Everything had to be arranged with the utmost secrecy.

My contacts outside the prison said that they would make all the necessary arrangements. I asked them to buy a number of the electric batons used by the Chinese police, insisting that they chose batons that bore the police insignia and that showed signs of use. I gave them the name of an old Chinese guard who could get anything for you if the money was right. I knew that he'd have a way of getting some old electric batons and, sure enough, he did.

A few weeks before the date I was due for release, I was summoned for another interrogation. Paljor and two other officials were waiting for me in a bare room thick with the smoke from their cigarettes. Paljor pointed to a chair, indicating that I should sit down.

"As you're leaving us soon," he began, "have you got anything to say?"

"No."

"You've always been stubborn," said Paljor. "Like a bull. You've always refused to reform."

I said nothing.

"Do you know Lhalu?" asked the Tibetan officer sitting next to Paljor. Lhalu was a former Tibetan government official who had been arrested in 1959 for leading the revolt against the Chinese. He had since been released and the Chinese had given him an honorary post in their administration.

"I interrogated Lhalu," the officer continued. "If someone like Lhalu can reform, then so can you!" After a pause, he repeated the old line about the Communist Party's benevolence and how those who reformed were always treated leniently. "Your obstinacy is useless," concluded the officer. "Your hope of a free Tibet is no more than a hollow dream. Look at Lhalu! He is serving the motherland! He holds an important post in the Chinese parliament!" The officer was implying that I too could look forward to such a glittering career.

Once more I told the story of my life, from the day I was first arrested right up to my beating by Paljor. I even told them the story about my Rolex, reminding them that I still had the receipt. Eventually, Paljor asked me straightforwardly where I wanted to go and I told him I wanted to return to the monastery.

I knew I had to convince the authorities that I intended to go back to the monastery and devote my remaining years to the religious life. I thought that if I insisted hard on returning to Drepung, then the authorities were more likely to be satisfied that I had no intention of leaving Tibet.

"I am an old man and I wish to devote myself to the religious life," I told them repeatedly. "If I am not allowed to return to Drepung," I warned, "I will demonstrate outside the Jokhang!"

The officials listened to my threats with stern faces, then told me that the interrogation had finished.

My impending release was common knowledge among the political prisoners. Four or five days before I was due to be freed, a meeting was called in the main yard, with all our brigade sitting together in a row. I don't remember what was said during the meeting. I remember only the way my fellow political prisoners surged towards me when it came to an end, patting my back, holding my hands and passing me a long white ceremonial scarf or *khata*.

"*Gyen, ku-zug la thug-cha nang-ro*," they said to me – "Teacher, take good care of yourself." I was at once overjoyed and saddened: sad that I was parting from some of the finest and most courageous people I have ever met. The guards stood at a distance, observing this flurry of activity, then came over to break us up and march us off to our separate dormitories. I was very moved.

It was customary for a departing prisoner to give a tea party for the entire brigade, so I took about thirty small bags of powdered milk and all the butter I could find to the kitchen and asked the cooks to make tea for everyone in our brigade, and for all the criminal convicts too. It really was coming to an end.

On the morning of 25 August 1992 I got up early and slowly rolled my bedding into a neat bundle. One of my cellmates fetched tea from the kitchen and woke the others. Ignoring my prison uniform, I dressed instead in a brand-new *chuba* my relatives had sent me, the traditional robe worn by lay Tibetans. The *chuba* was huge and one of the other prisoners had to help me tie the long silk sash around my waist to hold the folds of the robe in place.

We all chatted for a while, drinking tea. Yulu got up and placed his wide-brimmed felt hat on my head. He took a step back and looked at me approvingly.

"Now you look ten years younger," he said.

Suddenly the door opened and two officials came into the dormitory, accompanied by two guards. One of the officials was our brigade leader and the other was Tashi Kezhang, who had once responded to our complaints about the use of electric batons by saying, "The government spent a considerable amount of money on these weapons so that we could beat you with them and that's just what we've been doing."

But Tashi now adopted a polite manner and announced, rather mockingly, "Sir, we have come to send you on your way!"

The brigade leader picked up my bedding roll and Tashi took hold of my thermos. My cellmates rushed forward and placed long *khatas* around my neck. Then, without any further ceremony, I was led out of the dormitory and the compound, into the main yard. Some of the nuns working in the nearby greenhouse saw me and waved. I waved back at them.

We went into the main office and I signed my release papers.

"We have no objection to your returning to Drepung," said the brigade leader. "But you still need to obtain permission from the Religious Affairs Bureau and the monastic authority."

"Thank you," I said, knowing that it would be no problem to get the agreement of the monastery now that I had the prison authority's approval.

With the *khatas* still draped around my neck, I made my way slowly from the office to the main gate, escorted by two guards. The gate was already open and beyond it I could see a number of people waiting for me – my nephew Lobsang and a group of friends.

I walked on through the gate, out of the prison. That was all it took, just a few steps. The moment I stepped outside, my friends rushed forward and draped more *khatas* round my neck, and someone handed me a cup of Tibetan tea. They offered tea to the two guards, but they shook their heads and went back into the prison. The heavy gate was pushed shut.

Lobsang was accompanied by Dawa, a former prisoner, and a tall man called Rinchen la, who, with his wife, had been very kind to me during my imprisonment. Rinchen had himself spent many years in prison and after his release had dedicated himself to helping prisoners and their families. They had spread out colourful rugs on the ground and brought baskets full of biscuits, dried meat and cheese. They invited me to sit down and began to feed me.

I must have drunk a dozen cups of tea that morning, sitting just a few feet away from the prison walls. Then my friends drove me to Shol, a hamlet just beneath the great Potala Palace. Lobsang lived here with his wife and my stepmother, and it was here that Lobsang did his work, making traditional Tibetan hats for sale at a market in the centre of Lhasa.

Some of the neighbours came out to watch my arrival. I went straight into the house to see my stepmother, who was by now half-paralysed and bedridden. The room was cold and dark and my stepmother seemed not much more than a shadow. Then my eyes grew accustomed to the dim light and I saw her raise her head. I moved towards her and touched my forehead against hers.

"So much suffering," she murmured. Tears were running down her cheeks.

Over the next few days many visitors came to the house, most of them former prisoners. I received a message that the plans for my escape would soon be ready. My instructions were to do nothing that would provoke suspicion and to pretend that I was indeed intending to return to Drepung.

I took a bus to my old monastery. It was still early when I got there and the air was full of smoke from the incense burners. Most of the ruins had now been repaired and the sun cast a brilliant light on the white-washed walls. Many of the young monks were in prison and the police were keeping a close eye on the monastery. They had set up a checkpoint on the road leading up to Drepung, where any monk leaving the monastery would have to show a travel permit.

I asked a monk where I could find the *zhuren*, the monastery's secretary, and he told me to go to the main hall. The monks had just finished the morning assembly and one of them pointed me towards the deputy *zhuren*, a stocky man whom I recognised as Kunchok Tashi. I remembered that long ago, before I was even arrested, Kunchok had been a skilled carpenter. But I was wearing a *chuba* and Yulu's hat and he did not recognise me.

When I handed him my papers, Kunchok smiled. He *did* remember me. He assured me that all my papers were in order and took me to see the *zhuren*, a monk called Yeshi Thangtok.

"When do you want to come back to the monastery?" asked Yeshi, after a casual glance at my papers.

"As soon as possible," I told him.

Yeshi told me to come back in a few days and I knew that this was so they could check with the Public Security Bureau. A few days later I was allocated a large clean room with a window overlooking the valley, and I informed the authorities that I would move into the monastery after the *Shoton* festival on 29 August. The *Shoton* festival marked the end of summer. All the people of Lhasa would pitch tents in nearby parks and hold lavish picnics. Hundreds of families would move into Norbulingka, the Dalai Lama's summer palace, for a performance of Tibetan opera lasting three days.

Traditionally, the festival was celebrated in Drepung by the unveiling of a huge *thangka*, a painting of Je Tsongkapa, the founder of the Gelugpa school of Buddhism to which the monastery belonged. The banner was over sixty feet long and all the monks would form a column and carry it on their shoulders. But this year the *Shoton* festival was the occasion of another protest. The banned Tibetan national flag was raised above the part of the monastery in which the Dalai Lama resided whenever he visited. Posters appeared on all the walls of Drepung demanding that the Chinese withdraw from Tibet.

So when I went back to Drepung with my belongings after the festival, I found the monastery swarming with police. All the monks were being questioned.

"There was some trouble during the *Shoton*," Yeshi Thangtok explained to me. "Come back in a few days."

Meanwhile, I was becoming increasingly anxious about my escape. Was it really going to happen? I just had to be patient and trust that my friends were making all the necessary arrangements. I comforted myself with the thought that they had already helped many other political prisoners escape to Nepal and India. Of course, I had to keep all this secret from my family. It was crucial that I didn't involve them in my conspiracy, for they would be the first to be questioned once my absence was noticed.

Then one night I heard a knock on the door. My nephew told me that there was someone to see me. Outside, the light of the moon revealed a young man wearing a cap and holding a bicycle.

"Are you Palden Gyatso?" he whispered.

"Yes."

"This is for you," he said, handing me a bag. The bag contained a selection of the torture instruments used by the Chinese.

The young man came back the next morning with the message I'd been waiting for. I told my family that I was finally moving to the monastery. My stepmother seemed happy. I took her hands and pressed my forehead gently against hers. I said my goodbyes.

The young man took me to a safe house in Lhasa, where I was met by the friends who had been organising the escape. They told me they'd found a driver who could take me to the Nepalese border and reassured me that he was a good man. It was at this point that the excitement really set in. I was going. I was going!

I was woken early the next morning and told not to switch on the light. A boy brought me a neatly folded set of clothes and I found myself putting on my first ever cotton suit. The suit was far too big for me and I had to roll down the waist of the trousers where the belt should have gone. A friend brought what looked to me like a rope with a loop at the end and placed it round my neck. So this was a tie! After Mao's death, ties had come into fashion and every last cadre wore a tie to show how modern they were.

"You look like a real businessman!" my friend told me.

Half an hour later I was sitting on the back of a bicycle being pedalled out of Lhasa.

I looked at all the old people doing their morning circumambulations of the Jokhang. The sun was just appearing above the high mountains. Smoke drifted from the incense burners that lined the Barkor. We passed through the centre of this great city.

At Bama ri, a couple of miles from the city centre, we came to a halt and my friend told me to wait for a truck. I had nothing but my clothes and the bag containing the electric baton, truncheon, knives and hand-cuffs. This was my strange luggage.

My friend left me and I stood by the road shivering, for the suit offered me no protection from the morning winds. A few trucks passed. Then, at about seven o'clock, a green truck covered with grey canvas pulled up beside me.

"Are you the prisoner?" the driver asked.

I nodded.

It was 7 September 1992. My instructions were to make contact with a trader based in Dram, the last village before the crossing into Nepal. The truck driver, a young man who looked as though he'd just woken up, told me that he was delivering goods to a Nepalese merchant and that the back of the truck was loaded with boxes of Chinese shoes and vacuum flasks.

My family assumed that I had moved to Drepung. The monastery assumed that I was still in Shol. But here I was in a truck heading out of Lhasa towards Nepal. I knew that it would be several days before my absence was noticed. After a few hours we drove past Panam and I could make out the distant shape of Gadong monastery perched on its hill. My younger brother was still a monk there. I had not seen him since 1962, when I glimpsed him in Norbukhungtse.

It took us two days to reach Nyalam, the last old Tibetan town before the crossing into Nepal. The driver must have noticed how anxious I was, for when we approached a road block he placed his hand on my arm in an attempt to reassure me. He stopped the truck, got out and disappeared into an office. A few minutes later he emerged with a Chinese official and I was relieved to see that they were laughing. The official indicated that a soldier should raise the barrier that blocked the road and we drove on slowly into Nyalam.

We stopped for breakfast and a rest, and the driver delivered some letters he'd brought from Lhasa. And in the late afternoon we set off again, driving down a steep, winding road, the mountainsides around us covered with forest and every view greener than in any part of Tibet I'd known. We stopped at a bend and the driver told me it was best that we get to the border at night.

I could see the lights of Dram in the distance. We waited until early evening before heading on for the village. Dram was a new settlement, the last checkpoint before Nepal and home to customs and immigration offices. The driver told me to pretend to be asleep while he went to find my contact. It wasn't long before he was back at the truck, accompanied by a burly man with long plaited hair and a small turquoise in his left ear. It seemed auspicious to me, that here was a man dressed in the old style. He took me to a house and offered me tea and noodles.

The burly man had to find a guide who would take me across the Nepalese border. The border was less than one hour's drive from Dram and all you had to do was cross Friendship Bridge, the bridge that took you from Tibet to Nepal. But I was told that it was too risky to drive. I would have to walk through the night to reach the border.

We couldn't leave straight away. I had to hide all day in a storeroom, emerging only at nightfall. This waiting went on for ten days. It took that long for my friend to find a guide willing to take me across. Then one night he came home with an elderly Nepalese man and told me to follow him. My nervousness was not helped by the fact that my guide spoke no Tibetan and I spoke no Nepalese.

I walked close behind him and soon we were out of Dram and in the middle of thick forest. We climbed steadily up a narrow path, pausing at about midnight to look down on the lights of Dram far below us. It began to rain heavily and my guide covered himself with a sheet of plastic. My friend, luckily, had given me a raincoat.

My guide walked quickly, turning around every now and again to check that I was keeping up. Soon I was soaked through and my shoes were full of water. We said nothing. But at dawn we crossed a rope bridge and my guide said simply, "Nepal."

We walked on and reached a small village later that morning, where I was delighted to find my burly friend from Dram waiting for us with my bag of implements that he'd smuggled over the border. We spent the night there and early the next day I was on the back of a motorbike being driven by a young Sherpa, heading for Kathmandu.

We rode all day and reached the capital that evening. The young Sherpa parked the bike right outside the reception centre for Tibetan refugees that the Dalai Lama had set up some years ago. These hours were all passing by as if in a dream.

I had not stopped being afraid. I knew that the Nepalese police had been handing Tibetans over to the Chinese and I was certain I'd be deported if I were caught. Nor was I alone in this predicament. The reception centre was full of refugees, people who'd escaped over the Himalayas from all parts of Tibet, many of them suffering from frostbite, some so severely they would need to have limbs amputated.

I was taken to the office of the United Nations High Commission for Refugees and formally registered as a refugee. I was given some money and a permit to travel to India.

Warned that I should leave as soon as possible, I wasted no time in getting on a bus bound for Delhi. Several days later I arrived at last in Dharamsala, the tiny hill-station built during British rule whose name alone had been a great source of inspiration to Tibetan prisoners, for it was in Dharamsala that the Dalai Lama had made his home in exile.

It was raining. The black clouds were reminders to me of the gloom and sadness that prevailed in Tibet, and I couldn't help comparing the damp fogginess of Dharamsala with the splendour in which the Dalai Lama used to live – the magnificence of Potala Palace and Norbulingka.

I had first seen His Holiness in Gyantse in 1951. Then, in the old Tibet, he was surrounded with great pomp and ceremony, though now I was simply led into a plain room by a lone attendant. It was as though I were being taken to see a humble monk. It was extraordinary to be in the presence of the Dalai Lama after so long. I immediately prostrated myself and presented him with a *khata*.

"Gyen Rigzin Tenpa's pupil," said the Dalai Lama. I was too nervous to look up. "You have faced much hardship."

I sat quietly on the floor. His Holiness began to ask me about my time in prison and I realised that he must have heard about me from other prisoners. He referred to many of my fellow prisoners by name, which gave me an idea of the genuine concern he had for us. Our meeting lasted for more than two hours and I was able to tell him about the enduring faith we had in him.

I was weeping when I left the room. That meeting had been my life's ambition. I was given a new set of monk's robes, the first I had worn since 1961, and in my new robes I made my way to the temple opposite the Dalai Lama's residence and offered a prayer that all should be released from suffering.

After my escape was announced in the press, I discovered that I had been adopted as a prisoner of conscience by Amnesty International and that a group in Italy had been writing to the Chinese authorities ever since I was arrested in 1983. In 1995 I was invited to Italy and introduced to the people who had written letters on my behalf for nine years. Despite the separations of language and culture and geography, I was deeply touched by their compassion and generosity.

That same year I travelled to Geneva to give evidence to the United Nations Commission on Human Rights. I was led into a huge assembly hall and sat down next to two young Tibetans who were to act as my translators. People were wandering around and chatting and I wondered how anyone would be able to hear what I was saying. I took a deep breath and began to read my testimony.

"My name is Palden Gyatso. I became a monk when I was ten years old."

Only when I finished did I look up and notice the Chinese delegation sitting in front of me, listening. They were listening! That gave me such a rousing sense of my freedom and I wished all my fellow prisoners had been there to witness it, for we had all dreamed of being able to confront our tormentors face to face and have them listen to our testimony. I was the first Tibetan prisoner to have had the opportunity to speak before the United Nations, so I knew that I was not just speaking for myself but for all Tibetans still in prison and for all Tibetans who had ever been in prison. The delegates heard only my voice, but behind my voice lay the suffering of the thousands of prisoners who had not survived to bear witness as I have.

The Chinese delegation made no reply to my statement, but some time later, in London, I was shown a letter that the Chinese Ambassador to Britain had written to a national newspaper. Mr Ma Yuzhen's letter read as follows: "Palden Gyatso was a criminal who persisted in anti-government activities. The crimes he committed include activities aimed at overthrowing the government, escaping from prison and theft. Palden Gyatso's story of how he was tortured by prison guards is untrue. Torture is forbidden in Chinese prisons."

Oppressors will always deny that they are oppressors. All I can do is bear witness and set down what I saw and heard and what the strange journey of my life has been. Suffering is written now in the valleys and mountains of Tibet. Every village and monastery in the Land of Snows has its own stories of the cruelty inflicted on our people. And that suffering will go on until the day Tibet is free.